THE DESCENT

A Novel by Tom Sylvester

Tom Sylvester

ADVANCE COPY
756 OF 1000

Penguin sketch courtesy of Don McMahon.

Author photo courtesy of Dave Roe.

ISBN 1-57087-135-3

Professional Press
Chapel Hill, NC 27515-4371

Manufactured in the United States of America

First Professional Press Edition: June, 1995

97 96 95 10 9 8 7 6 5 4 3 2 1

THE DESCENT

A Novel by Tom Sylvester

"True genious resides in the capacity for evaluation of uncertain, hazardous, and conflicting information."
—Winston Churchill

"Trust begets truth."
—W.G. Benham

ONE

TODD GRANT'S SHOULDER STRAPS resisted his attempt to lean forward and see through the murk ahead as the aircraft cautiously moved along taxiway Tango One. Washington Dulles International Airport seems to get more fog and drizzle than either Washington National or Baltimore-Washington International. Tonight was no exception. Todd was particularly anxious as his Captain, seated to his left, carefully corralled the wet, yellow centerline underneath the nose landing gear.

"Checked, Set," barked Doug Grimes as he responded to another checklist item called out by Todd. "Two hours of aviating in this crap and the weather hasn't come up one iota," Doug added with a glance toward Todd.

"The speeds are, uh, one hundred twelve, one fifteen, one twenty-two," Todd announced, ignoring Doug's follow-on comment. *"One more flight to go with this jerk,"* he thought to himself. His flashlight created a dim red glow on the airspeed chart on the lower right corner of his laminated checklist. The cockpit was quite dark and seemed uncharacteristically quiet, given the two loud GTS-331 turboprop engines just three feet beyond their side windows. Pilots joke that the three-thirty-one engines convert jet fuel directly into noise.

The Javelin wasn't a comfortable airplane, even under the best conditions. The crew had to keep the cockpit door behind the pilots closed in order to keep the bright cabin lights from killing their "night vision." Unfortunately, it also shut out the cool, fresh, dry air that normally moves from behind the nineteenth seat. The air conditioner in the rear of the commuter aircraft pushes cool air up the aisle and into the cockpit. With the door shut, the "front office" quickly became musty and stuffy. Add the considerable heat radiating from the plethora of avionics—plus an ever-present, *WD-40*-like odor—and the cockpit quickly became a wholly unpleasant environment.

"Twelve, fifteen, twenty-two—yep, yep, yep...," Doug pompously replied as he moved the plastic tabs known as "bugs" around the outside of his airspeed indicator. These bugs denoted the "go—no go" decision airspeed, the lift off airspeed, and the airspeed that would give the aircraft the best rate of climb should an engine suddenly fail after takeoff.

"Full boat tonight," he added as he turned the airplane cautiously and slowly onto another taxiway. According to the manifest, the twin engine jetprop was heavy with seventeen corporate duffers and their golf clubs and luggage, obviously heading for a weekend getaway near Hot Springs Airport in western Virginia. Also in back was a maintenance technician for their company, Bands Airways, which does business as TransGlobe Express. The technician was a last minute add-on to the flight, along with his very heavy toolbox and a cardboard box marked "Delicate Instrument! Handle with Extreme Care!" to fix another Bands Javelin aircraft grounded in Hot Springs.

"I don't see 'full boat tonight' on my checklist," chided Todd as he pointed toward the Cockpit Voice Recorder in the center console, otherwise known as "Big Brother." He didn't like Cowboy Doug and his non-conformist and easy-going approach to flying, particularly in light of *the accident*, just one month ago.

Todd continued announcing checklist items and Doug restlessly responded as they continued to taxi toward Runway One-Nine Left. The tension between them rose as he finally got to "Crew Brief," the last item on the taxi checklist. *The accident* was clearly on Todd's mind. He thought about how the lives of hundreds of people changed forever when fourteen passengers and two pilots never came home last month. His best friend, Scott Bradley, died in the crash.

"O.K. It's my leg. This will be a non-APR takeoff with no reduced-thrust settings due to the wet runway, ninety-eight percent torque, and standard company call-outs on takeoff. What's the RVR now?"

"Still six," replied Todd after glancing at the slip of paper that showed the Runway Visual Range—the runway's actual measured forward visibility—to be only six hundred feet. The weather was barely good enough to takeoff, but they needed three times the visibility that they currently had in order to land back at Dulles. They would have to land at another airport if an emergency arose after they accelerated past the *go—no go* decision speed during the takeoff roll.

"If we have any problem, we'll let ATC vector us to National Airport for the ILS 36, since we can't get back into here. Otherwise, we'll climb out on runway heading to four thousand, then as filed. Questions?"

"Huh, maybe he'll straighten up his act," thought Todd. "No questions, taxi checklist complete."

"Wouldn't wanna drive home in this crap. Didja ever lose sight of the road while driving in weather like this? Kinda spooks ya. Ya just kinda keep driving in the same direction, hopin' nothin' pops up in front of ya...."

By now, Todd was ignoring Doug's prattle. He strained to see ahead, yet his mind kept wandering back to *the accident*. *"Bullshitting, just like this,"* thought Todd as he recalled listening a couple of weeks ago to the cockpit voice recorder's version of what it must be like to die in a plane crash.

After receiving their clearance from the tower to take off, Doug lined the aircraft up on the runway centerline using the ground steering lever with his left hand as Todd announced the last items on the Takeoff Checklist. Long gone were the thoughts of those passengers seated behind them. They were alone up front. Todd pushed the speed levers forward to the "flight" position as the Captain also pushed the throttle levers, resulting in a doubling of the noise and vibration. The aircraft was crying to have its brakes released, and the cockpit became filled with adrenaline. "Lights...On, Speeds...High, Caution Panel...Clear, Takeoff Check...Complete," announced Todd. Doug released his feet from the top of the rudder pedals, which released the brakes and allowed the aircraft to lunge forward into the darkness ahead. He could see the runway edge lights out of the corner of his eye, but divided his attention primarily between the aircraft flight instruments and the centerline lights. These lights appeared a couple hundred feet ahead and accelerated before disappearing underneath the airplane. Faster. Faster.

"Power set," called Todd as the engine gauges indicated the target torque setting for this takeoff. "Seventy knots," said Todd anxiously after he noticed Doug had already lifted his left hand from the ground steering lever to the control yoke just moments before and a few knots earlier than the required seventy knot call-out. The airplane, however, was going fast enough now for steering with only the rudder pedals. *"Cocky Sonofabitch,"* Todd thought of Doug's I-can-do-it-without-you attitude. The airplane continued its acceleration down the gloomy centerline. The airspeed indicator hit one hundred twelve knots, which resulted in Todd's call: "Vee one, rotate." V_1, the *go—no go* speed, had passed. They were going to fly, no matter what.

At V_1, Todd instinctively placed his left hand on the power lever, replacing Doug's right hand that had now joined the other on his yoke.

Doug pulled both hands back on the yoke; the aircraft rotated up about seven degrees, became airborne, and instantly disappeared into the clouds.

"Positive rate," called Todd as he noted the rate-of-climb indicator now showing a climb.

"Gear Up," called Doug as Todd took his left hand off the power levers and pulled the landing gear lever out and forward.

Suddenly, a loud bang was heard as two bright red lights began flashing on the glareshield panel. This was immediately followed by a sudden and severe yawing of the aircraft to the right and a loud fire bell coming from under the Copilot's seat. The yawing hurled the two pilots to the left from the centrifugal force of the aircraft instantly rotating horizontally to the right about thirty degrees.

"Gawd dammit!" Doug cried as he desperately jammed the left rudder pedal forward in an effort to maintain control of the aircraft.

Tom Sylvester

"I have a fire on the right engine. Confirm!" Todd shouted as he scoured the engine gauges.

Doug, with his eyes glued to the flight instruments, said, "Uhhhhh, confirmed.....shut down right engine!" He immediately knew which one had failed by the old pilot adage, "Dead leg, dead engine." He was pushing hard with his left leg to counteract the now unbalanced power from the two engines. His right leg was not exerting any pressure; i.e., it was "dead." Thus, he already knew it was the right engine that failed. Besides, he was low, slow, on one engine, and wasn't about to move his eyes over to the engine gauges to confirm what he already knew.

"RIGHT POWER LEVER—IDLE, CONFIRM!" Todd barked out the commands, and awaited Doug's confirmation before he pulled back the lever. His initial disbelief was now dissipating, yet his adrenaline continued to rise.

With a very quick glance at Todd's hand on the right power lever, Doug replied. "Confirmed—and how 'bout chillin' out a little." Doug's response had a noticeable change of tone in his voice as he stabilized the aircraft.

"Right Feather Lever, Turn and Pull—confirm!" again cried Todd.

"Cuuunnn-FIRMED," said Doug sarcastically in an exaggerated game show announcer voice. His eyes remained glued to the flight instruments, but he was now in full control of the wounded aircraft and had established a burdened climb on the remaining engine.

Suddenly, the gauges froze and the cockpit was instantly quiet. They both assumed a relaxed frown as a light in the rear of the simulator came on.

THE SIMULATOR INSTRUCTOR rotated his seat away from the computer screens that controlled the simulated emergencies and said, "Come on Doug, cut the bullshit." The instructor, who also happened to be the manager of training for Bands Airways, was seated behind Todd. But Todd couldn't see him because of a partition of circuit breakers directly behind his seat. Doug could see the instructor, but he chose not to.

The instructor continued, "I can't sign you off to fly again until you start abiding by our Flight Standards Manual's sterile cockpit rule. No talking AT ALL, except for stating the memory items for the Engine Failure on Takeoff emergency. You know the feds aren't gonna let up until we prove we're a safe operation."

Doug looked straight ahead and said, "Hey, I don't know why I should have to spend my day off in this vomit box when I wasn't anywhere near *the accident*!" He then slowly and disrespectfully turned his head to the right and awaited a response to his rhetoric.

"I know you can get out from under a vee-one cut or any other emergency that I throw at you, and you both will get signed off. But take the sim a little more seriously—heh!? O.K.!?"

Doug listened because he had to.

"Out of the two hundred and eighty pilots on payroll here, a few of you cowboys just don't seem to get it. Since *the accident*, the feds are looking for any reason to shut us down. Don't risk the whole company's future by being unprofessional."

Todd's chest was still pounding as the cool air entered through the opening simulator door. He, like most pilots, always treated the simulator as though it were real. The next pair were waiting to begin. Todd's armpits and lower backside displayed the evidence of his workout. He wasn't listening to the simulator instructor's sermon to Doug. His mind was on *the accident* as he got up from the Copilot's seat and readied the cockpit for the next victims. *"It just didn't make sense. They were better pilots than that,"* he reflected.

Sixteen people, including Captain Bill Payne and Scott Bradley, Todd's closest friend since he started flying for Bands...gone. It had been a month, yet he just couldn't shake the grief he felt. He glanced at his watch, which read 12:15 a.m., early Sunday morning. They were already eating into the 12:00 a.m. to 4:00 a.m. simulator session. He thought, *"I wonder if K.W. is waiting up?"*

Tom Sylvester

He walked out of the door in the back of the now stationary simulator, said hello to the next crew, whom he didn't recognize. He had been with Bands for only seven months. Except for Doug and the instructor, the next victims, and a technician behind the glass window in the computer room facing the floor of the simulator room, the facility was vacant. He walked across the metal drawbridge to the walkway that extended to a metal door that separates the gymnasium-sized, HALON fire-protected simulator room from the adjacent classrooms and offices. He walked down the empty classroom hallway, then through another metal door, around a corner, then with a *tank-tank-tank* sound of his topsiders touching the black metal stairs he went down to the first floor of the sim facility. He walked past the fifteen instructors' office cubicles that separated the classrooms from the common vending area.

Todd placed his flight case on top of one of the dinette tables, then took two more steps to the RC Cola machine. He managed a sentimental smile as he searched for the place to insert his crisp, perfect dollar bill. His smile then faded in close cadence with his dropping forehead as he side-stepped to the adjacent Coke machine, which welcomed his paper money. It was so late and quiet now that the sound of the can clanking its way out of the machine somewhat annoyed him. He quietly sat down, as he always does after a flight and organized his flight case. He replaced the approach charts and maps that he had used in the simulator to their respective binders.

After rubbing his eyes, he then annotated the company duty and flight time form, and made notes in his agenda about the number and type of approaches he had accomplished for translation later into the logbook he always kept at home.

"Cheated death again...," snapped Doug as he caught Todd by surprise and then continued to the glass entrance doors, where he slapped the red button, releasing the magnetic door locks to the secure facility. Doug had walked down to the floor of the simulator room, where the technician had printed profiles of the approaches they had just survived, then walked along the bottom hallway, thus bypassing the noisy metal stairway.

"See ya," he said as he pushed on the door and walked out.

"Later," said Todd. He was polite, in spite of his feelings about the lax Captain. All was quiet again, except for the effervescence resonating from inside the Coke can. After about a minute he finished his paperwork, looked at his watch, then hurriedly gathered his case and the walked out into the quiet, sticky, mercury-vapor illuminated parking lot to his car. Doug had already disappeared.

• • • •

About a half hour after Todd Grant pulled out of Darchoult's Javelin Simulator Facility about two miles north of Dulles Airport, Chris

Thomas was slowly pulling her wheeled luggage bag and flight case to her car in the east employee parking lot at the airport. Her white pilot shirt, wrinkled from her thirteen hour day that began just after lunch on Friday, remained nonetheless neatly tucked. The late summer heat takes its toll on the Bands pilots. The ramp area was a hundred and two degrees at 4:00 p.m., with no wind to even stir up the heat. The temperature inside the aircraft is usually cool when the freon unit in the rear of the aircraft is on. However, because it uses so much electricity, either the engines must be running or a ground power unit must be connected to the aircraft for it to be operable.

As a hub server, the commuter airline's aircraft would go off to the smaller cities such as Charlottesville, Scranton, or Salisbury and pick up people who would then catch the big jets at Dulles to far away places. After landing and once the passengers disembark, the Javelin aircraft is without air conditioning for about twenty minutes, since a ground power unit is not allowed to be hooked up to the aircraft while the aircraft is being refueled. Meanwhile, pilots had to remain in the aircraft in order to pick up the newspapers, coffee cups, and other trash in addition to obtaining their next flight's clearance, and setting up their navigation equipment for the next flight. Even with the front windows and rear door open, it was a sauna in just a few minutes. Multiply the event by five times a day, and the resultant "body annealing" takes its toll.

Now that it was well after midnight, the temperature had dropped to a musty seventy-six degrees and dew had appeared on all of the cars in the lot.

Chris's dark blonde hair, although brushed, was dirty and oily now. She didn't bother to put any makeup on for the short walk through the terminal. She finally felt better, though, since she had finally been able to wash the sweaty grit of a hot day's flying from her face and arms.

Although tired, she was awake enough to notice a hand print on the front hood of her car hood when she arrived. Did someone steal her battery?

She quickly threw her flight bag into the back seat, hopped in and put the key in the ignition, expecting silence.

It started.

"Whew," she muttered to herself as she backed out of the "Outer Mongolia" gravel parking lot and pulled out onto the service road. Across the street and beyond the tall chain-link fence was a large German C-130 military cargo plane that gleamed from the street lights and ruled the general aviation ramp where the small Cessnas and Pipers were neatly arranged.

She took the first exit off the deserted Dulles Access Road and then took Route 28 South towards Centreville. Several large companies had built impressive new buildings along the left side of the road, their logos showing their proper place in prosperous Fairfax and Loudoun

Counties near Dulles. Soon, the road became darker as farms and intermittent housing developments replaced the larger buildings. After going about a mile and a half, a bright red light on her dash startled her: **OIL.**

"Damn," she said loudly, with her eyes now focusing on the engine temperature gauge. Maybe she could make it to the corner about two miles ahead. No chance. The temperature needle was moving steadily to the red line on the gauge. She turned the car off, then slowly pulled over to the shoulder as the car decelerated.

When the car stopped, the noise did also. All noise. She sat in silence for a minute, considering her options. She turned on her flashers, which illuminated a pulsing orange on the trees on both sides of the narrow road and the backside of a "Speed Limit 45" sign about a hundred yards behind her. She opened the door—this action set off a rhythmic chime, just out of phase with the flashers, indicating that she had left her keys in the ignition. She removed the keys, which silenced all but the faint *tunk-et, tunk-et, tunk-et* sound of the flashers.

After about a minute, car lights from behind began to highlight a heavy row of pine trees on the other side of the road. Suddenly, the dark wooded road became blindingly bright as the car came around the corner and the driver hit his high beams. She squinted into the headlights and motioned with her palm down to knock it off, but the bright lights persisted as the car slowed, then quickly stopped about twenty feet behind her car. Dust from under the front wheels rose up into the car's bright lights.

The door opened and she heard the loud music of a country-western radio station escape and echo off the nearby tree line. His silhouette emerged alone from the driver's seat.

She walked toward his car to escape from his blinding high beams. Right as she was about to explain her predicament, she felt a terrible blow to the left side of her face and a flash of light that knocked her to the pavement. He sucker-punched her! She let out a painful grunt as she tried to gather herself. Dizzy and dazed, she tried to flee, but her arm missed the pavement as she tried to get up and she went down again, this time into the pea gravel and bits of broken asphalt that lined the road's shoulder. As she started to let out a scream, his boot caught her just under her cheek bone and sent her head back—her limp body following—to the pavement.

The man picked her up, dragged her to her car, then propped her across her open door. He quickly ran to his car, backed it up about forty yards, then accelerated into her. Concurrent sounds of a muffled thump, breaking glass, and tearing metal pierced the woods. She and her car door hurled together along the side of the road. Her forward motion soon stopped, but the door continued to bounce wildly and disappeared into the trees.

He never slowed down.

THREE

TODD arrived home at Severna Park, just north of Annapolis, at about 2:00 a.m. He made good time, even with the pit-stop at his favorite all-night doughnut shop for some chocolate cake doughnuts to keep him awake for the hour-long commute. Kelly, his wife of two years, was asleep on the sofa. She had obviously tried to wait up for him. She was beautiful by all definitions and standards. Some of her short black hair, stylishly cut straight back, lay forward and covered her perfect and fair complexion. Her vividly blue eyes were to remain hidden from view until morning. She wore an extra long T-shirt that said "Kiawah Island" and a had a picture of an alligator in front of a lazy sunset, all in pastels.

Instead of waking her, he grabbed the remote from on top of the kitchen counter. He turned down the volume of the TV, then turned it off. He then turned off the light and quietly crept into the apartment's only bedroom.

He closed the door to the bedroom in slow motion. The only light that was on was the lamp on her makeup table. He took off his shirt and pants and went into the bathroom to brush his teeth and wash his face. His athletic body was moving slowly from the day that started twenty-one hours ago. He was to have the day off, but the company called and demanded that he fill-in for a simulator cancellation. Thus, they wouldn't lose any precious time getting all of their pilots requalified as a result of the FAA's Action Order following *the accident*. Moments later, he emerged from the bathroom, turned off the light without a sound, then sat quietly on a wooden stool at her makeup table. He looked at himself without emotion for a few slow seconds, then removed a picture from the corner of the mirror. The picture brought back memories of how things were just a couple of months ago....

... "Bogie in the no-fly zone," shouted Todd to Scott Bradley as a sparrow passed high over them. Suddenly, from out of the sun, their radio-controlled airplanes screamed down on the unsuspecting bird. The heightening shrills of the chain saw-sounding engines added to the drama. Their ground-based tactics obviously gave the airborne advantage to the bird, but they had fun trying to engage the "enemy," nonetheless. The bird gracefully turned away as models awkwardly looped and dived in an attempt to bring down the intruder. Once the bird had successfully evaded, they both turned their aircraft back south toward Bay Bridge Airport.

Tom Sylvester

The airport was about the best place to fly model airplanes, since it had closed two months prior to most flights. A Piper Warrior lost engine power on final approach, landed short and rolled into the side of the house of an elderly woman. The newspaper reported that it had upset her. An attorney and member of the Citizens Against Bay Bridge Airport, or CABBA, filed a restraining order prohibiting flights over her house until she got over her "trauma." A district judge from the eastern shore mandated that the only takeoffs and departures had to be to the West, over the Chesapeake Bay and away from the woman's home.

The FAA said that the *one way in—one way out* operation wouldn't cut it from a collision safety standpoint, so the only flights allowed would be departures of existing aircraft based at the field, which is exactly what the CABBA people wanted.

The local pilots were wise to their plan and most chose to leave their aircraft there, rather than abandon the airport. The ensuing waiting game allowed a nice smooth runway available to the model airplane flyers. A handful of them stationed themselves about midway down the 2,800 foot asphalt runway. Four cars parked on the parallel taxiway, about sixty feet from the runway. All had their trunks or rear cabs up. Three people sat on lawn chairs, two observing the flights and one reading a thick novel. The one with the novel was an attractive young blonde woman, wearing Ray Bans to cut the glare from the noon-time sun.

"Does she have the stats?" Todd asked Scott as they both looked skyward towards their respective aircraft.

"Yes, she's been briefed. Do you think it's time to test her?"

"I was disappointed in the last one, you know. She said I was from *Vanilla*, Arkansas."

Scott never dated anyone for any extended length of time. Dating to him was nothing more than a game. He always ended any involvement before things got too serious. His true love was flying. However, the facets of dating involving the chase and the conquest were important and desirable, because they offered pure and personal competition.

One of his tactics in the game was to make his date feel privileged to receive an invitation to functions with his inner circle of friends. He insisted that she know all there is to know about them. He gave her the *Mary Poppins* treatment, without regard to whether she really needed it or not. He made her strive to look good when she was with him. Though, in many cases, he should have been the understudy. So, prior to meeting Todd, she was expected to know Todd's wife's name, where they grew up, his interests, and an obscure item of trivia, which was always a surprise to Todd. Scott went to great lengths to get the lowdown on his best friend, Todd. He started calling Todd's mother in Manila, Arkansas to find out embarrassing tidbits. After she ran out of ideas, she referred Scott to some of Todd's high school and college buddies. This trivia became an inside joke between Scott and Todd. Scott's *date d'jour* was simply the medium.

The last woman that Scott introduced to Todd asked him how he got his clothes back after he and his high school sweetheart dashed from the city pool when the police followed up on a report of some midnight swimmers. Even Kelly didn't know about that one.

Scott's dating practices were always initially successful, but dating to him was just a way to pass the time until he could go flying again.

Scott was O.K. He had a knack for making anything or any event enjoyable. Todd was already eager to test the new blonde for the bonus trivia.

"Emergency Descent!" Scott shouted as the whine of the two engines overhead became a single whine. He had run out of gas and was going to make another ceremonious dead-stick landing.

"OXYGEN MASKS—DON.

MICROPHONE SWITCH—SELECT MASK.

GLIDE—ESTABLISH.

SPEED LEVERS—HIGH.

GLIDE AT ONE HUNDRED THIRTY KNOTS.

REFER TO ENGINE AIR RESTART PROCEDURE," shouted Scott as he simulated the emergency decent checklist from the Javelin aircraft for this most captivating event.

"I shall alert the media...," announced Todd as he continued to grasp the transmitter box with both hands and look skyward toward his own airplane.

"She won't restart! I'll have to masterfully land her on this small, quaint airport below! I'm so glad I'm my pilot today."

"It's gotta stop right here," announced Todd as he pointed with his left foot to the asphalt directly in front of them. He was still looking up at his own aircraft while Scott's slowly and quietly descended toward the airport.

"Stewardess, please dab my sweating forehead, for I am now to save the lives of literally *none*dreds..."

The model suddenly dove, then pulled up into a gentle barrel roll and lined up on the runway's final approach course. The maneuver brought a harmonious sound from the now ten or so onlookers: "Woooo!"

"Whah ja do?" Todd asked as he continued to focus on his own airplane.

"Abbu Nidal was trying to hijack me, so I skillfully rolled him into the ceiling, breaking his neck, before turning final. How *do* I *do* it?!" The model airplane then touched down on the centerline of the runway, but stopped short of the intended point, obviously because of the last minute "anti-hijack" maneuver.

The loud cheer from the small crowd occurred at the same time that Todd's aircraft also ran dry. Scott turned and curtsied, then walked over to his plane.

"Emergency Descent!" Todd announced with the same enthusiasm as Scott had before him. As Scott turned off his radio transmitter, he joined Todd, chanting:

"OXYGEN MASKS—DON.
MICROPHONE SWITCH—SELECT MASK.
GLIDE—ESTABLISH.
SPEED LEVERS—HIGH.
GLIDE AT ONE HUNDRED THIRTY KNOTS.
REFER TO ENGINE AIR RESTART PROCEDURE."

Todd raised the nose and allowed the aircraft to stall, then enter a spin. "She's Breaking Up. She's Breaking Up...." Todd cried.

"Who's the pilot? A brave soul, I pray," queried Scott.

"Why its, yes its, Todd Grant, a man barely alive." Todd said.

"We can rebuild him," Scott continued, now standing close to Todd and also looking up.

"Too doo doo doo doo. Too doo doo doo doo..." Together they produced a stereo *Six Million Dollar Man* sound effect. Todd recovered from the spin, flew overhead in a tight turn, touched down on the centerline, then rolled the airplane right up to their feet.

"Yo' mama!" Todd said as he accepted a high five from Scott.

"That was great!" A female voice spoke from behind them. *"The blonde speaks,"* Todd thought to himself.

"I'm Bambi. You must be Todd. Scott's told me all about you," she said as she extended her hand.

"Bambi?" Todd thought to himself as he glanced at Scott then back to her. *"Could this be Scott's first beautician?"*

He decided to preempt an embarrassing situation ahead and try to guess what trite trivia Scott passed along to her: "I didn't do it-I swear! Anyway, I *thought* she was a mannequin. The store manager believed me..." Todd said, glancing at Scott for a reaction.

"Nope, that's not it, Todd," Scott said as he and Bambi smiled at each other. The three then began walking back to their cars. Scott gave a military salute to a boy who, with his dad, was heading to the runway with their own model airplane, ready to fly.

"What's Kelly up to today?" Bambi asked, saving the trivia bonus for later. She was obviously both lucid and well briefed.

"She's back home studying. She'll be starting law school once I upgrade to Captain."

"You know, Bambi just completed her first year of law school at George Mason," Scott said.

"How 'bout that!" Todd said to Bambi while indicating approval to Scott. Todd was relieved to know that Scott had not broken his streak of medical students, lawyers, and MBA types that usually showed up with him.

"Let me show you what I have here..." Scott said to Todd, turning away to another model airplane.

"Excuse me..." Todd said as he smiled and rolled his eyes to Bambi. She gave him a mirrored smile, acknowledging his wordless communication of Scott's obsession with airplanes. She turned, went back to her lawn chair and continued with her novel.

"Bambi?!" Todd said to Scott, now out of her earshot. "You know, Bambi was a *boy* deer!"

"That must be why whenever I see those scanty shorts on her I think *Oh Boy*!"

Scott then changed the subject to something more interesting to him. "Look at this. I put an *Instamatic* camera in the bottom of this Tri-Pacer." Scott lifted the model and turned it upside down, showing a hole in the bottom of the fuselage. "I connected the fifth channel to a servo which presses on the camera button. Wanna smile for the camera?"

"Have you any way to advance the film in flight?" Todd poked, already knowing that the answer was no.

"I always get the picture the first time." They headed out to the runway to join up with the father-son team who were already airborne.

"Let me take the first picture," Todd insisted.

"Here 'yar," said Scott, kindly mocking Todd's faint southern accent as he handed the transmitter to him. "Just flip this down to take the shot," he said, pointing to a plastic tab on the front of the transmitter.

"Dad!" the boy yelled, who was standing a couple of feet to their left. Scott instinctively dove for the boy, grabbed the transmitter from him, and jammed the control stick to full forward and left. The airplane, which had reverted into a steep, inverted spiral, went down behind a small building next to a harbor on the other side of the airport. Suddenly, it emerged and ascended, inverted, back up to a safe altitude. Scott rolled it upright, then turned it back toward the airport. The boy's father had been eyeing Bambi instead of his son's flying.

The boy and his dad thanked Scott as Todd, accustomed to Scott's flying talent, brought the camera plane into the air. After a couple of overhead practice runs, he took a picture of two good friends, waving skyward...

...Kelly entered the bedroom and saw Todd staring at the bird's eye picture of him and Scott. Todd's eyes were glassy and tired. "Are you back on line, R.C.?" she asked softly, knowing it wasn't what he wanted to talk about.

He looked her way and said, "Sorry if I woke you, K.W."

Tom Sylvester

K.W. stood for "Kelly-Wo!" The first time he saw her, she was walking through Indian Mall in Jonesboro, Arkansas when they were both in their second year at Arkansas State University. He was waiting in the food court for a 1:30 p.m. Saturday show at the theater. She was carrying two large store bags and wearing an outfit that melted everyone's Orange Julius.

He had to meet her. So he walked up to her, holding his half eaten nachos and diet Coke, and said, "Mary?! Gawd, you just keep getting more beautiful."

She, of course, was not fooled by his lame approach and gave him an *I know what you're up to* smile.

"Oh, gee. You're not Mary, now are you," he said in a feeble attempt to recover.

She quickly said "No. Now quickly, what's Mary's last name?" She then paused, allowing him to become even more uncomfortable.

"Uh, Hadda. Mary Hadda" Todd grimaced and shook his head slightly as he realized what he said.

"As in Hadda Little Lamb?"

"You idiot. Come on Todd, think," he thought to himself, then said, "Uh, no, not Hadda, I meant to say Hatfield."

She was enjoying every bumble. "My name is Kelly."

He looked hard at her and said, "Kelly." Then after a long pause, he shook his head slightly and said "...wo!" Her beauty had first stolen his quick wit. Now, he couldn't seem to speak at all. Still in catch-up mode, he continued. "Kelly-Wo. Interesting name. How 'bout if I just call you K.W. for short." After another obvious delay, he managed: "Uh, my name's Todd." There they stood, motionless, facing and admiring each other among the busy mall traffic.

She said "Yep. Real cute there Todd, *if that's your real name*. Actually you are *Really Cute*. Real Cute. How 'bout if I just call you R.C.?"

He smiled. Finally, he mustered: "I guess the *You-Look-Just-Like-Mary* skit wasn't very effective." He then waited for a response.

She said, "It appears that you are not a very good liar." Then she watched him squirm for more conversation.

He said, "So. K.W. How about an *instadate*. Movie starts in ten. *Terminator Two*. I already have a ticket for you right here. 'Course, I'll have to get one for myself."

She said, "Get one more for *tee two* in ten—A.S.A.P., R.C., O.K.?"

Her response coupled with her beautiful smile stunned him. He found himself just staring at her in amazement. Then it sank in that she had accepted his offer. Still shell-shocked from her beauty, he managed: "Great, K.W. Hold this—be right back."

She had to quickly put down her bags to receive his nachos and diet coke. He excitedly bolted for the ticket booth. She stood there for a moment, smiling at his thoughtlessness. Then she pushed her shopping bags with her foot to a nearby table on the edge of the food court, sat down and looked at his nachos. She then smiled, ate his nachos and drank his coke.

The resulting "K.W." and "R.C." were never used in public. It became their own affectionate nicknames.

Kelly spoke softly, "Sorry I couldn't stay awake. I got a call from College Park earlier today. They've agreed to let me start in December, but it's the last delay they'll allow. Susan talked 'em into the delay. She actually talked to the Dean of the School of Law...." She sensed that he was depressed again. "How's the upgrade looking?"

Todd stared at the picture, then quietly said, "Looks like I'll be a Copilot for a while longer. They've frozen all pilot upgrades until everyone gets back flying. Now that I'm back on line, the folks in crew scheduling will build me a schedule starting on Monday. They said to expect to take Sunday off. Nice of them, eh, seein' as how its, uh, almost three a.m."

Todd slowly leaned forward in the small chair to replace the picture on the edge of the vanity's glass. Kelly glided closely behind him and pulled off her T-shirt. He noticed her naked body in the mirror, but didn't immediately react. She looked down and smiled when she noticed his rear tan line, positioned well above his low riding underwear. Though he hadn't been shirtless since before *the accident*, the evidence of a previously active outdoor lifestyle persisted.

Dropping her shirt onto the carpet, she softly began rubbing his shoulders. He was quite tense, but welcomed her warm massage as he settled slightly in the chair. He closed his eyes when her hands moved down his chest, stopping there to pull him gently back into her bare breasts. Her hands then moved slowly down his flat stomach and beneath his jockey shorts. She kissed his neck softly as she held him with both hands. He turned around and kissed her lovingly.

Minutes later, they moved over to the bed and made love—slowly, softly, tenderly—in consonance with the tone of the evening.

She fell asleep in his arms. In the darkened stillness, a tear rolled down Todd's face and onto the pillow.

FOUR

THE BRILLIANT SUNSHINE of late Sunday morning was too much for Todd's eyes. He held his hand over them as he drifted barefoot to the sidewalk and slowly lifted the *Washington Post* from the cracked concrete. He wasn't sure exactly what time it was, but knew that if the dew was gone from the paper's plastic wrapping, yet the concrete was still wet beneath it, that it must be fairly late in the morning.

"You fly for TransGlobe, is it?" Ted Behlman asked, sending sound waves bouncing off all the surrounding gray brick walls. Ted was an older, single man who lived just adjacent to Todd's in the South River Apartments in the small community just north of Annapolis.

"Yea, Ted. Whassup?" Todd replied.

"Big stink about *the accident* in the *Post*."

Todd immediately ripped the plastic from around the newspaper, allowing it to unravel. There it was—the all too familiar photo of the tail of the airplane, floating upright in the ditch with no sign of the rest of the aircraft.

That particular photo had been used as a logo for the accident. A woman, who turned out to be the wife of a local tobacco farmer, saw the tail section flutter down and believed it to be a Cessna or some other small plane crashing. She got to the wreckage just before Randy Baldwin arrived. Baldwin, a small-time freelancer, also spotted the falling debris as he was driving toward Charlottesville for a State Senator's meeting. He didn't realize it at the time, but the picture he was about to take was going to change his life. The photo would make the cover of both *Time* and *Newsweek* and go on to win many awards. The wife reached the wreckage first and realized that it wasn't an entire airplane, but merely the tail section of a larger one. Baldwin stopped his car on the side of the road, about three hundred yards from the wreckage. He whipped out his camera, snapped a telephoto lens on it and took a clear, but long-ranged picture of the panic-stricken woman crying next to the TransGlobe logo on the aircraft's vertical stabilizer. Great photo. Lots of emotion on the woman's face.

The accident set into motion a flurry of articles and news reports about the relative safety of small commuter aircraft and the competence of their crewmembers. For three straight days, it was the lead story on all three networks. It made the news every night for a week on the local Washington stations. Some of the victim's relatives had filed huge lawsuits even before all of the bodies were removed from the wreckage. This set into motion substories about tort reform and liability limits. One article was titled: "Don't Play Lotto—Just Have

Mom Die in a Commuter Crash." The public was eager for more information and the media needed to fill space in an otherwise slow week of news. The interviews with witnesses, the expert commentary and analysis, the investigative reports. *The accident* turned out to be a sensational hit for the media.

The heading above the picture in today's *Post*, which covered the bottom half of the front page, read "NTSB Blames Poor Pilot Judgment for Crash." His heart sank. Without a word he walked back into the apartment. Ted wasn't offended. He understood.

"'Morning, R.C. Would you like some..." Kelly began.

Todd held up a finger, paused, then said, "Looks like the NTSB's *prelim* says that Scott flew it into a thunderstorm on climbout. Just broke up. Uh. They, uh, can't point to really bad weather where he was, but it apparently was bad enough to break it up in flight."

"Poor Scott. I'm just glad he's not here to witness the lynching of his character."

"I wish I could talk to him—ask him what happened. The CVR, er uh, the Cockpit Voice Recorder indicated six successive beeps on the stall warning horn before it broke apart," he restated from the article. He looked up directly at her. "Must have been pretty bad up and down drafts to cause that." He then looked down again.

"Also says the Bands stock price has gone all the way down to six and a quarter," he continued. "I don't know how they're gonna come out of this. Maybe we should just pack up and move back to Manila. I've got enough turboprop time now for the majors to take an interest in me. Better to be looked at as an *em*ployed crop duster than an unemployed commuter pilot."

"Are you quite finished with your daily sob therapy routine?" she announced. "Look, just deal with it. Big Lake Aero will always be there for you. I'm getting used to Washington and actually kinda like it here. Once I get started again in school we'll both be back on track. I've waited for a year and a half for you to start actually earning a living as a pilot. So quit it with the *I'm-giving-up-and-going-home* attitude. You're too close to getting hired by the majors to give up now."

"I jist wanna..."

"You just want to feel sorry for yourself. That kind of talk is just counterproductive. I know what you are going through. "What do you think Scott would say to you?"

"I know what he'd say," said Todd with a noticeable change in tone. "He'd say, 'Hey, Todd, you just moved up one notch on the *best pilot* list.'"

"He *was* good, wasn't he."

"Almost as good as his best friend. Hey, when was the last time you grabbed the lawn chair and went with me to Bay Bridge Airport?"

"Sounds great. You make the sandwiches, *Chef Boy R.C.,* and I'll get the sunblock, boombox, and the laptop."

"What do you need the computer for?"

"I want to run some numbers on our budget, now that you are going to be a Copilot for a while longer."

"Gee. It's Sunday, K.W. Take the day off," said Todd as he headed for the kitchen. He opened the pantry right as the phone rang.

"Yea, you're right," she said, as she approached the small computer on the bookcase opposite the entranceway into the kitchen. Instead of grabbing the computer, she instead grabbed a legal textbook and stuffed it into her beach bag.

"Hello," said Todd, answering the phone after the third ring. After a couple of seconds he grabbed his agenda. "Yea," he said as he flipped it open. "Sure am."

He grabbed a pencil and started marking on the pad next to the Rolodex file on the countertop. Todd always was neat and precise. He would never scribble directly into his agenda-he'd translate it later once all the information was given to him.

"Fifty-five-oh-four, with a two-thirty show time, got it."

Kelly looked at him and stopped what she was doing.

"All right. Later, John," he said, then hung up the telephone and glanced over at her without emotion. Finally, he said, "Two-thirty show time *tomorrow* for a two day trip. Today is ours."

"Great. Let's have some fun. Toy airplanes for you. Sunshine for me. Then, maybe a nice, late afternoon dinner at Charlene's Crab Bar overlooking the bay."

A SLIGHT MAN IN HIS MID TWENTIES was sitting alone in a squeaky chair on rollers. The wooden-floored room was small and stale, littered with electronic equipment, fast-food Styrofoam containers, and dirty clothes. Two old wooden tables with film developing equipment and a couple of cameras on them were in the far corner of the room. Nearby lay a three-inch thick pile of black and white photos, loosely stacked with post-it notes attached to some. He ran his left hand through his uncombed brown hair as he as adjusted a knob on a voltmeter with his other. Both hands then moved up and down his face as he pondered whether the contraption was ready for testing.

He aimed the desk lamp at a small plastic toy penguin for a last minute inspection. The legs were missing. However, the wings that circled on each side of the bird when the metal twist knob in the back was pushed in were still there. The legless penguin was glued to a one-inch square piece of balsa wood. Surrounding the penguin was a small but wide, blue rubber band, underneath the wings and around the back of the black and white bird. Bracing up the rubber band was a tiny piece of balsa. This balsa brace kept the rubber band from collapsing the twist knob into the toy bird, which would start the rotation of its tiny wings. A white filament wire touched the balsa brace. One end of the filament connected to a five volt power supply, which would not be the power source used when the gizmo is installed in the aircraft. The other end of the filament was not yet connected to the power supply box.

One of the wings had a thin wire attached to its end. An aluminum foil-covered balsa block, glued along the balsa base and aligned with the path of the circulating wing, was in place. Test leads from the voltmeter connected to both the foil and the wire on the wing.

He took a deep breath, then touched the wire from the filament to the power supply box. A bright white fire instantly snapped the thin balsa wood brace, collapsing the rubber band onto the twist knob and forcing it into the back of the bird. The wings went into motion, with the right one contacting the foil which was connected to the voltmeter. The needle on the voltmeter alternately swung from zero to five volts.

The man smiled, then pushed his chair back from the table, swung it around to another table where a large, white three-ringed binder lay. The cover showed a picture of the Darchoult Javelin, the commuter airplane that Bands Airways flew. The inscription across the top read:

"Darchoult Aeroplane Company." Just below the picture were several lines:

Maintenance Manual - Electrics
Book 2 of 5
Lighting, General
Stall Annunciation, Stick Shaker/Stick Pusher
Fuel Controls, Engine Computer
Station 110 Panel

Along the bottom was the airplane manufacturer's Munich address, telephone, fax, and Telex numbers. He opened it to the section entitled: Signal Summing Device (SSD), Stick Shaker/Stick Pusher. He unfolded the electrical schematic, revealing the voltage drops across various poles. Motionless, he studied the page for about two minutes, then flipped back to the installation diagrams in the back of the manual.

The aircraft's navigation and communication electronics were in the nose section of the aircraft, which is forward of the cockpit panel. The rest of the aircraft's electronic monitoring and control systems are either inside the pedestal between the pilots or inside the divider panel between the pilots and the passengers.

Every place on any aircraft is defined by its position in inches from the front of the airplane. This is done so every installed component on the aircraft can be precisely computed into the total weight and balance values for the complete aircraft. The divider panel where the SSD was located was one hundred and ten inches from the front of the aircraft. Thus it was called Station 110. Just as *Q-Tips* are seldom called cotton swabs, Station 110 was never referred to as the divider panel. It was *Station 110.*

He knew from his systems training in the aircraft that the SSD was located close to the boost pump relay on Station 110. Measuring the scaled distance, he determined how long the thin wires must be in order to connect the toy penguin to the SSD and the boost pump leads. He should have taken notes the last time he made them.

• • • •

Todd stared straight ahead. Though he wore his Ray Bans, Kelly could still notice his troubled squint from her vantage point in the passenger seat.

"You tell me, K.W., how he can fly into a cloud—not a thunderstorm—just a cumuliform cloud, obviously going slow because he was in a climb, and have the aircraft break apart in flight. I've seen the development test films on that aircraft. It's built like an M-1 tank. To climb into a cumulous cloud at a hundred and sixty knots would be about as risky as hurling feathers at a shot put. Sumpin' jist ain't right."

Kelly turned away and gazed out the passenger window of his car as they drove along Route 50 through Annapolis. After a noticeable pause, she slowly rotated back, crossed her legs, and looked straight at him. After a couple more long seconds, she said, in an *I'm-going-to-change-the-subject* tone, "What did you make us for lunch?"

"Sorry, K.W. I just can't let it go."

"You're gonna get ulcers before you're twenty-five."

"You know, the only thing important to him in his whole existence on this planet was that he be thought of as a great pilot. You and I know that he lived and breathed airplanes, and we both know that he was almost as good as *me*, but we're now in the minority. He's been editorialized as an undertrained, overworked, and inexperienced aviator. I just can't take that. I'd write the *Post* to counter them, but it would be my word against the NTSB's expert testimony. Who would you believe?"

"You," she responded with a smile.

"You're just saying that because I'm R.C. and you like my cooking."

"Maybe you're right. So what is today's culinary creation?"

"Uh," he glanced into the back seat where the brown grocery bag of lunch items lay, then noticed the doughnut bag from the night before on the floor behind her seat. He thought for a moment, then said "Donking Doughnuts," with his eyebrows raised.

"Dunkin' Doughnuts?!"

"Nope. Here, steer for a second." He reached behind her seat as she frantically reached for the wheel. He pulled out the sole, hard doughnut from the bag. Next, he reached into the brown grocery bag and pulled out a clear sandwich bag with one of the Turkey Pita sandwiches he had made for their lunch and removed the bean sprouts. He placed them atop the doughnut and stated: "I present to you the Don King Doughnut!"

She smiled and punched him in the arm, making Don's "hair" fall off.

"Sure, it's unattractive. But it's well promoted," he continued as they shared a familiar laugh together.

The car arrived at the Bay Bridge toll plaza at the western edge of the Chesapeake Bay. Kelly always enjoyed the ride over the bridge. The weather was perfect, too, with the skies an uncharacteristically deep shade of blue. A cold front passed through at about daybreak, clearing the air of almost all of its humidity. Plus, since it was Sunday, the bridge traffic was heavy in the *other* direction with people returning from the Atlantic beaches. Todd looked at the attendant's name tag and paid the dollar toll. Then he handed her another buck, saying, "Annie, do you think the people behind us could stand a sudden act of kindness?"

She smiled and nodded as he quickly accelerated to gain distance and anonymity.

"Scott got me doing that," he answered rhetorically. "He said he probably pays about ten bucks a year in tolls. So even if he doubles that amount, it won't break him. He said it sends his happyometer to the red line."

"And I bet the people in the car behind him got their needles pegged, too. But remember, you only make nineteen thousand a year, *bud*. And that extra dollar came from *your* discretionary funds. You know what they say, *Lack of* money is the root of all evil!"

After a pause, her smile faded to just a hint as she realized the reason for his copycat kindness. "I miss Scott, too."

"Yea, I gotta clear his name. I owe it to him."

• • • •

The usual crowd of RC modelers grew considerably in many weeks since Todd had last been to Bay Bridge Airport. It simply wasn't the same with Scott gone, but it was still fun—and good therapy. Todd's car pulled up beside the one belonging to the man who's son's airplane was saved by Scott a month and a half ago. As he got out, the man recognized him and said, "Hey. Glad to see you back here. I'm sorry about your friend."

"Thanks. Yea, he was one of the good guys. What's with the crowd?" he asked, changing the subject.

"More and more people are finding out about this place, but it's starting to irritate Jake McFadden. Say, did your friend really fly into a cloudburst? I thought you guys had radar to keep you away from cloudbursts."

"Who's Jake McFadden?" Todd asked, ignoring the rest of his rambling. Todd lifted the trunk of his car and pulled out the fuselage of his Wind Drifter radio-controlled glider. Kelly was already setting up camp close to the action.

"Airport manager. He's pissed because the CABBA people reported to the FAA that an airplane took off over Old Lady Trenton's house last night. That's good news for us, 'cuz that means the airport'll stay shut down longer. He was just over here and said his fuel sales are zero and bills are coming due. Someone took the airport car late yesterday and didn't log it out. He's worried about the airport going broke. He's a mess. He was just over here talking about charging us a fee for using his airport. Hell, it ain't his airport. He should vent his anger in the direction of the CABBA folks, not us!"

"Yea, he's lucky that there's at least some kind of flight operations going on here!" Todd said with a smile.

"As a matter of fact, see that blue and white Cessna gathering dust over there? Tail number is November Echo Sierra Sierra," the man asked.

"Yea."

"That's mine. I'd like to fly it, but I'll be damned if I'm gonna let the CABBA people run me out of here. I'll wait as long as I have to. Hey, once the airport reopens, if you'd like to take it around the patch, just gimme a call. My name's Paul Ness."

Todd looked at the airplane's registration number then smiled: NESS—November Echo Sierra Sierra. "Wow, you don't often see vanity plates on airplanes! Thanks a lot, Paul. My name's Todd Grant. That's my wife, Kelly," he said pointing in her direction after shaking hands with the man. "I bet it's been a year since I've flown a light single engine plane!"

Todd smiled as the man walked off. Todd turned and took out his Hi-Start, the rubber slingshot device he uses for launching his glider. He walked about one hundred yards toward the bay side of the runway, then walked across the runway and staked one end of the Hi-Start into the ground. He unraveled the one hundred and fifty feet of surgical tubing along the other side of the runway, then continued unwinding the some three hundred feet of string attached to the end of the tubing. The end of the string had a parachute attached to it with a metal ring on the top of the parachute. Walking back across, he announced: "Is anybody on channel fifty-one?"

After no one spoke up, he grabbed his glider, gave it a gentle toss to test fly it, then walked back across the runway with it. He picked up the end of the Hi-Start, and slipped the ring on top of the parachute around the hook protruding from underneath the glider's belly.

"Well, here goes..." Todd thought as he stretched the Hi-Start back about two hundred feet. With the transmitter in his left hand and the glider in his right, he gave the glider a *Hail Mary* hurl. The glider leaped skyward in a high arc. He slowly lowered the nose as it reached apogee. The glider then moved forward and, with the line becoming slack, the ring slipped off the back of the hook. The parachute was now free to inflate, which pulled and straightened the line out in the direction of the wind for the next launch.

With the glider almost stationary into the gentle breeze about three hundred feet up, Todd walked backwards to his lawn chair next to Kelly's and sat down without taking his eyes off the glider. The chairs reclined about thirty degrees back with the seat just a few inches above the thick, green grass.

"Now. This is mellow!" he said as he reached for his Ray Bans. He sat back with the transmitter in his lap and reached for an R.C. cola from the cooler.

"I love you!" Kelly said, looking directly at him.

Surprised by the comment, he looked over at her, then back up to the glider. He made a couple of slight movements with the control stick on the transmitter, then laid it on the grass. He slowly leaned over to her as the glider floated high overhead, now pilotless. He moved in close to her with both hands supporting him. As his lips neared hers, he said with a soft smile, “You just like my cookin’!”

TODD'S IDENTIFICATION BADGE slid through the wall reader. Todd clipped it back on his shirt, then entered a four digit code into the adjoining keypad. The door clicked. He pushed it in and entered the crew lounge.

The lounge was considered part of the SIDA, the Security Identification Display Area, where everyone had to display their badges on their upper torso or—security issues aside—risk a thousand dollar fine for them and a ten thousand dollar fine for the company. The rear doors in the lounge opened out to the noisy aircraft ramp. He looked in his folder on the hanging file for any notes or messages, then went around the corner where the tables and couches were, to fill out his paperwork for the day's upcoming flights. The room was rather large, but the walls needed a fresh coat of paint and the furniture was a throwback to the early seventies. He glanced around the room and didn't immediately spot anyone he knew, nor an open space on any desk to do his work. Due to the limited amount of office space at Dulles, all of the airport employees at Bands used the pilot lounge. The mechanics, baggage handlers (a.k.a. rampers), flight attendants, gate agents, and dispatchers all commingled. The resultant flurry of activity made Todd look right past Steve Sanders in an effort to find a spot to sit down.

"Earth to Todd. Come in Todd," said Steve, standing up from his precious spot at a large work table.

"Hey Steve! How ya been!" Todd replied with a genuine smile. Someone needed to get by, so Todd moved in toward the table on the other side of Steve's now vacant chair.

Steve gave Todd a long delay, hoping he already had found out. After it was apparent that he hadn't, Steve responded. "Guess you haven't heard about Chris Thomas," he said, now with a serious tone. Todd's smile began to fade as he recognized that the news was not going to be good.

He continued. "She got hit by a car and killed on Route 28 Saturday night."

Todd's mouth opened slowly and slightly by the shock.

"She must have had car trouble, 'cuz her blinkers were on. She got out right as a car came by and took her and her car door a couple of hundred feet down the road."

Todd's eyes filled with tears as he stood and listened. Another death of a close friend.

Another pilot got up just to his left as he finished his paperwork and added: "Pity, she was an easy lay."

Todd immediately pulled his left arm up and ripped it across the pilot's right temple, sending him airborne and landing across the lap of a ramper. The unannounced concussion of the blow sent shock waves throughout the room, followed by a loud shrill of agony by the pilot. A rush of movement spread through the crew lounge, like a child running through a flock of pidgins. One lone ramper remained still, like he had witnessed the whole event as though it were on TV. As quickly as everyone moved, everyone became still. The small, inlaid diamonds on Todd's wedding ring gashed the pilot's upper face and sent blood gushing all over the pilot and ramper. The ramper immediately pushed back in his chair and shoved the pilot onto the dirty carpet.

Everyone was quiet and still.

"You didn't know her," said Todd calmly, fighting back both the rising adrenaline and tears. Todd looked down at his wedding ring and started to tremble slightly. The pilot was grunting in pain as the room remained quiet with the exception of the aircraft engine noise outside.

A few more seconds of high tension passed as he continued to fight the tears.

"She was very unhappy. She was very lonely," he said softly, then turned and walked down the hallway towards the weather room.

When he was near the end of the hallway, he heard: "Come back here, dickhead! I'll kick your ass!"

Todd stopped, drooped his shoulders, then turned and walked back. Upon reentering the room, the bloody pilot leaped at him. Todd leaned slightly left and down, then sprang forward as he swung his right fist squarely into the middle of the pilot's approaching forehead. The force of his punch was so great that it reversed the pilot's forward momentum in mid-air and sent him back to the ground, motionless.

Tears were now streaming from Todd's eyes. He thought nothing of the incident that had just occurred. He nervously touched his forehead with his left thumb and index finger while looking down. "Forgot my bags," he said in a low tone. He grabbed them and left the room slowly.

No one dare spoke.

• • • •

Todd was paired with Chris Thomas last June. He knew in advance that she was beautiful, smart—and also promiscuous. It made him nervous. Not that anything would happen, but that he might have to face rejecting her if she came on to him. On their first overnight, they met for dinner in the lobby of the Richmond Airport Ramada. Across the street was Gorge's Ensalada, an upscale Mexican restaurant, where he first had a chance to really talk with her. As they were seated in a corner booth, they noticed a small cadre of cameramen loitering at some tables near the entranceway. A family of six were seated next to their booth and were also looking towards the front entrance. Todd asked the hostess, "What's all the commotion about?"

She said, "The governor is here tonight to have dinner with some tobacco industry executives."

"Be sure to stick 'em in the smoking section, all right?" Todd said pleasantly.

"Third time I've heard that joke tonight," the hostess replied grumpily, then walked away.

Todd stuck his tongue out at her and made a face. Chris laughed quietly to herself. He put his elbows on the table, jammed his chin into his palm cradle, looked at Chris and said, "Well, that was a fun day. I love those smooth, foggy approaches where the airplane just slides down the glide slope and pops out of the clouds with the runway right there in front of you."

She said, "Well, you sure fly smoothly. How much time do you have in the Javelin now?"

Todd found himself looking at her and liking what he saw. Maybe it was the soft, low light from the warm, decorative lamp above their booth, or that this was the first time he had seen her in street clothes, or maybe he just felt completely at ease talking with her. She wasn't a low class hussy with an attitude. "Oh, 'bout six hundred," he admitted in a humble voice. "And you?"

"Oh, 'bout three thousand," she said in his same tone.

"Dayam! How come you're not flying the heavy metal airplanes for the big boys yet?"

"My husband won't let me."

Todd gave her a puzzled look from across the booth and leaned forward. "Your husband!?"

Todd then realized that he had spoken much too loudly. The family of six, sitting directly next to their booth, became quiet. All of them acted as if they didn't hear him, but fooled no one. Having realized what he had just done, he started to apologize to her, but she was quicker to respond.

"Yes, and I've told him all about us and that the child is actually yours!" she said with a straight face.

"Child!?" he blurted. He was slow to catch on.

"Yes, when you left to go to the seminary I decided to go ahead and have your baby. I named him after you. Oh what a relief it is to finally bring it out in the open."

Todd stared at her as he caught on, but kept his astonished look. Finally he chimed in: "Bless you my child. But, what about my parish?"

The family of six had stopped eating altogether and were focusing on their every word. Chris and Todd slowly turned their heads toward the family in unison and smiled, to let them know that they had just been had. The family, caught eavesdropping, all simultaneously looked back down at their plates and continued eating.

Todd was no longer nervous. She was smart, good natured, and yet presented no threat to his marital fidelity. He leaned closer to her, now aware that his voice carried and said, "Now, why won't he let you fly for the majors?"

She became serious. "He and I don't get along well. I mean he used to be sweet and kind, until I got a job here and he couldn't get a flying job anywhere. He couldn't handle it. He's really smart and talented, but I think he's lost a lot of his self respect, seeing as how I'm a Captain now and he's gone nowhere in the past two and a half years."

"What's he doing now?" Todd asked with genuine interest.

"He's fixing VCRs for SunVisor Videos and flight instructing over at Hyde Field," she answered.

"Can't you get him an interview with Bands?"

"He got one on his own merits last year, but, uh, he'll never be a TransGlobe Express pilot," she again answered, knowing that she'd have to explain further. "He, uh, the interview didn't go well at all and I guess he lost his temper and physically threatened the Chief Pilot."

"Wo!" Todd said, prompting her for more.

"Yea, he has a bad temper. I probably would have left him after the first time he hit me, but..."

"He hits you?! We're not playing the eavesdrop game again for the Walton's over here are we?" Todd tried to ease the growing tension.

"Yea, I moved out last month after a particularly rough night at home. I'd divorce him, but he knows that I fudged my logbook by a hundred and fifty hours two years ago in order to meet Band's minimum requirements for getting an interview." She was really confessing and Todd was really feeling sorry for her. "The Chief Pilot doesn't even know that I'm married, much less to him. If they found out that I had lied to them—that I only had three hundred and fifty hours of multiengine time when I got hired—they'd fire me right on the spot."

"They've got a lot invested in you now. You're a Captain with a clean record and several check rides under your belt. And, you were legal as far as the FAA is concerned. That multiengine time is just an arbitrary number that *the company* set. It's not like you lied about having your commercial pilot's license." Todd wouldn't normally try to rationalize her action. But her husband had her trapped. He had beaten her. *"Who could do such a thing,"* he thought.

She looked down at her hands, clasped together on the table top. "They would—and should— fire me for that, just out of principle. I've given it a lot of thought. If they were to keep me then they would send the message to everyone that its O.K. to lie to get hired, but only if you get caught later on."

She then looked directly at Todd, and without emotion said: "You know, *Father Todd*, you're the only one I've confessed my sins to. Please don't let anyone know about this. Flying is my only joy in life right now."

"Let us pray, my child," he said as he grasped her hand in a priestly manner. "*Domiknuckle de husbandes in de jawbone. Alle jerkus is de mannus. Gripus scrotum and yankum. Amen.*"

The governor moved through the front of the room as photographers flashed away, but they paid no attention to the commotion.

She laughed with her eyes shut. When he finished the pseudo prayer, they looked at each other and smiled. He liked her and wanted her to have a friend she could trust.

• • • •

"Grant. Come here, please," said Charlie Brooks, the station manager for Bands at Dulles. His tone was controlled and tempered. He had with him a bloodied mess of a person, holding a small, wet towel over his left eye. All three went into the small, unremarkable office where Charlie dwelled. Charlie's office didn't seem to match him. He dressed well and presented himself as a polished professional. You got the impression that his office was just a staging area for him to go do bigger and better things.

"This isn't a school yard, Todd. What happened?" he asked calmly.

"Maybe you'd better ask him first. I'll fill in whatever details he decides to leave out."

Todd was still angry, but was cool headed enough to know that they were both wrong and it was better that the other guy admit his guilt first.

The pilot, Gary Heinmann, had a yellow and blue knot forming in the middle of his forehead. It became all the more noticeable when he looked down and began to speak: "I, uh, I guess I kinda insulted Chris Thomas. 'Said she was an easy lay. Maybe that was kinda inappropriate, given that it's only been two days. I guess I was wrong."

Todd couldn't believe his ears. This was too easy. Here he was, admitting guilt to inciting the fight. *"What an idiot,"* he thought to himself.

"How's the eye?" Todd asked the pilot without offering any more about the incident.

"Looks like you caught me right on the brow. I'll need a butterfly bandage to close it, but the airport nurse says my eyebrow will cover the scar. I guess I'm lucky," he said like a henpecked husband.

Charlie spoke up, "Well, you're going to the Mediquik Clinic to get that stitched up. A ramper will take you in the baggage truck to avoid the gate area. Take off your epaulettes and wings. We don't want any passengers to see you. I'll fill out an irregularity report, whereby both of you will have the opportunity to add anything that you feel is pertinent, and you both will sign it. I've called crew scheduling. They've called up two reserve pilots. Both of you are going home for the day. They will call you later today to reschedule your trips. Stay by the phone."

The injured pilot nodded, then walked out without a word. Todd put the notepad that he had been using to document the meeting back in his shirt pocket. Charlie moved to intercept Todd before he, too, left the room.

"Todd, Gary is a troublemaker. Has been from the git-go. He knows he's on thin ice around here. But you. What really made you so mad?" Charlie asked with concern.

"I find out ten minutes ago that a friend of mine, a *close* friend of mine, died violently over the weekend. How could he be so callous as to think no one would feel any loss? Sure, I know her reputation. She was loose. But I flew with her for a month and got to know her in a different way than some of the other guys. She was a good person with a good heart. She had a lot of trouble in her life. Some people drink to make their troubles go away. I guess she had other methods."

"Don't worry about the report, Todd. I told scheduling that you were taking a sick day today and would be returning home. I don't want you flying people around today only half-focused."

"Thanks, Charlie." They shook hands and Todd left the office. He grabbed his bags, exited onto the ramp and through the operations office door, thus bypassing the pilot lounge.

SEVEN

KELLY looked up toward the opening door. "What are you doing home?" she asked as she put down her text book. Todd closed the door behind him. She was still wearing her blouse from work, but had replaced her skirt with a pair of running shorts. She continued, "Crew scheduling called and said they would call back later. What's going on? Aren't you s'possed to be on a two day trip?"

"I had a bad day, K.W.," he began. He dropped his bags. Then, standing alone in the middle of the room, he explained about Chris and the fight. After a couple of minutes he finished and just stood there, emotionless.

She got up, walked over to him and gave him a slow hug. He lowered his face into the side of her neck and held her tightly. They both remained motionless for several seconds.

Suddenly, the phone pierced the silence and startled both of them. They looked at each other, then laughed for being so jumpy. Todd turned and reached for it.

"Hello. Grant's," he announced with an almost cheerful tone. He raised his eyebrows as he glanced at Kelly and returned the phone back to countertop. "Why can't they just say 'Sorry, wrong number' instead of hanging up?"

"Folks up here jist ain't as poe'light as weeuns is," she said southernly as she slid slowly back to him and gave him a soft kiss on the cheek. The phone rang again, which made both of them again jerk clumsily into each other. Their resultant laughter was even more pronounced than before.

"Even these Yankee phones are inconsiderate," she said with a smile.

This time Todd picked up the phone, but didn't say anything. About five long seconds passed as Todd and Kelly waited out the time by staring at each other with sinister smiles. Finally, Kelly heard a loud "Hello?" coming from the earpiece close to Todd's right ear.

"Who's calling, please?" Todd asked politely as he continued to stare at Kelly.

"John Briggs. Is Todd there?"

"Hey John, whuz goin' on," he responded. Since John was one of the dispatchers and schedulers for the company, Todd automatically reached over to a notepad and pulled it close.

"Not much, you brute. How's the hand?"

Todd smiled, acknowledging Kelly as she turned and walked towards the kitchen and also because of John's comment. "Fine. Need someone to kick some butt? Just call 1-800-TKO-TODD."

"Proud of you, boy. Gary's such a jerk."

"I really shouldn't have unloaded on him. I haven't been pulled into a brawl in years. By the way, did you just try to call me?"

"Yea. I called. You answered. We're still on the line. Are you sure he didn't get a lick in? Make you dizzy?"

"Smart ass!"

"Nope, wasn't me. Hey, you interested in picking up the balance of your trip tomorrow at 11:15?"

"Sure!" Todd said excitedly. In one fluid motion he switched the phone to his left ear, holding it up with his shoulder, and pulled a silver pen from the left pocket of his untucked shirt.

"Great. You'll take the second and subsequent legs from Rick Donnelly when they come back from Pittsburgh. Some of the flight numbers and times have changed slightly from the lines that you have—got a pen handy?"

"Yea. You can just fax the stuff to me, though, if you'd prefer."

"You have a fax machine at home?"

"Yea. Same phone number."

"O.K. I'll get it to you in a minute. By the way, I marked today as a scheduling cancellation for you and a trip drop for Gary. I.E., you get paid for the day and he doesn't."

"With a simple tap on your keyboard, you take away the spoils of my day," said Todd half-reverently.

"Hey, after all, you didn't start the fight—and he needs another one-two punch from us at scheduling for making us pull up two reserve pilots today."

"Actually, I did throw the first punch."

"Hell, you threw *all* the punches. But I've known Gary for two years. He had it coming."

"Well, thanks for looking out for me, buddy!"

"You bet, killer! Stop by and see us over here at corporate!"

"Sure will," said Todd. He put the phone back in its cradle on the breakfast nook, then walked around to the kitchen and unbuttoned his untucked shirt.

"*John* sure is poe'light," said Todd. "He's giving me a pay credit for today, see'in as how it wasn't my fault."

"You slug a guy because he mouths off to you and it's *his* fault? C'mon. You really believe that?!"

"That's typical lawyer cross examiner stuff. Don't highlight the fact that I just got the news of Chris's death. Couple that with...uh." He paused, then said, "Yep, you're right. I should have slugged him with insults. They hurt longer."

"Speaking of cross examiners, tomorrow I finally get to wear that suit you got me for my birthday."

"REALLY! The outfit held in escrow until you finally made the varsity! Pity the sucker who's across the table from you tomorrow."

"I'm just there to flip charts and look pretty."

"I've always told you that you are most beautiful when you are in your birthday suit!"

"Well, they won't be seeing *that* suit tomorrow! Hey, 'you still mad at that guy now?" she asked, sensing that he was now relaxing.

He leaned close to her face and began to talk slowly and softly: "He's a bone head. A chowder head. A pickle-faced, stump-water sippin',..." Kelly smiled. "...nose drippin', nut scratchin', sack of chicken turds." Todd looked at her, then a slight smile appeared on his face.

"How colorful."

He stood there for a moment, almost as though he needed to collect his thoughts as he became more serious. He leaned away from her and talked much faster. "He's such a coward. He wouldn't dare say something like that to her face. And with her gone, he thought he was perfectly safe to say anything he wanted. Gawd. I can't believe she's dead." He froze for a second, realizing he had unwittingly changed both the subject and his mood.

Again, he spoke: "Well, the first punch was out of anger. The second was out of contempt for him and every one who only saw what they wanted to see in her. First Scott. Now Chris. My God, I just never imagined that I could lose two close friends in such short order." A rush of sadness swept through him.

She again made her way over to him and started to lean his way. He stopped her, turned, and took the phone off the hook.

TODD arrived at the 490 L'Enfant Plaza at precisely 9:15 a.m., as planned. His show time at Dulles was 11:15 a.m., which allowed him plenty of time. Although he had never been in the building, it's location was easy for him to remember: two blocks south of his favorite spot in Washington—the Smithsonian's Air & Space Museum. He parked on 7th Street, the north-south road that goes between the NTSB offices and the museum. He walked south on 7th, then jaywalked across the side street that fronts L'Enfant Plaza and entered the building at the Promenade Level. The building, called 490 L'Enfant Plaza, displayed no evidence that the Headquarters of the National Transportation Safety Board was located inside. He passed through the double doors and up to the area where a receptionist was talking to a security guard. Several sign-in binders lay open on the countertop.

"You a pilot?" the young, very attractive black woman asked from behind the counter. Todd was wearing his uniform since there was no convenient place to change into it at Dulles.

"Uh, yea. Can I go get a copy of a preliminary accident investigation report from the NTSB?"

She swung a binder around towards him and said, "I figured you was a pilot. You'd think they'd be lots of pilots comin' through this building, see'n as how the FAA is always comin' through here and all. I don't never see none, though."

"Summer hire," thought Todd. He glanced to the three-ringed binder with a piece of paper that said "NTSB" cellophaned to it and began to sign in. "Yes ma'am, but I bet a lot of those guys *are* pilots, too. They just don't dress the part," said Todd with a polite smile.

"You show' do look sharp!" the receptionist responded with an inviting tone. The security guard, having clearly been outclassed, walked away.

The receptionist, in spite of her weak verbal skills, was otherwise bright and pleasant. Todd looked up from his writing and said with a slight blush, "Well, aren't you nice!"

"Don't you never get scared, flyin' round in tah-nadoes and lightnin'?" she asked sincerely as she handed him a visitor's badge.

"No, 'cuz we have a radar screen in the airplane that tells us where the nasty weather is. We just steer away from the bad stuff." He immediately was reminded of *the accident.* The smile on his face quickly diluted to a fake smile. "What floor is the NTSB on?"

"Five. Take them elevators right there," she said as she pointed to her left.

Todd couldn't help himself as he began walking away: "Think I'll just take *one* of them. No sense hogging all of 'em."

She shook her head as she smiled and turned the binder back around towards her and read his name.

••••

"Hey, Susan!" Kelly said cheerfully as she passed by Susan's office. Kelly was dressed in a very conservative business suit. Today would be her first day to sit at the defendants table in an actual court case. She was trying not very hard to allow Susan not to notice her new outfit.

Kelly's law firm was about the most pleasant work environment that anyone could imagine. Her boss, Susan Bartlett, made her feel right at home and took her under her wing. Kelly was given much more authority than a legal assistant normally would.

"Hey council!" Susan called toward the now empty doorway.

A shy smile reemerged, followed by the rest of her.

"We find for the defendant!" Susan said proudly. "That's what they'll say before you even sit down! Knock 'em dead!"

Susan, ironically, was not a lawyer. She was a CPA and had fallen into her job by chance. The law offices of Banks, Yang, and Costello, P.A. moved in across the hall just as her accounting firm moved to downtown D.C. She wasn't willing to commute from Bowie, Maryland to D.C. every day and knew that BYC was in need of an office manager. They reluctantly hired her, thinking she was both over- and misqualified for the work that they had intended for that position. But now, after ten years, wouldn't trade her for ten lawyers.

She practically ran the firm. She chaired the weekly management meetings, assigned cases, and tracked billings. She, long ago, was given unlimited authority to direct the workloads of the lawyers. When personal computers first came on the scene, she took several courses and soon became quite PC literate. She then took programming courses and wrote a very robust program for tracking the firm's progress. Among her thirty-four lawyers, she could instantly tell who her best performers were, ranked by win/loss percentage, speed to settlement, jury vs. judge win/loss ranking, and of course: billable hours. She was the one responsible for the firm's new, cost effective voice mail phone system.

She actively pursued new clients, namely large real estate firms, which are always ripe for legal representation. At her five year point with the firm, she was promoted to partner. One would think that many of the *partner wanna be*'s would have been furious that a CPA and office manager be promoted to partner, but they threw the biggest and wildest party for her that the firm had ever seen in its sixty year history.

They knew that it was her that brought a sixty-five percent increase in earnings to the firm and that they all benefited from the success.

Kelly admired her and they became close friends. She thought Susan was a perfect businessperson in every way. She always acted in a professional yet pleasant manner. She was well groomed and always looked like she just came from the salon. She never lost her temper, nor chastised someone in the presence of another. She politely quelched any negativisms that tends to creep into an office environment and always remembered everyone's birthdays and anniversaries. Everyone knew the company's goals, as set by her, and their respective contributions needed to achieve them. She was a slave driver, but no one felt the whip. She always reminded the workaholics that they weren't allowed to work past dinner time unless it was absolutely necessary. As a CPA, she approached work analytically. She showed them how to be more productive without ever feeling overworked. She also effectively nudged the underachievers to pull their fair share of the workload. The other partners in the firm were perfectly happy to let her handle the day to day grudge work, which allowed them more time to concentrate on those facets of the law that interested them the most.

It was Susan who convinced the University of Maryland's School of Law to extend the date when Kelly was to begin her studies. Susan saw a lot of promise in the Arkansas State University undergrad. She saw the promise of an intelligent and charming young woman and wanted her to succeed. She allowed Kelly to prepare cases, take depositions, research related rulings, and many of the other tasks that a young attorney would be expected to do.

With the latitude afforded by Susan, Kelly was quick to pick up the language of law and soon became respected in her own right around the firm. She conducted mock cross examinations with experienced lawyers and sometimes brought them to their knees. When she did lose, however, it was always the last time under those circumstances. She quickly became known as a legal magnet.

"Thanks, Susan." Kelly responded to the complimentary pep talk. "I hope I can," she continued but was interrupted by a voice from the receptionist down the hall: "Kelly, call on three-one."

"Duty calls," she said as she bolted to her cubicle with a familiar *gotta go* look on her face. She swung around her desk, and slid her agenda next to her picture of Todd, which was the only evidence of a life away from her work. Without sitting down, though the chair was directly beneath her, Kelly then leaned over her neatly arranged stacks of papers, grabbed the phone and punched the second button, labeled "4231" with the red LED flashing above it. A click was heard as the line came alive and she heard a familiar sound of sixty hertz interference. The base unit of their portable phone at home sat on top of their microwave oven. Anytime the microwave was on and someone was talking on the portable, a dull hum came over the line. She quickly summized that it was Todd, calling from home. Why was he home—and cooking?

"Ms. Grant," she said cheerfully, knowing it was Todd. She listened in silence for a second or two and heard what sounded like a large dog bark in the background.

"R.C.?" she asked, now unsure.

"I guess Todd ain't gonna be screwin' Chris no more, huh!?" the male voice said quietly.

"Huh?" she said, stunned. "Who's calling?"

"Gotta give him credit—he's smart; no one would ever suspect him," he continued softly then hung up.

"Hey, HEY, WHAT THE," she said even though she knew he was no longer on the line. She held the phone up and tried to calmly decipher what had just occurred. Grabbing her pen, she flung open her agenda and transcribed the short conversation, noting his inflections and the dog. She obviously knew that the call's intent was to damage Todd. She had always completely trusted Todd, yet her mind started racing, evaluating the possibilities.

After she finished the note, she laid her pen down and rubbed her shaking hands together. She then immediately pressed line five-five on her phone, got a dial tone, then frantically called home. After a couple of rings, the answering machine picked up. She hung up without leaving a message.

• • • •

Todd walked out of the elevator holding a single piece of paper in his hand. Walking directly back to the receptionist's desk, she noticed him right away and said loudly, "That sure was quick!"

He acknowledged her with a smile as he moved closer. Nearing the counter, he reached into the left pocket of his pilot shirt and pulled out his pen, then entered "09:27" into the *time out* block of the sign-in log.

"What was you visitin' the NTSB for?" she asked in an attempt to restart some conversation.

"Just checking on what they came up with about an accident a month ago."

"Ja get what ja want?"

"Na. Couldn't get past the secretary in Public Affairs. She, uh, just gave me this." Todd produced a single piece of letterhead bond with the words **National Transportation Safety Board News Release** printed in large blue letters across the top, followed by a black subtitle: **Preliminary Findings: Bands Flight 2234 Aircraft Accident, Prince William County, Virginia.** Below the subtitle was a narrative that was essentially the same information that he read about in yesterday's *Post*. "They don't let you see anything until they're fairly sure that they've got something figured out," he added.

"I know a guy up there. He'll tell you wha'chew wanna know."

"You sure he wouldn't mind talking to me?"

"Let me call him up."

"Well, thanks. Thanks a lot."

She picked up her phone and dialed a four-digit number without looking it up. After a moment, she said, "Hey James, its Keisha. 'Sup? Hey, I got a handsome looking pilot down here that wants to find out what y'all know about an accident. Can you talk to him?"

She listened for a second, then said to Todd, "You ain't part of a lawsuit or insurance claim or nothin', is ya?"

"No, Keisha," he said to her without emotion. "My best friend was one of the pilots in the accident."

"Naw. His best friend was the pilot," she said back into the phone.

Todd listened to her conversation with James: "I know, but he's a nice guy... Listen, James, talk to the boy," she said with conviction. "Just to let him know what y'all are working on, that's all," she said more calmly. "Yea," she said. "Yea," she said again, this time glancing up at Todd.

She rotated the phone one hundred and eighty degrees up, while still listening through the earpiece. "Is there a case number on that?" Kiesha asked Todd, pointing to the news release.

He stood there looking at her, not expecting any cooperation from James on the other end. Then when it sank in, he said "Uh, let's see...." He raised up the news release and found **Case No. 93-072102** in the upper right hand corner of the page. "Yea. Ninety-three dash oh seven two one oh two," he said to her.

She repeated the number to James, then after a pause said, "No way!" After yet another pause, she then said "Well, all right!"

She continued talking into the phone: "Naw. Well, yea he is. But don't worry, I see a wedding ring on his finger." She smiled at Todd. He looked away and smiled. "Hey, you know it. Later!" She said. Then she hung up and wove her fingers together proudly on her desktop.

"He said give him a couple of minutes, then go up to fifth floor again. Take a left out of the elevator and through the doors that say Office of Research and Engineering. Third cubicle on the right. He's James Hatch. He's a *metaljist*."

"A, uh, metallurgist?"

"Yea, he said he did some stuff with that crash and he'll tell you a little bit 'bout what he knows."

"Hey, that's great, Kiesha! You don't know how much I appreciate it."

"James is pretty sharp. College boy and all. And he's a sharp dresser. Lot of these guys wear, like, leather patches on the elbows of their jacket sleeves. They all lookin' like Ward Cleaver. But James—he's GQ—he's always stylin'."

"Well, I'll just go up there and see who's stylin' and who ain't," he said with a smile.

"Here. Take your visitor badge again. I'll take care of this," she said as she opened some White-Out to erase his sign-out time on the log.

• • • •

"Dispatch. This is John," said John Briggs into the phone from his chair in the room behind the large glass window. Two other people were behind computer screens in this room that more resembled a war room than just another office at Bands Airways Headquarters. The rear wall consisted of a huge, white, dry-erase board. The board had many sections, each containing rows and columns of data. Some dealt with aircraft in need of service. Other sections had station manager names and phone numbers. Yet another had statistics and goals for aircraft availability, on-time performance, and revenue yields. One side wall was lined with two large printers that were mindlessly pumping out page after page of fanfold paper. Just adjacent to them was a six-foot high rack of radio equipment, with several metal conduit lines extending from each console into a hole in the ceiling. The other side wall consisted of filing cabinets and another, but much smaller, dry-erase board above them that had nothing but these words, neatly printed in bold black letters: **Poor planning on your part does not necessarily constitute an emergency on my part.**

"John, this is Todd Grant's wife. Has he checked in yet?"

"Hi, Kelly. Uh, just a second." He tapped on his keyboard, then waited just about long enough to read what appeared on his screen, then said, "Uh, no he hasn't. Ole' killer's not due to check in until eleven fifteen."

She thought about the ramifications of him now being referred to as *Killer*. "Uh. It's kinda important. When he does check in, would you please have him call me at work. I'll be here until twelve fifteen."

"You bet. Take care." John hung up the phone and annotated a note: *CALL KELLY AT WORK BY 12:15* next to Todd's shift number on the computer screen, in case one of the other dispatchers answered Todd's check-in call.

TODD knocked softly on the open door to the cubicle office. The office was extremely small, yet neatly arranged. The room was barely large enough to contain a wooden desk and chair, one five-drawer filing cabinet, a guest chair, and a credenza. Perpendicular to the desk was a computer resting on the end of the credenza. Its placement allowed the man to rotate from his desk ninety degrees to his right and be in position to begin typing. The brightly colored, fine quality video display, and nearby paper markups evidenced a report being edited.

His desk was neat and orderly. Next to the desk, a polished ceramic pot contained a large, deep green, leafy plant.

The walls were merely wood veneer partitions that extended up about six and a half feet. One wall had a matted and framed lithograph of Michael Delacroix's Mount Vernon that Todd recognized. Another had a similarly framed litho of a New England cityscape by another painter that was equally appealing. A small bookcase held some mechanical engineering textbooks and three computer books: Word for Windows Users Manual, CompuServe Guide for Members, and Understanding Microsoft Access. Todd immediately got the impression that the man was thorough, organized, and enjoyed working in a comfortable environment. His office was essentially no different in size and shape than any other, yet it exuded pride and organization.

"James?" Todd asked.

A slim, young black man looked up and smiled through his round, wire rimmed glasses. He appeared poised and confident as he rose from his chair, exposing his conservative, custom-tailored Brooks Brothers suit. "Mr. Grant, come on in," he said.

Todd clearly remembered that Kiesha had not given him his name. He must have called back down to the desk to get it. As Todd entered the room, an unusual odor hit him, which must have made him flinch slightly.

James said, "Sorry about the smell in here. I came in on Saturday, removed the top of this desk, brought it out in the main hallway and refurb'd it."

"You did that?! Wow. Looks great!" Todd said with enthusiasm. The top of the desk was a deep, polished cherry finish. It was immaculate.

"Thanks. A week ago I found this desk down the hall in a vacant cubicle and did a midnight Chinese fire drill with my old one. This one is solid mahogany with a dark cherry finish."

"That must have been difficult to get such a beautiful finish."

"The toughest part was finding out what the original finish was. I got the GSA contract number from the placard inside the top drawer. From there, I researched the number over at GSA headquarters during my lunch hour and found that it was made by Birnham of High Point for a 1968 GSA schedule. After a couple of calls, I found out that they went out of business in seventy-six, but sold the drawings to another company down in North Carolina that never produced a single one of these desks. I glad-handed a foreman down there to look up the stain type on the old manufacturing drawings that Birnham used on this. Two lunch hours and six bucks on my Sprint card. It was really quite simple."

"You did all that just to get the original finish?"

"Actually, the only part of the desk that was damaged was the top. The rest was O.K. As you probably know, most stains tend to darken with age..."

Actually, Todd *didn't* know that, but nodded anyway.

"...so I added three drops of black dye to the pint of stain to compensate for the natural darkening. I then stripped, sanded, stained, and varnished it, then brought in back in here yesterday. It's dry enough to use now. But, unfortunately, it still reeks of varnish." As James explained the new desk top, Todd came up to it. He lightly moved his index and middle fingers over the top back edge of the desk and slowly sat down in the guest chair as he listened.

"I think you're in the wrong line of work. It's magnificent," he said sincerely. Todd looked around and noticed a wooden plaque on the wall opposite where he was sitting. It had gold lettering in an elegant serif font that read: **A pint of sweat will save a gallon of blood. - George Patton.**

James swung around in his chair and opened the bottom drawer of the filing cabinet. The open drawer revealed some thirty neatly arranged hanging files. Given the labels on the other drawers, there were probably well over a hundred active accidents that he was investigating. "Everyone needs a hobby. Here's what we have on Bands Twenty-two Thirty-four," he said with no transition. Leaning forward, he handed Todd a bulging manila folder filled with site reports and photos, witness depositions, radar summaries, computer printouts, materials lab results, and toxicology reports. "I did the yield testing on the failed structural components."

"Yea. Kiesha said you were a *metaljist*," Todd joked.

James chuckled and replied, "She has a lot of promise in her. She's very bright. And an utter knockout...." James paused, and looked right through Todd as though he was forming a mental picture of her. "I've been tutoring her on some freshman math and science courses. She's doing night school at the University of the District of Columbia."

"The lobby is certainly a pleasant place to pass through with her down there," Todd said, then changed the subject. "I've read the press release and the *Post* story from yesterday. I'm troubled that the investigation seems to be zeroing in on pilot error."

"Which one was your friend, Bill or Scott?"

Todd was surprised that James knew the pilot's names. "Uh, Scott."

"Scott was the pilot flying that leg as I remember."

"Yea." Todd was amazed that James was so familiar with that particular case, in light of the large filing cabinet.

"Well, the one thing we are quite confident about is that the aircraft experienced structural failure. The rear fuselage tore apart and separated from the rest of the aircraft, just aft of the rear door. What was left of the forward and rear spars of the wing showed a plastic deformation consistent with a high-g pull-up. Also, the inner elevator hinges displayed axial stress fractures and the outer hinges were simply destroyed. I ran the yields on the metals of both the wing spar and the elevator and its hinges. There was no evidence of corrosion or interstitial impurities." James flipped through some papers, found what he was looking for, then swung it around for Todd to see. "Here." He pointed to a computer graph, labeled *Yield Stress Analysis, Port Outer Elevator Hinge, Bands 2234.* "We tested this hinge in the materials lab, and found that it failed when the aircraft hit eight point nine g's." He quickly flipped five pages back and said, "Now here. The wing spar tests showed plastic deformation consistent with a nine g pull-up."

Todd looked at the graphs. Less than two years ago, he graduated with honors with a degree in Electrical Engineering from Arkansas State. His parents encouraged him to use the degree to get a nice job as a design engineer for an aerospace company or something related to aviation.

In fact, the reason why he had a fax machine at home is because he built one for his Advanced Studies 400 project. He researched and found the standard data format for ANSI's Group II facsimile transmissions. Then, he designed a protocol and architecture for capturing the data from the phone line and sending that data directly to a laser printer. The curriculum only required him to produce the logic and circuit diagrams and other supporting documentation. The course didn't offer the hardware to build an actual working model of each student's project. But, he went ahead and built one at his own expense. It didn't have much memory and used an outdated microprocessor as its brain. The total: $137. The cost was equivalent to three hours of flight in a Cessna, which proved to be a tough financial decision for him. The machine was slow by today's standards and had no capability of sending faxes. But it did show his instructors that he had a real talent in tackling tough technical projects.

Todd was not one that would be content being an engineer in some avionics design department. He had to fly. The money and security of being an electrical engineer were a lure, but flying was always his only love.

As a junior, he had to take one compulsory course in mechanical engineering, called *Statics and Strength of Materiels*. Therefore, the graphs weren't entirely foreign to him. He decided to try to speak James's language: "At what g would this spar normally go from elastic to plastic deformation?"

James took the clue that Todd was knowledgeable about this field. He then proceeded to explain, in very complex terms, the science of dynamic structural loading. Todd followed him to a point, then became comfortably confused. The more complex the science became, the more confident Todd became in James's analysis. James was both erudite and thorough.

"But what made the airplane load up to nine g's?"

A voice from the doorway interjected. "That's the question we'd all like to answer."

Todd turned far around in his seat and looked at the short, stocky man leaning on the door, arms folded. The cartoon-like man was more like the bureaucrat image that Todd expected: Off the rack pants, pale blue oxford shirt, polyester tie, and penny loafers.

Todd stood, eyebrows raised. James said, "Todd Grant, this is Bernard Rudd..."

Bernard Ruddman interrupted: "Hi. Barney Rubble." The man smirked as he leaned away from the doorway and extended his hand to Todd.

"We've met. Bedrock Lanes, League Night," Todd said with a sly smile as they shook hands firmly.

Barney smiled back as James continued: "Barney is the lead investigator for the Bands accident." Todd was again impressed with James's attention to detail. He must have called Barney to let him know that he was coming up.

"Nice to meet you. I'm impressed by the amount and quality of analysis conducted by the Board so far."

Barney said, "Folks at Darchault and Bands Airways have been really helpful and cooperative. We've pretty much figured out *how* it fell out of the sky. Now's the tough part: *Why*. It could be the thunderstorms, could be the aircraft design, could be PIO, or any combination."

"Pilot Induced Oscillations?" Todd asked to confirm the acronym.

Barney nodded as James asked, "You two are pilots. You tell me. Could a pilot actually induce a nine g load on an airplane?"

Todd answered. "I can't imagine nine g's resulting from PIO. And he'd have to be someone with considerably less experience than Scott. Like maybe a student pilot that flew into severe turbulence or something like that."

"I kinda agree with Todd," Barney added. "But think about it for minute. You hit an air pocket and the plane pitches up slightly. You push the nose down right as you hit the backside of the air pocket and the pitch down effect is amplified. You pull up rather violently right as you hit another updraft and before you know it, you're pulling several g's. You can see the synergism."

Todd looked directly at Barney. "But you, and I, and anyone who has just a few hundred hours under their belt figures it out that the best way to deal with moderate or higher turbulence is to just hold a constant pitch and ride straight through the bumps."

"So you tell me, Todd. Why did the aircraft experience nine g's? There's evidence to support the PIO theory. We heard the stall horn go off six times in the cockpit, just prior to the loud grunts and the *Oh shit, we're dead* comment."

"I know, I heard the tapes two weeks ago," Todd said, clearly shaken by the haunting memory of the recording.

The crew was alive during the entire five thousand feet uncontrolled dive to the ground. The sobbing, the utterances, the outward futile strains to try to effect the aircraft's control: All of this was recorded and played back at the press conference two weeks after the crash. Todd attended that press conference, held just down the hall in the NTSB auditorium. The press were given a paper release of the pertinent cockpit comments from the pilot flying (PF) and the pilot not flying (PNF), with time sequences along the left hand column. The time sequences up to when the aircraft broke apart were printed verbatim in almost every newspaper in the country:

11:50:52.4 **PF** "Select ten mile mode and see what's close in" [reference to radar range selection]
11:50:58.3 **PNF** "Where's the smooth air?"
11:51:01.3 **PF** "The pax are gonna puke, Bill."
11:51:01.7 *grunting sound from* ***PF***
11:51:01.8 **PNF** "Let's see, suggest fifteen degrees left, Scott."
11:51:02.6 **PF** "They're gonna blow chunks."
11:51:03.1 **PF** "There's five." [required five thousand foot call-out]
11:51:03.9 **PNF** "Passing five thousand, boost pumps comin' off."
11:51:04.5 **PF** "O.K."
11:51:04.9 **PF** "[*expletive*] bumps."
11:51:05.2 *stall warning horn*
11:51:05:7 *grunting sound from* ***PF***
11:51:05.9 **PNF** "The hell?!"
11:51:06.0 *stall warning horn*
11:51:06.4 *grunting sound from* ***PF****, followed by* "Oh, [expletive]..."
11:51:06.8 *stall warning horn*
11:51:07.4 **PNF** "The [*expletive*] is going on?"
11:51:07.6 *stall warning horn*
11:51:07.8 **PF** "[*expletive*], [*expletive*], gimme a hand."
11:51:08.2 **PNF** "Here..."
11:51:08.2 *stall warning horn*

11:51:08.4 *grunting sounds from both pilots*
11:51:08.7 **PNF** "Up, no, [expletive]"
11:51:09.0 *stall warning horn*
11:51:09.5 *sudden, loud metallic noise*
11:51:09.6 *begin 34dB increase in cockpit noise level.*
11:51:09.7 *unintelligible remarks from crew members*
11:51:12.1 **PF** "[expletive], Bill, gimme idle power."
11:51:12.3 **PNF** "Oh, no."
11:51:13.8 **PF** "Oh [expletive], we're dead."

The sequence of events shown on the paper copy was not nearly as horrifying as hearing the playback of the actual cockpit voice recorder. It revealed the desperate emotions of the two pilots struggling to keep the airplane under control. The press refrained from reporting the comments made by the crew following the "Oh shit, we're dead" comment. After it was apparent that the crew had lost all control, their last utterances filled the press room with tears. Every one in the room, shocked by the realism of the playback, wanted to just rewind the tape and somehow undo history. They all felt the same helplessness that Scott and Bill must have felt. And no one in the room felt it more than Todd. He had sat in the first quarter of the half empty auditorium. He was not expecting to hear Scott's voice that day. As they began the tape, he slumped forward, with his face in his hands, and hung on every sound. They played the entire last seven minutes of the flight. By the end, tears were appearing between his fingers.

Now, two weeks later, he was again reliving the event.

"I'm sorry," said Barney, realizing that he struck a nerve with his callous comment. "I am as frustrated as you are. Please understand that we don't take our causal conclusions lightly. The ramifications of our conclusions affect the airplane manufacturers, the airline companies, the insurance companies, and the litigation attorneys. But, most importantly, they affect the families of those lost in the accidents, especially the families of the pilots."

"I know. But I know Scott's capabilities."

"You know, they *did* do some things wrong. They're supposed to have a sterile cockpit below ten thousand feet. And there they were bullshitting about the passengers getting sick. Also, you can't have two people try to fly the airplane at the same time."

"Did y'all look into the Stall Warning System and Stick Pusher?"

Barney hesitated, then said softly, "Unfortunately, the aircraft hit the ground, full of fuel, at over three hundred and fifty miles an hour. There was virtually nothing left. The only reason we got the voice recordings is because the box is bolted inside in the tail section. We figure the tail finally separated from the rest of the aircraft at about fifteen hundred feet up. It fluttered away and landed pretty much intact."

"I know, I saw the front page of *Newsweek*. Look, I just want to offer any help that I can that might be useful in getting to the real truth."

Barney leaned away from the doorway. "Todd, I'm truly sorry about Scott. Personally, I hope it's not his fault. But I have to be completely fair in my analysis. If there was a smoking gun, we probably would have uncovered it by now. There was no bomb. There was no one else in the cockpit. Both engines were operating normally. Those conclusions come quickly. This accident investigation will be much more difficult. If we conclude with a reasonable certainty a cause or set of causes for the accident, it will be only after eliminating all other possible causes. And even with the unusually high press we've been getting on this, we won't get pressured into making a quick judgment. We'll give it everything we have, you have my word."

Todd said, "I know the airplane systems and our company procedures quite well. I can't guarantee that I'd be fair and impartial, but I can still offer expertise."

"Thanks, Todd. And we welcome your assistance. Give James your phone number and if we have a question we think you can help us with, we'll sure give you a call." Barney shook Todd's hand and left in a hurry.

Todd turned and looked at James. "My offer for help is sincere. Y'all need anything at all, please let me know."

James stood up. "I sure will Todd. Don't mind ole' Barney. He's actually among our best. He never forgets anything. He's logical and intuitive. I firmly believe that if Barney had been around when Amelia Earhardt's plane went down, he'd have solved it in no time."

"Thanks, James," said Todd as he ripped a page with his name and phone number printed neatly on it from his memo book. He turned toward James as he placed it on James's new desktop. "I feel very confident in the Board's capabilities."

"We've got some good people here with a lot of talent."

"Like Kiesha," Todd said, smiling.

"Like Kiesha," James repeated with the same smile.

KELLY arrived at the Anne Arundel County Courthouse and immediately excused herself from the two attorneys that she was accompanying to go to a pay phone in the east end of the large echoing entranceway. She dialed her work number and asked the secretary if her husband had called. He had not. She then stuck another quarter in the pay phone and called the apartment. No message from Todd there either. In one fluid motion she dropped the phone back in its vertical cradle and trotted across the marble foyer. She had to tell him about that phone call.

• • • •

"You think we oughtta bring in Stu Varney?" Barney Rubble asked from James Hatch's doorway.

James looked over from his computer. "Hard to say. He *did* ask about the Stall Warning System."

"Yea. And when I mentioned that the stall warning horns were rhythmic, he played real dumb."

"He seems sincere."

"Or he just wanted to know what *we* knew."

"I guess we should give Stu a call."

"All right. You have everything documented?"

"Of course," James said as he flipped his Rolodex open under "F" and searched until he found: FBI Air Piracy and Sabotage. Stu Varney. (202) 555-7313.

• • • •

Todd arrived at Dulles at 10:50 and drove to the employee parking lot just south of the Red Satellite Lot. The shuttle van delivered him at the main terminal at 10:55, which gave him twenty minutes to get to the operations office at the other end of the terminal and report in. He normally arrives thirty minutes before his scheduled show time, which is always one hour before the flight departs. However, his visit with the NTSB had taken longer than he had originally planned. He had cut into his safety margin. At 11:05, he called the flight dispatch office at Bands's headquarters from the check-in phone in the operations office.

The company set up a special phone there, which was down the hall from the pilot lounge. Next to the phone was the password of the day, taped to the Formica counter top. All pilots had to call from that particular phone when checking in because they otherwise wouldn't know the password. The company had experienced a rash of canceled flights because pilots were calling from home and saying they were at the airport, only to then get stuck in traffic or have car trouble. The company decided that since a couple of the pilots weren't being honest about check-ins, that everyone had to use a password found only in the operations office.

The passwords took on a life of their own. They actually provided a medium for some humor, something everyone needed in view of *the accident.* The more offbeat they became, the more everyone got a kick out of them. "BANANAS GIVE ME GAS." "ADRIENNE!" "I WISH COTTON WAS A MONKEY." The people over at the dispatch office often ran bets on them. Once, they bet a case of beer over how many pilots pronounced the password DUODENUM as *doo•wah'•deh•num* versus *du'•oh•dee'•num.*

The Bands management also had *Caller I.D.* installed by the phone company at the flight dispatch office, but opted not to use it nor let anyone know about it, since the password practice seemed to work and they didn't want to otherwise alienate the pilot group from the company management.

Todd spoke into the phone, "Hi John, it's Todd, checking in. LOSE THE MUSTACHE."

"LOSE THE MUSTACHE!" John Briggs said loudly, as though he were announcing it to everyone in the room. Another dispatcher sitting next to him rolled his eyes. "Todd, Todd. Here you are. Eleven Fifteen. Your Captain is Paul Stewart. Shift fifty one fifty three. He'll be coming in from Pitt at...." Todd could here John typing away at his keyboard. "...at, um, at eleven forty in aircraft 977TE. Gotcha. Oh, hey, your wife called. Wants you to call her by twelve fifteen."

"O.K. Thanks. Hey, I didn't know you were growing a mustache."

"Nope, it's Daryl over here. He's pretty shook up though, now that sixty people so far this morning have told him to lose it." Daryl rolled his eyes again.

"Love those passwords!" Todd said, smiling, then he hung up.

He went back down the hallway to the door to that opens into the passenger gates and slipped his card into the reader. The door clicked and he walked around the noisy Gate A-Eleven area to a bank of pay phones, stuck a quarter in one, and called Kelly. Her office said that she had to leave for the courthouse early. The attorneys for the opposition had apparently decided at the last minute to accept the firm's offer for an out of court settlement. They wanted to meet at 11:00 a.m. to see if the settlement could be finalized before the afternoon session began.

He hung up then walked back to the pilot lounge door, inserted his card, then walked into the lounge. He picked up his bags, checked his file for any chart updates or company newsletters, then walked just outside the rear door to the ramp. There, he hopped up on a ground power unit, out of view from the passengers, and waited in the warm midday sunshine for his plane to arrive.

The ramp only had two airplanes on it. One had the rear door down. A fuel truck parked in front of it and a fat man got out slowly. As for the other, the right engine cowling was propped up against the right main wheel. The ramp was quiet. The midday push wouldn't begin for about fifteen minutes or so, with Todd's plane one of the first scheduled to arrive. There were no other pilots around, since he was showing up in the middle of a shift to pick up the rest of his schedule. He knew that soon the ramp would resemble an aircraft carrier, with every bit as much danger and almost as much noise. The commuter aircraft would be coming in from all over the region to make the connections with the TransGlobe jets, whose departures begin at 1:00. The noise and hectic activity were imminent. But, for now, it was quiet.

A loud conversation began increasing in volume as a couple of people neared Todd from around the corner near the Gate Eleven doors. Just as they were almost in site, Todd overheard one exclaim, "...and so Grant comes back. Then this guy, bleeding now, jumps at him. Then KAPOOSH! According to Greg, he nails him right here...."

Two young rampers rounded the corner of the building, with one holding a finger in the center of his forehead. He looked at Todd, moved his finger from his forehead and directed it his way, then said, "Hey, aren't you the guy?!" The ramper became more excited and said to Todd, "You're Todd Grant! You're the one that knocked that asshole out. I mean *clean* out! Where'd you learn to fight like that?!"

The other ramper turned without even slowing down and walked quickly into the pilot lounge. Todd and the ramper made eye contact, but the ramper looked away before vanishing through the doorway. The excited one stopped and said, "Wish I could have seen it!"

Todd turned his head from the now empty lounge doorway to the excited ramper and said, "Really wasn't much to see. The whole thing's kinda a blur to me now."

"I bet *everything's* a blur now to that assbite Gary—and that'd be fine with me. That sonofabitch wrote me up once for helpin' some lady down the airplane steps. He said it was the gate agent's job—we're too dirty and sweaty to help out, he said. Hell, she had a connection to make and we couldn't find a gate agent anywhere."

"Sounds like to me you did the right thing," Todd said, noting the ramper's genuine initiative. Todd looked back towards the empty doorway.

"Sounds like you did the right thing, too!" The ramper replied with a little shadow boxing. The ramper then turned and headed for the pilot lounge door. Looking forward he said with a smile, "Gawd, I wish I'd seen that....KAPOOSH!" He then disappeared.

Todd had fought as a freshman on his fraternity's boxing team. At a hundred and eighty pounds, he was certainly not a heavyweight. But, he fought heavyweight because he was the biggest guy that his frat had to offer. He also never lost. He was quick and strong, which were good qualities. More importantly, he had brains and balance. He wore out the huge guys from the jock frats. He had a keen sense of leverage that allowed him to use the opponent's momentum to take the opponent off balance, allowing him an opportunity to score.

At the end of his freshman year, he recognized that the inherent dangers associated with boxing conflicted with his desire to maintain a valid pilot medical certificate. So he gave it up— undefeated.

The recollection of yesterday's fight brought back the horrible fact that Chris was gone. She was really gone. He planned to check the pilot information file in operations for any word on her memorial service, but the call to Kelly got him sidetracked. Three weeks ago, Bill and Scott's families scheduled the memorial services for the weekend. That way, more pilots could attend since there are fewer flights on weekends. It really didn't matter, though. Seventy percent of the pilots at Bands attended the memorial services for Bill and Scott. Dozens of flights were canceled because the pilots called in sick. The company didn't even question it. Chris's service would probably be scheduled for this weekend, too.

Bill's service was first and held at a small Methodist church in Sterling, Virginia, about four miles north of the airport. The church couldn't seat all who attended. The scores of pilots in attendance all wore generally the only suit they owned—their dark interviewing suit, with black polished shoes, white dress shirt and red silk tie. This was the mufti required to get a pilot job. After that, it went back in the closet for use again at a much later time. No one thought that their suits would be used for this type of occasion.

Bill's service was dignified and relatively painless for the pilots. Bill was, like Scott, unmarried. Bill's parents and two sisters had just returned from laying him to rest near their home in Butler, Pennsylvania. The service up there happened while they were still in a state of shock. Now, it had been a week since *the accident*. Seeing all the bright young pilots at the service reminded them of how senseless it all was. It was just too much for them. All of the pent-up emotions were released by the family at the service. The weeping was so loud and so severe that the pilots in attendance reacted with the opposite emotions of strength and support.

It wasn't that way at Scott's. His started at four that afternoon at Saint Paul's Episcopal Church in Old Town Alexandria. The services were scheduled to begin at different times to allow everyone the opportunity to attend both services. Everyone did. For some reason, the news media poured out for Scott's. You could almost convince yourself that it was because the church was physically closer to the local Washington press corps. In reality, it was because his name, and not Bill's, had been splattered across every magazine, newspaper, and television screen for the preceding week. After all, he was the one at the controls when it went down.

The press corps were not allowed on the church property. The Alexandria Police set up big yellow DO NOT CROSS tape all the way around the building to keep them away. Unfortunately, this made the service that much more of a spectacle.

Inside the spacious church, the pastor led the congregation in an opening hymn, followed by the Lord's Prayer. Then he began his eulogy. Every eye focused on him as he began speaking to directly to the pilots:

"In the early days of World War II, a young British aviator by the name of John Gillespie Magee, Jr. wrote a poem to his mother just after landing his Spitfire following a practice flight. It was a picture perfect morning and he wanted to describe to her his feelings about flying. I think the poem is also indicative of what Scott thought of flying. It goes like this...

Oh, I have slipped the surly bonds of earth
And danced the skies on laughter-silvered wings;
Sunward I've climbed and joined the tumbling mirth
Of sun-split clouds—And done a hundred things
You have not dreamed of—Wheeled and soared and swung
High up in the sunlit silence. Hovering there,
I've chased the shouting wind along and flung
My eager craft through footless halls of air.
Up, up the long delirious burning blue
I've topped the windswept heights with easy grace,
Where never lark, or even eagle, flew;
And, while with silent, lifting mind I've trod
The high untrespassed sanctity of space
Put out my hand, and touched the face of God."

The pastor paused for a long moment, then continued. "Two days after writing this poem, John Gillespie Magee, Jr. was killed when his Spitfire collided with another over southern England. His mother received the poem the same day she got word of his death. Many have been inspired by the words of that young Spitfire pilot.

Much has been written and reported of the events of last week with Scott. What has *not* been written is the kind of love and compassion for flying *and* for people that I knew existed within Scott.

I bet not one of you knew that Scott volunteered at least twice a month as a Big Brother to some of the most destitute and hopeless young boys in Alexandria. He would take six or seven kids across the Wilson Bridge to Hyde Field and arrange for them to sit in some of the airplanes. He'd explain what the dials did and how the controls worked. Then, they'd design paper airplanes and compete against each other, using basic aerodynamic principals. He promised ten boys last spring that whomever gave him a report card with at least a 'B' average would get an hour's flying time in one of those Cessnas. Did you know that he spent over four hundred dollars fulfilling that promise, because every single kid came back with at least a 'B' average. Every single kid. He, single-handedly, changed the direction of their lives."

Todd remembered looking around at the people around him. They had all put on their Ray Bans, supposedly because the late afternoon sun was shining in through the stained glass. He started to pull out his, but Kelly stopped him and held his hand tightly. The Ray Bans only covered the eyes. The red faces and tear marks down their cheeks gave them away.

It was funny, Todd thought. He and Scott played the *Guess Todd's Past* Trivia game for ages, yet Todd never knew that Scott volunteered to help underprivileged kids.

By the time the pastor had finished, everyone was smiling for having known Scott, and at the same time crying for having to say good-bye. Todd handled it all fairly well to that point. Then the pastor announced the closing hymn. It was one that he remembered Scott singing while slumped in an easy chair and gripping a beer by the bottle neck over at Todd's apartment one late night. Scott had a wonderful voice and loved the hymn. He even wrote away to the Air Force Academy gift shop and purchased an album recorded by the Cadet Chorale that had that particular hymn on it.

The pastor continued. "Scott's favorite hymn couldn't be found in this church. I had to call Father Joseph at the Andrews Air Base Chapel and have him send over all the Armed Forces Hymnals that he could muster. There should be one in front of you. Would you please open to page one ninety-two, 'Lord Guard and Guide the Men Who Fly', and sing verses one and four. Scott's listening, so sing it proudly."

The congregation of pilots rose noisily in the echoing chapel, but no one looked around. Every pilot looked down at his hymnal and scanned the verses. Many were surprised to discover that there was an anthem that was for pilots, albeit Air Force pilots. They studied every word, since they didn't dare look around. The organist completed the slow-paced introduction, then everyone began singing:

Lord, guard and guide the men who fly
Through the great spaces of the sky
Be with them traversing the air
In darkening storms or sunshine fair

Aloft in solitudes of space
Uphold them with your saving grace

O God, protect the men who fly
Through lonely ways beneath the sky.

By the time the song was over, few were still singing. The singing became too difficult. Their lower lips stiffened and their foreheads tensed. Tears dripped onto hundreds of Ray Bans.

The sound of the approaching turboprop engine brought Todd back to the present day. He took off his sunglasses, wiped his eyes, then his face, and put his sunglasses back on. He jumped off the power cart and lifted his bags as he noticed aircraft 977TE taxi by and head to the far end of the ramp. Soon, he would be in the air. He could always find happiness there.

ELEVEN

KELLY looked over at Jeff Caldwell as the group walked out of the administration office. "I've got to make another call."

Jeff was one of the two attorneys she was accompanying to the courthouse. He was younger than the other attorney, but clearly more poised and in charge. He, like Susan, had taken an special interest in Kelly. He also recognized that since Todd was still in the "minor leagues" as a pilot and Kelly was just about to enter law school, they had no money for entertainment. So Jeff often invited them aboard their large boat earlier in the summer to motor around the Chesapeake Bay with his wife and two small kids. Todd said Jeff was the first "normal" lawyer he'd ever met. They all became good friends.

"The conference room is the third door on the right from the top of the stairs. We're starting in ten. Is something wrong?"

"No. I'll be right there."

Jeff gave her a casual salute, then turned and walked away with the older attorney a pace behind him toward the stairway. She returned to the same pay phone in the foyer and put in another quarter, then dialed her office again.

"Sandy, this is Kelly. Has Todd called?"

"Yea, he just did. He said he'll call again when he comes back through Dulles later this afternoon."

"O.K. Thanks," she said, then hung up. She knew before she made the call that she wouldn't be able to reach him. She was simply nervous about the earlier call and would just have to wait until later to discuss it with Todd.

She walked briskly upstairs to the conference room. Only Jeff and the other attorney were present. "Where's Campbell and Campbell?" she asked.

"They know they're licked. They've still got four minutes. They'll show up in about three and a half and say that their client just can't come up with the full three million and would we be able to accept two point four? Then I'll say 'blow it out your ass. It's three or we walk down to the courtroom.' Then they'll bitch about it for show, then cave in. I've played this game before." The three smiled. They were going to settle and they had the upper hand.

About a minute later, two older gentlemen—nice men—walked in and introduced themselves. Kelly and her two attorneys stood up. "Sorry if we've kept you folks," the older of the two began. "I just got off the phone with the CFO of KayBax. He just can't find three million in cash without closing down the company. He wanted to know if we can work out some other acceptable terms. Maybe stocks, capital equipment, something."

"Nope. I guess you'll just have to tell him to close it down."

"Think of all the workers that'll be put out on the street if we do that."

"You really don't expect us to believe that, do you now, Thompson?" Jeff asked, indignantly. Both were now standing squarely at each other, with the conference table the only intermediary.

Thompson leaned forward slightly. "You know that KayBax has been on S&P's watch list for more than two years. Do you think they'll be able to generate that kind of money and still stay solvent? Here are their financial disclosures. See for yourself." Thompson got increasingly irritated the more he talked with the young attorney. He slung the envelope across the table, and would have fallen off had it not bumped into Jeff's leg. Jeff didn't flinch.

"Blow it out your ass, Thompson. It's three mill or we walk down to the courtroom." Kelly almost laughed when she heard him actually say it. No one had even sat down yet.

"We'll need some time to figure out how to get the three million to him, but we'll try," Thompson said as he and the other attorney finally pulled out a chair and sat down.

Jeff reached into his briefcase and produced manila folder similar to the one just hurled at him. He slung it at Thompson. This time, Thompson flinched to grab it. "Bruce Dodd is now a paraplegic because of KayBax. He has the rest of his life to sit on his ass. I don't. Review these agreements and payment schedules, and sign them in ten minutes, or we go to court. We'll leave you alone to peruse them."

The trio left and closed the door. Jeff started to smile. As they got a safe distance from the room, Kelly said, "Jeff, you really scared me in there. You were kind of brutal. You certainly gained no friends."

"Someone said, 'If you want a friend, buy a dog,'" he said with a smile, then continued. "I interviewed with them eight years ago. They turned me down. They said I was talented and bright. However, I lacked the assertiveness that their firm was looking for in a litigation attorney. Wanna know who told me that?"

"Thompson?" she asked, pointing behind her as they continued walking away from the conference room.

"Uh huh. I can just hear the general council for KayBax telling Thompson when he gets back: 'Son, your firm just doesn't have the assertiveness that we're looking for.' Then he'll yell over at his secretary and say 'Gladys, get that young Caldwell boy on the line over there at Banks, Yang, and Costello.' You know Kelly, a smart person once gave me some advice that I'll never forget. I remember the words exactly. He said 'Never back down. Never show weakness or fear. Always act like you are made of steel.'"

The three arrived downstairs by now and were able to chuckle freely over their victory.

• • • •

Todd lay his case underneath the left wing of the Javelin after the propellers stopped. He grabbed a small screwdriver and began his walkaround inspection as the rampers opened the rear door and the gate agent assisted the passengers down the steps. Todd checked underneath the left wing and into the wheel well. Numerous hydraulic, electrical and pneumatic lines were neatly secured along the top and sides of the well. The Javelin, like most modern commuter aircraft, was a flying computer. Each system, whether pressurization or hydraulic, electrical or power plant, had its own monitoring and control systems. These computers kept the hydraulic pressure from either going too high or too low, or kept the engines from overpowering or flaming out. Most of it was automatic and could be monitored from the cockpit. But both pilots had to know how to manually control those systems should one or more of them fail.

He worked his way around the front of the left wing and up to the propellers where he rotated and inspected each one. As he was just about to turn towards the aircraft's nose, he made eye contact with the ramper that earlier kept walking when the other stopped to talk about the fight. The ramper quickly turned away and reached for a bag to hand down the steps to another. This time, however, he faced away from Todd.

Walking around to the other engine nacelle, he used his screwdriver to open up the oil cap and oil filter bypass access panels. After inspection, he checked the propellers and the leading edge de-ice boots and the stall warning sensor. He finished the walkaround at the back of the airplane by stepping back and looking up at the tail section, which rose some eighteen feet above the ground. To the passengers, it was a tiny, nineteen seat airplane. To Todd, it was both art and science. The rampers finished unloading the bags from the inbound flight and were just finishing up putting the bags aboard for the outbound. He looked around for the ramper that was avoiding him and saw him in the truck that was used to pull the bag carts. He was writing something on a clipboard and didn't see Todd as he climbed up the steps and into the cabin. The ramper that talked to him earlier was locking the baggage door. Todd looked at the nametag sewn on his shirt.

"Hey Mark. Who's that ramper that was with you earlier? He kinda gives me the creeps."

"Ben Robertson. Yea, he's an odd one. Never smiles. You're the third person to ask me about him."

"How long has he been working here?"

"Couple of months, I suppose. He's a part-timer. Gives everyone that evil eye. He's really not a bad guy, though. He never bitches pay or work hours. But then again, he never really says anything positive, either. Hey, if you don't like him, just nail him right here!" The ramper smiled and pointed to the middle of his forehead.

"You're not gonna let me forget about that, are you," Todd said, smiling back.

The ramper brought his cuffed fists slowly up to a guard position, then slowly jabbed toward Todd's face. "Kapoosh," he said softly.

Todd shook his head ruefully and turned around towards the cockpit where the two pilots were finishing up the flight log for the trip. Now that he would be relieving Rick Donnelly, Paul Stewart would close out the flight log and begin another sheet with Todd listed as the Copilot for the rest of the shift.

"Hi, guys," Todd said as he approached the cockpit. The two turned around and smiled. Todd continued: "No Mohammed Ali jokes, O.K.?"

"You bet. Wouldn't wanna get you upset!"

"I don't think I like the reputation I'm getting."

"We were thinking. Are you available for hire? We both have people we'd like to punch out from time to time."

"I'm very expensive."

"Well, forget it then. I thought you'd do it mostly for the thrill."

"I get more than my share of thrills, thank you."

TWELVE

SUSAN BARTLETT was clearing her desk and preparing to leave just as Kelly got back to the office. It was six o'clock and, as was customary, half of the office lights were turned off. This was "first call" for all of the workaholic lawyers that they better be getting ready to go home. Billable hours were not to be accrued at the expense of the family. Jeff and the other attorney went straight home from the courthouse, since both of them lived in Annapolis.

Jeff was particularly anxious to get home because he had to pack for a two-day conference in Florida that he would be leaving for the following afternoon. He had racked up enough frequent flier miles to take his wife and son along and would be taking an extra three days off following the conference for a mini vacation.

Kelly's apartment in Severna Park was closer than her office in Bowie, but Todd was away and someone had to scan the signed agreements into the computer and put the originals in the office safe.

"I guess Todd's out of town," Susan Bartlett said as Kelly walked by her door without slowing.

Kelly backed up. "Susan. Sorry I didn't notice you. Yea. He's off on a two day trip. Hey, do you have a minute?"

"Sure." Susan motioned her in as she went around her desk and sat down.

"I think this is kinda serious. I got a phone call earlier today from a guy that accused Todd of sleeping with a female pilot who was killed in a hit and run accident over the weekend. He also made it sound like Todd was responsible for the hit and run. You and I know Todd. One, he's not a good enough liar to get away with having an affair. And of course he wouldn't hurt a fly, much less run someone down in a car. I just wonder what he did to make someone make those kind of accusations."

"Did he know her well?"

"Yea. He flew with her for the month of June. She was separated from her husband and she had a reputation of one who slept around. Todd became a friend of hers. He told me about the kind of miserable life she had and felt sorry for her. He felt like he was someone she could confide in. But, I'm positive that he never slept with her."

"Does Todd have any enemies?"

"Yea. And he was who I first thought about after I got the call. Yesterday, a pilot made a lewd comment about this girl just after Todd was told about her being killed. He decked the guy in front of a whole bunch of other people."

"Well, that's easy. The guy's obviously trying to make life tough at home for Todd. I wouldn't worry about it much. Still, there are a lot of crazy people in this world. Be careful if you get any more threats, particularly with Todd away. We always have a room for you at our place if you want."

"I never really thought about *that*. Sorta gives me the willies." She paused, then dismissed it: "Na. I doubt he'd try anything. He's gotta be stupid anyway, thinking that he wouldn't be suspected. Todd will take care of him when he finds out about the call."

"So Todd doesn't know about the call yet."

"I've tried to reach him a few times today, and I'm sure we'll catch each other later tonight."

"You be sure to tell him to settle his dispute with this guy with non-threatening *words*. If the guy *isn't* as stupid as you think, he could still have Todd up on charges of battery. He has to walk a fine line to resolve this."

"Poor Todd. He's been through a lot." She touched her index finger, followed by the others as she listed his reasons for unhappiness: "First he lost Scott. Then they blame Scott for the accident, which deeply hurt Todd. Then, another friend of his dies. He gets into a fight at work. And now, accusations are being made about his marital fidelity and more."

"How are *you* handling all of this?"

"O.K. I guess. But, we're a team. When bad things happen to Todd, I feel the pain as well."

• • • •

About an hour after her conversation with Susan, Kelly pulled into her open garage just as the late summer sun was beneath the horizon. She gave her apartment window a good look. The apartment complex, though old, was surrounded by a safe neighborhood. She normally didn't think much about the safety of her home, but her conversation with Susan spooked her. If someone was furious enough to make that kind of accusation, would they try something more harmful? The lights were out, as they were supposed to be. However, it didn't diminish her anxiety. Her mind was swimming as she slowly unlocked the door and turned on the light. Everything looked in order, except for an open drawer in the far corner of the room next to the bookcase. It was where they kept stationary, pictures, greeting cards, and letters. The drawer where they kept their checkbook and important documents was closed.

As she walked toward the open drawer, she didn't notice the piece of paper laying upside down in the output tray of the laser printer. She looked in the drawer and saw nothing unusual. Just as she closed the drawer, the phone rang. *Must be Todd*, she thought as she raced to the phone.

"Hello."

There was a moment of silence on the other end of the line.

"I think you should know that Todd has been unfaithful to you."

The voice was not the same as the one earlier today. She held her breath and her knees became weak. After a moment, she summoned up the strength to speak, although not confidently: "I don't believe you. You'll have to give me proof."

"I'm afraid I have no proof. I just thought you needed to know. I'm very sorry, Kelly." Then he hung up.

She shuttered. It was definitely not the same person that had called before. His voice was sincere and non-threatening. He mentioned nothing of the hit and run. As she hung up the phone, she noticed the answering machine had a message on it. She grabbed her pen and wrote a note, quoting the complete conversation that just occurred. Voice style and inflection. Everything. She then pressed the button and the recorder's beep sounded, followed by a foreign tone. The tone sounded again. Then, the electronic clattering of a fax message was replayed. The fax machine that Todd made in college was designed to always listen for a tone, then receive the fax and direct it to the laser printer. The answering machine couldn't tell that it was a fax coming in, so it recorded the gibberish like any other message.

She looked over at the laser printer and saw the piece of paper. She then glanced at the bookcase where their laptop normally sat in it's case. Todd had it. When he had the laptop, he usually faxed her notes rather than leaving messages.

She grabbed the paper and turned it over. It said: `"K.W. I would rather tell you in person rather than by fax, but I think it's better than finding out from someone else. I slept with Chris Thomas a few times in June. I'm truly sorry. I didn't kill her, though. I swear. I'll call you later and tell you everything. I love you deeply, R.C."`

She started shaking and crying uncontrollably as she read it again. "Oh, dear God," she said out loud in a broken voice. "Oh, no. Please, God."

• • • •

Todd had, by now, completed leg four of six for the day. The shift began out of Pittsburgh, then Todd picked up the remaining five legs. He went from Dulles to Kennedy, Kennedy back to Dulles, then Dulles to Salisbury, Maryland. He had forty-five minutes in Salisbury, so he decided to give Kelly a call from there, rather than back at Dulles. He would only have fifteen minutes at Dulles before heading out on his last leg to Syracuse, where he would stay overnight. The Grants were on a tight budget and long distance calls were seldom made. Though they lived in Severna Park, some thirty five miles east of Washington, they had a Washington area phone number. Dulles was fifteen miles *west* of Washington, but had pay phones that accessed Washington numbers. Since a call could be made for just a quarter, he normally called her only when passing through Dulles. He knew, however, that she had tried him earlier today and he wanted to be sure to catch her before she went to bed.

Paul stayed in the airplane to work on his timesheet. Todd walked from the airplane about fifty feet across the asphalt ramp towards the brand new terminal at Salisbury.

The town of Salisbury is in the heart of Maryland's eastern shore, midway between the Chesapeake Bay and the Atlantic Ocean. The airport was pleasant and serene. There was never a hustle and bustle in Salisbury. With the rural sky still a bright orange from the now absent sun, it reminded him of lazy summer sunsets back in Manila, Arkansas. It put him in a good mood.

The inside of the terminal was bright and cheerful. A theme restaurant at the end of the terminal was closing for the night. Only a couple more inbound commuter flights were due after 9:00 p.m. Todd's flight was the last one outbound and was only booked for four passengers. The restaurant owner would always walk over to the TransGlobe Express counter and ask the ticket agent about the outbound loads. If there were more than ten passengers booked, he would stay open a while longer. It was the outbound people that normally ate there.

The pay phones were straight across the hall from the restaurant. He went to the first one and called home. The phone was busy. He hung up the phone, then picked it up and tried the call again. Still busy. He walked over to the restaurant and said hello to the lone waitress that was turning chairs upside down on their respective tabletops. He helped her with the last of them. "You think I could get your last cup of coffee before you turn off the pot?"

"Sure," she said cheerfully. "Just walk around and pour yourself one." She pointed around the counter to the large coffee machine as she headed for the kitchen.

"Thanks a lot," he said with a smile. He'd have some coffee, then try to call Kelly again in a couple of minutes. He poured himself a cup, replaced the carafe, then walked around to the front of the counter and hopped up on a stool. After a minute or so, the owner came up behind him and said hello. Todd said hi and thanked him for the late coffee.

"So, I guess you only have four booked out of here tonight."

"Yea. I can always guess our loads outbound by the number of chairs you have turned over in here."

"Yep. When you are booked for more than ten, I make about sixty more dollars. It's worth it to check your bookings."

"Sure is nice out here. This is one of my favorite airports. The eastern shore is always calm and, well, slow paced."

"Have you ever spent any time on the eastern shore?"

"Not much. Although, for fun I'll take my RC model airplane and fly it over at Bay Bridge, now that it's closed."

"Yea. I feel bad for ole' Jake McFadden. First, they shut down his airport. Then someone steals the airport car. Then he has to lay off his staff of flight instructors and fuelers. We've got about six airplanes tied down out here that used to be at Bay Bridge. And that's only because Easton Airport ran out of ramp space at *their* airport. Jake's losing money fast and he's not a happy camper."

"I hear the county government has finally filed a counter suit against the CABBA organization."

"Yep. But every day that passes brings Jake one day closer to bankruptcy. You know, the county may own the airport, but Jake owns the fuel business and flight school." The owner got back to work as he chatted.

In the hallway, a man turned on a floor polisher that broke the silence of the terminal. "Nice talking with you, but I know you've gotta close down here and I need to make a call. Thanks again for the coffee." Todd slid a dollar bill under the saucer, then shook the owner's hand.

"You take care now."

"You too. I hope we get more than ten booked tomorrow night!"

"I could use the customers!"

Todd walked back over to the phone and dialed home. It rang twice, then Kelly answered. "Hello, " she said defensively.

"Hey, K.W., whassup?"

"Go to hell, Todd. How could you sleep with Chris, you son-of...," she said, then broke up into tears.

Todd held the phone closer to his ear. The floor polisher was interfering with his conversation. "K.W., what are you saying?"

She hung up on him. His heart started to race. He looked at the man who had his back to him as he polished the floor. He quickly ran down to the next group of pay phones where it was a little quieter and called her back. After four rings, the answering machine picked up. After the beep, he said, "Listen K.W., pick up the phone. I didn't sleep with Chris. Something's terribly wrong here. Pick up the phone. Damn it, Chris—Er, eh, Kelly. Pick up the phone." He waited for a couple of seconds. "Come on. Damn it K.W.! It's not true." He waited another two seconds, then he slammed the phone down. He stood there and faced the phone. His chest tightened as he ran his hands through his hair.

He walked purposefully back to the airplane. It was now almost dark and the ramp was glowing from the yellow stadium lamps atop either end of the terminal. He looked at his watch. He still had twenty five minutes until departure. *"Calm down,"* he thought to himself. *"It's Gary. I'll kill the bastard."*

He walked up the rear steps of the airplane and entered the cabin where Paul was sitting, now working on next month's bid sheets.

"Did you get a hold of Kelly?" he asked cordially.

"That sum' bitch Gary called her and told her that I slept with Chris Thomas."

"You're kidding!" He put down his pen. "What'd she say?"

"Not much. She said she couldn't believe that I slept with her, then she hung up on me. I tried her again, but she wouldn't pick up the phone. I muh na kee'l that sum' bitch Gary." As he got more and more angry, his southern dialect became more pronounced.

"You need to report him to the police or something. He's always been an ass, but this time I think he's flipped."

"I really need to talk to Kelly. I wish I knew what he said to her. Gawd dammit. You'd think she knew me better than that. I'm mad at her for even *listening* to him, much less believing him."

• • • •

Kelly threw the answering machine across the room. The phone dangled behind in trail. The other end of the phone cord, connected to Todd's fax machine snapped at the connector, sending a clear piece of plastic ricocheting off the countertop.

She was still sobbing wildly. She wanted to believe Todd, but she just couldn't. Who else knew that she was K.W. and he was R.C.? No one. Who else even knew they had a fax machine. Very few. Why would two different people call her. It couldn't have been coercion, because the second guy felt bad even telling her. Todd had the computer. He must have sent the fax. He must have slept with her.

But why did he recant his story just then? Was he just waiting until he got home to admit guilt? She found herself moving around the apartment nervously. She walked into the bedroom and called her parents in Arkansas. No answer. She again cried and lay down on the bed. He had violated their trust. Their marriage was over, just like that. "Oh God, no," she muttered into the pillow.

Todd called again three times that night.

No one answered.

THIRTEEN

THE MORNING SUN was bright through the small skylights in the lobby. "Hi, Kiesha, I'm here to see James Hatch," the tall, thin man of forty said to her. His sunglasses still covered his eyes which were looking down to his shirt pocket to find his FBI badge.

"Hi, Stu. I'll sign you in." She slapped a visitor's badge on the counter top.

"Thanks, how's school?"

"Got a B in calculus. Who'duh thought?!"

"Hey, that's super! See ya later." Special Agent Stuart Varney walked down the hall, removed his sunglasses, and punched the "^" button on the elevator panel and waited. The NTSB offices were like his second home. He had been there on countless occasions. This was his third trip regarding the Bands 2234 crash. As the elevator doors closed, he brushed off his coat and straightened his tie. It was unneccesary, though. He was always immaculate.

The elevator doors opened and Stu made a left down the wide hallway, then a right down a much more narrow one, where he arrived at the office.

"James, gawd it stinks in here," he said as he entered and sat down in his office without knocking.

"The smell of quality workmanship." James reached beyond the papers he was working on and ran his hand across his desk top.

"Hey! Wow. Looks nice."

"Thanks for coming over. We're gonna pull you into the Bands Twenty-two Thirty-four investigation after all. I had a pilot come in here and ask questions about how the investigation is proceeding. He was also at the press conference when we released the CVR tapes."

"Tell me more."

"Guy's name is Todd Grant. We don't know anything about him except he claims to be a friend of the Copilot killed in the accident. He brought up the Stall Warning System during our conversation with him. Barney was in here also."

"Why did he come to you? Why didn't he go to Barney?"

"He sweet talked Kiesha into calling someone up here, and she thought of me."

"Hmm. So this penguin theory of yours may have some merit?"

"You Fibbies. You know everything. I haven't yet finished my analysis, but I think so. If it was an act of sabotage, we need to find some more of the materiel. We have a partially melted plastic wind-up toy penguin with a piece of seared wire on one wing and that's about it.

The wires to where it was connected must have been extremely thin and simply disintegrated in the explosion and heat. We were fortunate that the toy was found at all. I'm trying to figure out, using spectroscopy, the wire type and gauge connected to the penguin. We know that the insulation was quite thin, leading us to believe it was the kind of wire that they use for low voltage applications, like computer wire wraps and such. If I find that, I can find other similar wire residues on the other components at Station 110."

"Station 110. That's where a lot of the plane's computers and electrical junk is located?"

"Yea. You're obviously keeping up with your homework."

James and Stu, although from altogether different backgrounds, were vigorous competitors. They were both full of tenacity and drive. They probably wouldn't be such good friends if they worked in the same organization.

James continued. "The Fuel Crossfeed Controller, the main Electrical Bus Relay, Boost Pump Relays, the Flight Management and Air Data Systems Computers, and the Stall Warning System—you know, the thing that rang out six times on the voice recorder—all are located on Station 110."

"You found over a hundred pounds of two-ounce items at the crash site. What makes you think a toy penguin is responsible? There were three kids on that flight. It could have been one of theirs."

"You don't normally see wind-up penguins with their legs removed. That takes the fun out of the toy. And more importantly, the wire taped to one of the wings was put there deliberately. Here let me show you something." James reached in his desk and pulled out a new toy penguin and wound it. "I got this at the Imaginarium Store at Tyson's Corner Mall last week. Dollar fifty nine, plus tax. They didn't carry this particular one at Kay Bee's or Toys-R-Us. But they had it at both the Imaginarium Store and Kiddie City. I bet if I searched an area within twenty minutes of my home in Reston I could find a dozen stores that carry these wind-up penguins."

James reached for a pencil and held it above one of the wings. "Watch this." He pushed in the metal knob in the back of the little penguin and the wings started rotating slowly around in a circle, tapping the pencil every second. He put it down after six taps, and it continued to wriggle on its side on his new desktop.

"Now," James said excitedly as he reached down and pulled up a tape recorder and placed it on his desk, where he quickly punched the PLAY button.

"Listen," he said. They both listened and heard the six successive sounds of the stall warning system. James tapped his pencil on his desktop like a music conductor as they listened.

"Now. Being black, I'm supposed to have a natural rhythm sense and can, of course, hear the correlation."

"Well, *even I* feel the rhythm."

"So you agree."

"Yep. Todd Grant. We'll look into him."

"You want his phone number, Stu?"

He stood and smiled fatherly at James as he shook his head no.

James realized that his offer was inconsequential and shrugged his shoulders.

Barney Rubble entered the room from behind Stu and put both hands on Stu's shoulders and shook them lightly. "You boys got it figured out, yet?"

Stu turned around quickly, looked down at the short man, then smiled. "Barney! How are you!" he asked as though he had run into old schoolmate.

"If I was any better I just couldn't stand it! I just got my workload decreased by one case."

"How's that?" Stu asked as James rose from his desk and took off his thin glasses.

"The board voted to take me off the Bands Twenty-two Thirty-four case. Gave it to some young hot shot who's never led a full investigation before. His last name is, uh, Hatch, I believe."

James muffled a smile.

"Hey, I know a young black feller' around here—a metallurgist as I recall—named Hatch."

"Congratulations, James," Barney said with a broad smile emerging. "The board members all said that they needed a smart, thorough, take-charge kinda guy to handle the case full time, what with all the publicity surrounding it. I told them I knew of the perfect guy, but I was simply too busy with three other cases."

"Thanks, Barney. I won't let you down."

"I remember twenty years ago when I got some advise from *my* boss on *my* first case. He said you should always listen to as many people as you can. And when you *do* find the truth, you'll almost always be surprised who it was that finally led you to it."

Barney smiled at James, then at Stu, then back at James. He then patted Stu on the shoulder, then vanished out the door.

Stu gathered his notes and closed them in his briefcase. "I feel sorry for Grant. He's probably thinking he got away with it. Little does he know that he's now up against the J-Team! You're first case. And it promises to be a real lulu!"

• • • •

"Sandy, I'm not gonna be in today. Is Susan in?" Kelly sounded normal, though she hadn't slept at all the night before.

"Sure, standby just a sec." Sandy clicked the hold button on her phone, then punched 2-2 on her phone. Moments later, Susan was talking to Kelly.

"Are you sick?"

"No. Listen, Susan. I need to talk to someone. I've, uh. Todd's, uh..."

"Why don't you go straight to my house. I got in here way too early and skipped breakfast. I broke one of my own rules. Why don't we start the day together with some pancakes and relaxed conversation?"

"You're a saint. I'd like that. Would eight forty-five be O.K.?"

"You bet. See you then."

Kelly already had her bags packed and were in the trunk of her car. The fax message from the night before had been crumpled up, then uncrumpled on the kitchen table. The tear marks had dried and disappeared. "Screw you." was handwritten across the page with a red felt-tipped pen.

• • • •

"John, this is Todd Grant," he said from his hotel room in Syracuse.

"Hey, killer. What's new?"

"How many reserves do you have for today? If possible, I'd like to drop my remaining four legs after I get back to Dulles at two o'clock. I'd like to start my three days off a little early."

"Let's see, hang on."

Todd could hear John Briggs typing and humming to himself.

"Looks like you're in luck. But, this time I'll have to dock you, uh, four point six hours. Is that all right? Unless, of course, you slug Gary again," John said as he chuckled.

"Nope. But I *am* gonna go see the sheriff about him."

"Really."

"Yea. He called my wife yesterday and told her that I'd been sleeping with Chris Thomas. Now she's not talking to me. I guess I'll file a harassment complaint or something with the police. It's probably best to start a file in case he keeps pestering us."

"Hey, good luck, Todd. If you need anything, let me know."

"Thanks, John. You've already helped me."

• • • •

Kelly and Todd had been to Susan and John Bartlett's place many times. Her house had a kind of homey softness about it. It was elegantly appointed and yet had a livable feel to it. Kelly and Todd dreamed of buying a home like Susan's someday. It was a six month-old home in a brand new subdivision. Most of the vacant lots surrounding her house had signs that said the lot number and a large red "SOLD" sign at an angle across them. The two dozen or so finished homes were large and beautiful. This was the newest subdivision in Bowie, Maryland and was on its way to being *the* place to live. Susan's car was already in the driveway as Kelly pulled up.

As Kelly reached for the doorbell, Susan swung open the door. A cool breeze hit her, indicating the sliding glass door in the back of her house must be open. Susan motioned her in with a faint smile, then turned and went straight back down the hallway toward the kitchen. On the right side, just inside the door was the staircase to the upstairs bedrooms. The entranceway extended as a hallway directly to the kitchen and family room in the back of the house. The breeze brought with it the smell of bacon frying. Kelly walked toward the kitchen, which was on the left side in the back of the house.

"You like biscuits or muffins?" Susan asked with her back to her.

Kelly sat down at the large kitchen table and stared out through the glass door and watched a squirrel jump from limb to limb in the thick trees just beyond Susan's perfectly manicured lawn.

"That's a stupid question. I know you'd kill for my biscuits."

Kelly started talking: "You know, you hear stories about pilots. How they're often chasing skirts and generally living the macho lifestyle. I didn't think Todd was like that. Maybe his character just isn't as solid as I thought."

"Obviously more has happened since we last talked." Susan poured some milk and flour into the small amount of bacon grease left after she drained the pan. The gravy for the biscuits wouldn't take long.

"I got a second phone call last night. This time it was from a guy that knew me, I think. I didn't really recognize his voice, but he knew me—called me Kelly. He said he was very sorry that he had to be the one to tell me, but it was true about Chris and Todd. It was definitely not the same person that called the office yesterday."

"So this guy that got punched is bringing his friends in on the plot to destroy you and Todd. You still don't believe it do you?"

"That's not it. I got a fax from Todd last night." Kelly's eyes began to water. She paused. Susan placed the gravy on the back burner and turned around and faced her. When she realized she was crying, Susan walked over to her. Kelly looked up at her, then stood and hugged her, mainly because she didn't want to look her in the eye as she talked. "You know, maybe I'm just not strong enough to handle this. I feel like I've been shot in the chest with a shotgun." Kelly reached around Susan's neck and wiped her eyes.

"What did the fax say?"

"It um..." Kelly began to talk, then moved away from Susan and looked down as she sat back down. "It, um, said that...." Again, she lowered her head and motioned for Susan to continue cooking breakfast. "...that he'd slept with her a couple of times in June and that, essentially, it was just a fling and that he still loved me. I couldn't believe how callous his words were. Here he was, telling me about his being unfaithful to me, then finishing it off with a *we'll talk about it when I get home* style. Like hell he will."

"You sure it was Todd that faxed it to you?"

"Yep, we have nicknames for each other. I'm K.W. He's R.C. Names we've been calling each other since the first time we met. The initials have no relevance to our names and very few people know that we call each other by them. The fax started with 'Dear K.W.' and ended with 'Love R.C.'"

"Wow. I just never thought he'd do something like that."

"He called last night and denied sleeping with her."

"Doesn't that make you suspicious?"

"I don't know what to think anymore. He could be lying to me and really did sleep with her. Hell, he could even have killed Chris for all I know. You know, he hasn't been himself since Scott died."

"But on the other hand...."

"But on the other hand he did make a scene in the pilot lounge that would cause that jerk to do start a big rumor about him and Chris. But that guy couldn't have pulled off such a convincing fax."

Susan looked hard at Kelly as she served the meal and sat down. "You are staying here until you can get it all sorted out."

"No, but thanks, Susan. This is the first place Todd will think of when he finds out I've left. I'll rent a room at the Comfort Inn for a week or so."

"Absolutely not. Look, the people moving into the new house next door aren't gonna be in town until late Sunday. We've met them and they are super people. They asked us if we would watch the house for them until they get here from Texas. I'll call them and ask if we can keep your car in their garage. Todd will never know you're here. And furthermore, I'll bring some of your stuff here and you can work out of the guest bedroom upstairs. We'll tell Todd that you asked to use some of your vacation days."

"Susan, that's way too much of an imposition."

"Look, you'll need to have some time to clear your mind, establish facts, confirm suspicions, make decisions—whatever. You've also become too valuable at work to not be around at all. I'll schedule your day here so that you can get your work done and do what you need to do with your personal life. Staying here is the best option."

"Thanks, Susan. I'm sorry if I've disappointed you. I had hoped that you would come to depend on *me* for things. Now, I've become a burden on you."

"Look, I don't know whether you realize it or not, but you have become my closest friend next to John. I've admired you professionally from day one. But, more importantly, I enjoy being with you away from the office. This offer is not a professional one, it is a personal one."

Kelly's eyes filled with tears again.

• • • •

Todd arrived back at Dulles at 11:15 a.m. Paul Stewart taxied the aircraft to the gate as Todd completed the After Landing checklist and advised the company of their arrival time on the company's radio frequency.

Paul sensed how upset Todd was and, following the completion of the last checklist, tried to cut the tension: "Well, it's been a couple of hours now. Time to get a new Copilot."

Todd smiled. "The next one may actually be with you for the rest of the day!"

"Doubtful. Hey, I hope you and Kelly get it all straightened out."

"Thanks, me too."

Twenty five minutes later, Todd pulled up to the Loudoun County Sheriff's Office in Leesburg and went to the rear of the parking lot. The lot faced the side of the building with no windows. He had changed into a casual shirt, shorts, and tennis shoes on the way. As Todd entered the building, another car pulled up beside his.

Todd didn't know what to expect, as this was his first time in a police station. The receptionist sat in a separate room behind a Plexiglas window and spoke through a metal slotted hole in the center of the window. The foyer where Todd was standing was a mere eight by six feet. It had two small school chairs with flip-up desk tops in the right rear corner and a white door on the opposite wall to the left of the big Plexiglas partition. He looked up towards the top of the partition, all of which reminded him of a bank teller's cage.

"Can I help you?" a rough looking middle aged woman asked insincerely from behind the glass.

"Yes ma'am. I'd like to file a complaint against a guy who has been harassing my wife."

The woman turned away slowly. Maybe she didn't hear him. He leaned closer to the slot and repeated: "I'd like to file a com...."

"I heard ya the first time," she said as she reached into a drawer and retrieved a form, then slowly handed the form through the metal sleeve at the bottom of the window.

"Thanks," Todd said upon receipt of the form. "I'd also like to check the balance in my Christmas Club account." Todd raised his eyebrows and smiled.

The lady looked up at him without expression, then said, "When you're done with the form, let me know."

"All right," he replied. She obviously didn't see humor in much of anything.

Todd sat down and placed his sunglasses on the adjacent chair and his flight bag on the floor. He filled out the information on the top of the form, including his address and phone number as well as Gary's phone number, which Todd got from a company social roster in his flight bag.

He then had to decide what to put into the narrative section. He knew that the fight would have to be discussed. He also knew that Gary had admitted that he had provoked the altercation on the company's incident report and that, for his own protection, should attach a copy of it. He would describe the short phone call that he had with his wife last night where he was accused of sleeping with Chris and how he could suspect no one else but Gary of making such a call. After organizing his thoughts on his notepad, he carefully prepared a factual, detailed narrative.

After some thirty minutes, he returned to the woman behind the glass and slipped the form to her. Then he slipped a copy of the incident report under the glass and asked her to make a copy of it and attach it to the form. She grunted, got up and walked over to the copier, made a quick copy, stapled the copy to the form, then walked back toward the glass partition. About midway across the room, she yelled, "Sergeant Cripp!" This startled Todd, but he managed to calmly accept his copy of the incident report from under the glass. She told him to again be seated. He returned the report to his flight bag and sat down as he noticed her hand the other papers over the top of an opaque plastic partition to a large hairy arm that grabbed it and disappeared back behind the partition.

After about five minutes, he walked up to the glass and asked how much longer it would be. She said they were reviewing it now, and to sit down and just wait. After about ten strenuous minutes or so, a click sounded as an electric lock to the side door was released. A burly police officer appeared, complete with a Marine Corps-style hair cut and a well-polished badge. He also had a huge firearm holstered to a thick leather belt.

"Mr. Grant," he said in a rich, polite, baritone voice.

Todd stood as though being called to attention. "Yes, Sir."

"Come on back." The policeman held the door open as Todd grabbed his Ray Bans and his flight bag and walked quickly through the doorway and into a large, open office. They walked to the left rear of the office area. A hallway extended from behind the officer's chair to the left, out of view.

"Sit there if you'd like."

"Thanks," Todd said softly as he sat in the chair against the left wall across from rearmost one of the six desks. As the policeman walked around the back of the desk and sat down, he made eye contact with a man in a business suit who was sitting in the hallway with a yellow notepad, just out of Todd's view. The man had his right leg was crossed over his left knee and his pen was poised for note taking. The man's chair was positioned close to the corner of the hallway and, from there, the man could hear everything. The desktops in the processing area had no family pictures, no potted plants, no fancy desk clocks.

The desks were community property. They had no single owner and their starkness made them quite intimidating to the visitor.

"So, did you sleep with her?"

Todd was stunned and starred back at the officer, who maintained no emotion. "Could you be a little more specific?"

"Chris Thomas. Did you poke her?"

"What the hell kind of question is that?"

"You never said in your statement whether you actually slept with her or not."

Todd was furious. "You'll notice that I never said in there whether I slept with *your wife*, either."

"I don't like your tone, *son.*"

"Nor do I like yours—dad." Todd knew he was close to crossing over the line. "Listen, Chris Thomas was a friend of mine. She was married. I'm happily married. Enough said. So drop it."

"So you don't deny having slept with her."

"Listen *Pop.* For the record, I have neither slept with Chris Thomas nor your wife."

"When she died, where were you, *for the record*?"

Todd winced. "Why?" Todd's angered expression diminished.

"Call it lame curiosity." Another policeman entered the processing area from the rear hallway. Todd noticed that he had made a slight turn as though he were walking around something just out of his view.

"Ya'll think it was more than a hit and run?"

"We haven't ruled out anything."

Todd saw a slight shadow on the lower rear wall move ever so slightly. *Someone was eavesdropping!* He leaped up and walked around the right side of the desk and peered left. "There's a chair right here. You can hear better," Todd said loudly as he swung a chair in his direction.

"He's just waiting..." said the sergeant.

"*Daddy*, I wasn't talking to you," said Todd as his anger increased.

The man clicked his pen, stuck it in his shirt pocket, then rose. "Mr. Grant, I'm Inspector Dwight Conners," he said as he extended his hand. Todd started to shake it, then snapped his arm back.

"You guys are not being square with me. I'm leaving."

"We're not done with you," Sergeant Cripp said as he rose.

"*Yes!* You are, *pop,*" Todd said deliberately. He grabbed his flight bag, then walked over and pulled on the door to the entrance foyer. It didn't budge. "Open this gawd damned door, now!" Todd banged his fist against the door, sending an echo throughout the building. The sergeant looked at the inspector who smirked, then the sergeant walked slowly toward the door and stepped on a foot button near the baseboard. The door clicked and Todd left.

"He'll be back," said Inspector Conners to the sergeant who was walking back to the rear of the office.

"Why do you say that?"

The inspector held up Todd's sunglasses. "You don't think he'd want us to keep these, do you?"

"I guess not. So, how'd I do?"

"Well, I asked you to be combative with him. Anger a guy and he'll tell you all you need to know. But I could tell from the complaint form that he's very smart. He covers his bases well. He's alert and attentive. I think he knew something was up from the git-go. I say let's bring this Gary guy in and ask him what he knows about ole' Chris and Todd."

"So we didn't get anything out of this interrogation?"

"Oh, I wouldn't say that at all. Let's go back to my office and do some brainstorming." The sergeant nodded and walked back. The inspector reached over the opaque plastic partition and said, "Hey, Molly. Give these sunglasses to Todd Grant if he comes back for them. If not, call him later on and tell him we have them and he can come back and get them." The woman grabbed them and grumbled something back.

FOURTEEN

THE SPIRITED VOICE coming over the phone's earpiece reflected the excitement of the caller: "We got some good stuff!"

"So do we."

"You first."

"O.K." James Hatch sat back in his chair and flipped through some pages as he held the phone up to his ear with his shoulder. The offices were quiet, as most of the NTSB people in his area had gone to lunch. "First, the toy penguin was, in fact, wired into the Signal Summing Device. The SSD is the computer located at Station 110 that takes the input from the stall warning sensors on each wing and tells the stick pusher to drop the nose of the airplane in order to keep the plane from stalling."

Agent Varney said, "So, the stick pusher is supposed to automatically push the nose down if the airplane slows down too much?"

"Right. All big airplanes are required to have them. Some smaller airplanes also have them because of poor handling characteristics at critically slow airspeeds. The Javelin, for example, takes about seven thousand feet of altitude to recover from a full stall."

"That sounds like a *lot* of altitude!"

"That's a whole lot! Especially if you are flying below seven thousand. I've got more."

"Shoot!"

"Point two. The controller for the fuel boost pumps is located right next to the SSD. We found traces of two wires connected from there to the penguin. I was stumped so I called the people over from Darchoult to help me out. They said that the boost pumps are normally turned off when the aircraft is climbing through five thousand feet."

"Let me guess. They got the stall warning horn at about five thousand feet."

"Right. A relay in the boost pump controller normally sends five volts to a switch that shuts off the boost pumps. Looks like Grant took that five volt signal to the toy penguin and made it do the funky chicken with the stick pusher. This guy's a real live MacGuyver."

"I concur! We looked into his background and found him to be a summa cum laude in Electrical Engineering from Arkansas State. He wrote a senior thesis on something called Residual Voltage Effects on non-TTL Gates. His thesis was honored at an IEEE conference in San Fran the year after he graduated. He didn't attend, though. He was crop dusting in Arkansas. The guy is book smart and can practically apply those smarts. I found out that he made a fax machine from scratch."

"No way!"

"Yep. He's a MacGuyver all right."

"Well, Stu. What's the next step."

"How much more time do you need to organize your findings?"

"Better give me a few more days."

"I'll need a little more time, too. I don't as yet have a defensible motive."

• • • •

The Loudoun County homicide inspector entered his office. Sergeant Cripp was already sitting in a chair a couple of feet from the chalkboard. "O.K. Here's what we know thus far, Sergeant." Dwight Conners began writing on the chalkboard. He wrote in big letters: "Pebbles—."

"We know now without a doubt that Chris Thomas was murdered. She had tiny imprints of pebbles in her palm and scrapes on her left elbow and forearm. She was hit at some forty or fifty miles an hour and thrown into the ditch. She wouldn't get those kind of scrapes unless she went straight down on the pavement."

The sergeant spoke up. "Wait. She had car trouble, no oil in the tank, remember? Couldn't she have gotten those imprints by looking under her car for an oil leak?"

"It was pitch dark. She had no flashlight. She wouldn't have been able to see anything under there. I went there last night. She wouldn't have even tried to look under there. Which brings me to the next two points...." Sergeant Cripp leaned back and crossed his legs and Dwight wrote two more lines: "Paper Towel—" and just below it, "Blood—."

Dwight turned back to Cripp, who fidgeted slightly in his seat. "We found tracings of a paper towel that had been plugged into the oil drain. Someone unscrewed the drain plug and stuck a paper towel in it. After she started the car, enough oil pressure built up to pop out the paper towel and begin quickly draining the oil out of the car as she drove away."

"Did you find the paper towel plug?"

"Nope. Grant was smart enough to leave the real drain plug in the puddle of oil in the parking lot and grab the paper plug if it dropped out anywhere near it. We know he must have been waiting there in the lot, because he had to clean up his tracks and then follow her. But he was kinda stupid to think we wouldn't find minute paper fibers in the drain hole."

"How did he know how long it would take before she would have to pull over?"

"Don't know. I guess he figured it would run at least until she got on Route 28 South where it was good and dark. Now, about the blood." He pointed to the third bullet on the chalkboard. "We found some blood that matched hers about thirty feet in back of her car, along the shoulder."

"Was it from the scrapes on her arm?"

"Nope. Hardly any blood from those scrapes." He turned and wrote "Shoe polish—" on the chalkboard. "It was when he drop-kicked her. Her right cheekbone was crushed by a blunt object that left a residue of shoe polish on her cheek."

"A shoe!"

"We'll make a detective out of you, yet," Dwight said with a smile and turned back to the blackboard. He looked down at his notes as Cripp realized how inane his outburst had sounded. "After the kick, blood gushed from her nose and mouth and left a small puddle there and a trail back to her car. He must have propped her up against her car door because the blood dripped down her chin and onto her white pilot shirt while he went back to his car to ram her. She ended up face up and head low in the ditch. Now unless the laws of gravity don't apply when laying head low in a ditch, there's no way she could have gotten blood-soaked that way from being hit by the car."

Dwight drew a large circle around the bulletized lines and wrote "Murder:" directly above the circle. "Looks like ole' Todd Grant is smart, but he, nonetheless, left some great stuff for us to nail his ass." He then moved to the right and wrote "Motive:" and drew another circle just below it. "We need to fill in this circle."

"O.K. Just minutes ago, Grant said both he and Chris Thomas were both happily married."

"Nope," Dwight said as he scoured his notes.

"Whatta you mean, *nope*?"

"Nope. He said she was *married* and he was *happily* married."

"So."

"Well, that tells me that he knew at least something about her home life. Possibly the troubles she was having at home."

"You're digging."

"No. I'm trying to paint a picture. Who knows what. What happened when. Gathering crime scene evidence is straightforward. Trying to capture a motive is often much more difficult, particularly when the players may have been trying to cover up an affair in the first place."

"What about the way he quickly determined that we thought there was foul play involved? What about the way he got defensive and bolted out of here? If he didn't have anything to do with it, why didn't he cooperate more with us?"

"Well, you *did* ask him if he'd poked her! I would probably get defensive, too. What intrigues me is how *quickly* he angered and lashed back with the verbal abuse of your wife. He has feelings for Chris Thomas. That's obvious. I want to dig deeper and find out just what kind of relationship that they had. My initial guess is that he had a torrid fling with her that went sour and she was about to spring the news of the affair on his wife. I'd like to know if Grant's wife knew that Chris even existed. Also, does anyone else know about them?"

"I say we start with this Gary fellow that is supposedly harassing Grant. Could be that he's been framing Grant all along and *he's* our guy. Let's also talk to Al Thomas again."

"Yea. Maybe he's the jealous husband."

"Could be. What do we know about him?" Dwight moved over and sat down at his desk.

"He repairs VCRs at a video place in Alexandria. She moved out two months ago when they became legally separated."

"Who initiated the separation?"

"He did. Irreconcilable differences. She was always gone and he wanted her home making babies. She couldn't have kids and be a pilot, too. He said he still loved her, but came to realize that it would never work out."

"How'd he handle the news of her death?"

"He got real shook up."

"Imagine how shook up he'll be when he finds out she was murdered."

• • • •

The blue lights appeared in Todd's rearview mirror, but he didn't immediately notice them. He was scarcely two miles out of Leesburg, eastbound on Route 7. He was heading home, which was twenty five miles on the east side of Washington. He was twenty miles to the *west* of the Washington beltway. He had a long drive home, but it would give him some time to calm down and think about what to say to Kelly. He had just passed a scenic golf course on the right and noticed three ducks sail over the road in perfect formation. The road had few other cars in either direction in the mid afternoon, but would become much more congested when rush hour hits. Just as his blood pressure began dropping, he saw the lights.

"Bastards!" he said to himself as he slowed down, then stopped in the shoulder. They were gonna bring him back for more questions, he thought. The officer sat in his cruiser, seemingly motionless for what seemed an eternity. Todd rolled down his window and waited. The officer then slowly he got out and placed his right hand on his holster, then unlatched it. Todd noticed and placed his hands atop the steering wheel.

"I need to see your license and registration."

"You're not here to run me in?"

"That remains to be seen."

Todd reached in his back pocket and pulled out his billfold. The officer stepped back and held his hand on his revolver. Todd didn't make any sudden moves as he nervously leaned towards the glovebox and retrieved the registration.

He handed the two items to the officer and asked "What's going on?"

He knew he wasn't speeding. There wasn't a stop sign or red light to run anywhere nearby.

"We got a complaint of reckless driving on this vehicle about ten minutes ago. Have you been drinking, sir?"

"What!" Todd was stunned. "Hey, you think I don't know what's going on! You and Sergeant Cripp can both kiss my ass!"

"Step out of the car, sir."

"Damn right I will." Another police cruiser pulled up behind the first and the officer got out right away as Todd walked back behind his car. The officer looked at the floorboard in the back seat and said, "What's this?"

"What's what?" Todd asked, steaming.

"This." The policeman held up a huge Miller Genuine Draft bottle. It wasn't a bottle from a six pack. It was one of those big bottles that destitute winos and teenagers with fake I.D.s buy as singles from the liquor store.

"You fingerprint that bottle right now! You won't find my prints on it anywhere! Damn you! Why are you doing this!"

The second officer approached and said "Calm down, son."

"I'm not your gawd damned son! I want a bottle to pee into or give me a breathalyzer test—NOW! And I want the State Police here to supervise—NOW. I know what you're doing. You sum' bitches."

"Sir, I need you to—slowly now—move to the side of the police cruiser, spread your legs and place both hands on the cruiser. I'll ask you first, then I'll check. Are you carrying a weapon of any kind?"

"No. I'm not. But, I'm sure you'll come up with something." Traffic passed very slowly in front of Todd as the policeman frisked him. He was on display to the people driving past. A couple of young boys in the back of their parent's car had their faces to the glass and made eye contact with *Todd the Criminal.*

"He's clean," the frisking policeman said to the other.

"You sure?" Todd asked defiantly. "Wouldn't it be jucier if you were to find a machete in my tube sock."

"Mr. Grant. You are acting quite unruly and, as such, we have probable cause to believe you may be operating a motor vehicle under the influence of alcohol."

"Well, of course you do."

"You have the option of taking a field sobriety test here or having a blood test or breathalyzer test done at Physicians Hospital."

"I'll be damned if I let you be the judge and jury. Take me to the hospital. And I'm not kidding—I want another police jurisdiction to witness the test."

"We'll see what we can do, sir."

"Who's gonna watch my car? When are you gonna fingerprint the bottle?"

"I'll stay behind and watch the car until you return. Mr. Grant, it is unnecessary to fingerprint the bottle. The test you will take at the hospital will determine your sobriety. However, the Commonwealth of Virginia has an open container law and is enforced without regard as to who was actually consuming the alcoholic beverage."

"If you don't fingerprint the bottle, then I won't know which one of you cronies actually put the bottle behind my seat back at the police station."

"O.K. I'll pull up the prints on it while you're being tested."

"And who will supervise you? Is the fox guarding the hen house?"

"How about if I have the State Police do the prints?"

"That'll work. I'll wait here until they arrive. Not that I don't trust you."

"That won't be necessary. It is not our intent to unnecessarily detain you."

"You're not keeping me from anything. And you'll still have plenty of time to stop by Mr. Donut and munch on some Bavarian Cremes before your shift is over. So I'll wait."

After about an hour, Todd was returned to his car. His test had come up negative, of course, and the only prints found on the bottle were those of the officer who found the bottle. This didn't surprise Todd. These guys were professionals. They wouldn't think of leaving their prints on it. He got in his car and tossed the Summons onto the passenger seat. He was charged with operating a motor vehicle with an open container of alcohol aboard. It is no minor charge. He could be fined many hundreds of dollars and have many points assessed to his otherwise safe driving record, which could triple his insurance premiums.

But, by far, the worst part is that his flying career would be over. Four years of flying and very expensive training to get the Commercial Pilot certificate, then two years of hazardous crop dusting to build time until he qualified to get a Airline Transport Pilot certificate, and now about a year of poverty level wages as a Copilot on a small commuter airplane. He sacrificed both time and money in the hopes that someday he would be hired with a major airline and actually earn a living as a pilot. All of the dreams may have ended on Route 7 with a thirty-two ounce beer bottle.

He drove straight to Bands Airways headquarters and went directly into the Chief Pilot's office. It was now about five o'clock and people were just starting to leave. The Chief Pilot's office was one of about six offices on the first floor that faced out of the front of the two story complex. Todd was still in his shorts. Normally, he either showed up in his uniform or in a shirt and tie. This, however, was an emergency. He knocked on the side of the open door.

"Todd, you look comfortable," Bill Baldwin said.

"I've got big problems, Bill. Do you have a few minutes?"

"Sure." He motioned him in, then said, "Shut the door." Bill made it a point to get to know every pilot on the payroll. Todd was known by Bill as a bright pilot that would have no trouble transitioning to Captain.

"Bill, as you know, Chris Thomas died over the weekend. As you also know, I slugged Gary Heinmann when he made a lewd comment about her in the pilot lounge. Well, yesterday, he called my wife and accused me of sleeping with Chris. It must have been convincing because my wife won't answer the phone now. I went by the Loudoun County Sheriff's Department to file a complaint against Gary. But while I was there, I found out that they have reason to believe there was foul play involved and they ended up questioning me about it."

Bill put down his pen and listened as Todd continued: "I'm now to the bad part. After an uncooperative session with the people there, I left and was shortly thereafter pulled over by a policeman who finds an open beer bottle in the rear floorboard of my car. They gave me a blood test, which revealed no alcohol, but they charged me with an open container violation, which is reportable to the FAA."

"Wow. You've got big problems."

"I had them fingerprint the bottle. The only prints on it were those of the officer who found it."

"You need to call your union attorney, now! It's time to put those union dues that you have been paying to work. You know I have strict guidelines to follow if you are eventually convicted. I'll help you any way I can, but understand what I have to do if you don't win a dismissal. Our reputation has been damaged severely by *the accident*. The public and our management simply won't tolerate our having a convicted alcohol abuser among our ranks."

"I know, Bill. I just wanted you to know what's going on."

"I tell you what I *can* do, Todd. When is your vacation scheduled?"

"Early November."

"When is the next time you fly?"

"Friday."

"Effective Friday, you begin your vacation. I'll see to it that you have the necessary time off to take care of this problem."

"I'm gonna get it resolved *tonight*. I originally thought it was the Sheriff's Office using a harassment tactic on me. I don't think that's true anymore. It's Gary. It must be."

"My advise is to talk to an attorney. Don't dig a deeper hole by going after Gary by yourself. He's already done the damage. You've got a long time to rectify your feud with him. Focus on how to get that charge dismissed."

Todd stood without smiling. After a moment, he extended his hand, produced a smile and said, "Thanks for the advise, Bill."

• • • •

Almost an hour passed by the time Todd located Gary's apartment. Getting the address was easy enough. He walked from the chief pilot's office over to the Human Resources department and asked a friend for a copy of the latest list of those airlines that have jumpseat agreements with Bands. Then he asked the young receptionist, "Say Linda, do you know the area around here?"

"Yea, sorta." Linda smiled.

Todd reached into his shorts pocket for an address. He pulled out his notepad and searched the rest of his pocket for a nonexistent piece of paper. "I'm going to Gary Heinmann's house...uh, and I don't know where this address is....uh...." Todd searched all of his pockets and acted embarrassed when he couldn't find it.

Linda asked, "Are you always this organized?" Her comment actually hurt his feelings, because he was proud of how organized he really was.

"Shoot. I had it at the airport. He's gonna be ticked. I'm supposed to bring the charcoal. Shoot."

Linda tapped about ten keys on her computer. "10233 Golf Course Vista Lane, Apartment Ten Ten in Reston."

Reston was only a couple of miles from Bands headquarters. Todd scribbled the address onto his notepad, then asked, "Thanks. Where's Golf Course Vista Lane?"

"Take Route 28 South to the Dulles Toll Road. Take it towards Washington but take the first exit. Go straight until you see the Mobile station on the right. Hang a left. It'll be the uh, lets see..." Linda started counting her fingers. "...fourth stop light. It's just a couple of miles. Hang a left, then your second crossing street is Golf Course Vista Lane."

Todd scribbled the directions, then stuck the notepad into his shorts. "Thanks." Todd smiled and turned to leave.

"Don't forget this!" She held up the jumpseat listing.

Todd lowered his head. "And the charcoal. I can't forget the charcoal," he murmured to himself as he shook his head and left the building.

Todd spent the next forty to fifty minutes chasing down his address. There were *two* Mobile stations. She meant the second. He turned at the first. By the time he found the station, the sun was starting to get low in the sky and his anger was increasing. He pulled into the parking lot and into a reserved slot. He wouldn't be long. He walked about fifty feet to apartment 1010 and knocked at the door. A familiar face opened the door.

"Todd! Hey, come on in!" It was Edwin Smith, apparently Gary's roommate.

"Is Gary here?" Todd asked as he entered without smiling.

"Yep, he's in the back watchin' *Cheers*."

"Ed, I've got some words for him. I've been practicing these words all day."

"Tell it like it is..." Edwin said as he motioned him naively into the family area. Todd walked right up to the back of Gary's lounge chair, which was facing the loud TV that was airing a rerun episode. He grabbed a handful of hair and raised him up out of his chair with his left hand. Gary let out an awful yell and reached frantically for the hand that had pulled him up. In one motion, Todd swung him around and kicked him hard in the groin. As he bent forward from the pain, Todd pulled his head down to meet his upcoming knee. The succession of blows was over in milliseconds. The blow to Gary's forehead probably hurt Todd's knee more, but Todd was full of adrenaline and felt no pain. He let go of his hair as Gary recoiled from the second blow and went down backwards onto the carpet.

Edwin, not expecting to see a fight, started to move toward them, but Todd jerked quickly toward him and held up his index finger. "I'll be brief," he said to Edwin, which made Edwin stop dead in his tracks. He then turned to Gary, grabbed his hand as though he were going to help him up. Gary thought the fight was over and offered no resistance. Todd grabbed Gary's pinkie with the other hand and gave it a swift twisting jerk outward. An awful cracking sound occurred, followed by a shrill of agony and down he went again.

Todd spoke calmly. "Gary. If you *ever* wondered what it feels like to have a broken finger—now you know. Fifth digit, lateral separation of the third metacarpal along with a tearing of associated facia and ligaments. Can be quite painful."

Gary was crying openly, laying in a fetal position holding his groin with one hand and inspecting his finger with the other.

"Now. I'll give you a minute to collect your thoughts and allow you to decide for yourself how many more fingers I'm gonna have to break before you fess up." Todd wasn't even breathing heavily.

Gary had not yet been able to say anything. He had not even seen Todd's face yet. Slowly, he started to get up. Todd kicked him hard in the gut.

"Please remain as you are and listen to me. In the span of one day, you have made me lose the trust of my wife, the trust that has until now, never been tarnished. You've also quite possibly ended my flying career with that beer bottle stunt. My wife and my flying. That just about covers all that's important to me. You'll notice that I broke your *left* pinkie."

Gary started moving about as he struggled with the pain. Todd kicked him hard in the forearm. "Gary, please try to pay attention. I broke your left pinkie. Your right hand is still fully functional. Use the opportunity while it remains functional to go to the Loudoun County Sheriff's Office and describe, in writing, all of those things that you have done to me and my wife over the last day."

Todd slowly paced around Gary, who finally managed to look up at him. Todd continued, "Please don't underestimate my frame of mind right now. I've had a bad day. You, now have *also* had a bad day. Please understand that if you don't confess to everything—*to-night*, that it will take months to recover from the day that you'll have—*to-morrow*. Tomorrow, I will rip your lips off. Remember, that's the Loudoun County Sheriff's Office in Leesburg. They'll be expecting you."

Todd quickly, and yet without emotion, kicked him hard in the shoulder. The blow was so intense that it nearly lifted Gary off the ground. Todd then immediately turned and began walking toward the door. He glanced at Ed and said, "Sorry if I alarmed you, Ed. Please convince him that he goes to Leesburg tonight."

• • • •

The ride home was somewhat serene. Todd felt he accomplished his objective with Gary. He knew that the only way to have Gary confess was to be rough and ruthless to the point of being crazed. He wanted to let Gary know that he would never give up until he confessed. Todd believed it worked. The sun was right at the horizon, which still had westbound traffic backed up on the beltway. Fortunately, traffic in his direction was light and the only two things that consumed Todd's thoughts were: 1) his left knee, which was really sore from contact with Gary's forehead and 2) what he would say to Kelly when he got home.

Todd arrived home when there was only a sliver of light left in the western sky. He pulled into the covered driveway and noticed that Kelly's car was not there. His mind raced as he got out of the car and walked through the dark stillness to his apartment. The lights were out. She wasn't home. He walked awkwardly up the steps, as his knee was bothering him. He placed his key into the lock and gave it a turn. It didn't offer the resistance that it normally did, indicating that the door had not been locked. *She must have been so furious that she left without locking the door*. He walked in and hit the light switch, but nothing happened. He looked through the door to their bedroom and noticed that the alarm clock light was lit. The bulb must have burned out. A streetlight gave some light through the window on the other side of the room. He walked across the room to the table lamp and reached under it to feel for the switch.

His hair stood on end as he realized someone was approaching him from behind. He bolted left and down, but not quick enough for a large knife to miss him. It was hurled deep into his right shoulder blade, causing Todd to drop to his all fours. The pain was sharp and it all happened so quickly that he didn't know if he had been stabbed or shot. He knew another one was coming though, so he instinctively did an old wrestling maneuver. He extended his legs to either side of the attacker, then quickly twisted his body, pulling the attacker down by his knees. The move wasn't clean though, since his right arm gave way in the middle of the horizontal rotation. He was injured, unsure of his opponent, and his opponent was coming down toward him with a weapon. He moved with every ounce of energy he could muster and got clear just as the attacker made a swipe with the blade. He actually felt the wind of the blade as it was hurled by. He rolled to his feet and turned toward the oncoming silhouetted enemy and jerked both arms skyward. The attacker reacted by raising the knife just as Todd released a kick to his abdomen. But the knife came down just before Todd could retreat his leg and the knife sliced right across his shin. The attacker was still bending forward from the blow to his abdomen and didn't see the fist coming down onto his upper nose. The blow was so severe that his knees buckled and he dropped the knife.

Todd never slowed his counterattack. He drove his body into the attacker before the attacker had time to react. Todd rammed him across the dark room and through the window frame and screen. They both rotated out of the second story window. Todd frantically waived his arms to release the attacker and grasp anything that would keep him from also falling. The attacker did a slow, three-quarter back flip and wound up plowing face first into the tall shrubbery below. Until that point, the attacker had made no sounds. Once he hit the bushes, he let out a high pitched groan. Todd turned away from the badly damaged window and reached for the knife. He stopped midway down with a loud cry of agony. He twisted slightly and leaned slower and picked up the knife with his left hand. He was bleeding profusely from the shoulder. His leg, though cut, wasn't too bad. He hobbled to the steps with the knife in hand to contain the attacker until he could get help. *"My God, where's Kelly?"* Todd thought as he hurried down the steps as fast as his bruised left knee and sliced right shin would allow. Her car wasn't there, but what if someone else had driven off with her. What would have happened if she had shown up before him?

As he arrived at the bottom of the outside staircase, Ted Behlman was just opening his apartment door to investigate the commotion. He said, "Todd, what's wrong!? Todd! Hey!...."

Todd by now was running awkwardly around to the backside of the apartment complex. He arrived to find no one there. He scoured the area and concluded that he was gone before turning to go back. Just as he turned, he came face to face with Ted, which made Todd snap to an on guard position. Ted jumped back as Todd spoke: "Where's Kelly! Did you seen Kelly?!"

Ted stepped back, frightened at the look of a bloody man yielding a knife. "No, Todd. Calm down, buddy. I'll get a doctor for you."

Todd threw down the knife into the grass and walked toward his car. About halfway there, he tried to reach into his pocket to get the car keys, but his right shoulder wouldn't allow it. He reached across with his left hand and into his right pocket to retrieve them. In a matter of seconds, he was in his car and gone.

• • • •

The police got a full report from Ted. In fact, so did News Channel 4: "He was all bloody from head to toe and he had this *huge* knife in his hand. He looked like he was in a trance! He walked around from back there and asked me if I had seen Kelly run by..."

Ted squinted at the reporters in front of the bright camera lights. "I sure hope Kelly got away O.K. I've never seen Todd act so wild before."

The fax in the apartment was recovered as evidence by the Anne Arundel County Sheriff's Department. So was the answering machine tape. So was the knife. One of the young deputies, anxious to release some of the steamy details, told News Channel 4 about the admission by Todd via fax that he had slept with another woman. He also told them about the hand-written response of "Screw you." across it. After some pressing, he told them the name of the other woman was Chris Thomas.

To News Channel 4, this was not just a ho-hum domestic dispute. This was ratings news. This was Emmy news. They had an hour and a half before the Eleven O'clock News, which gave them plenty of time to piece together that the "other woman" had been suspiciously killed by a hit and run over the past weekend. The frenzy of phone calls eventually found their way to Loudoun County and to Dwight Conners at his home. He issued an arrest warrant that night for the murder of Chris Thomas and the attempted murder of Kelly Grant.

• • • •

Todd stopped by a critical care clinic, but opted not to go in. With all the trouble that he had today, including the fight with Gary, he couldn't chance it. He knew that the clinic would have to report the knife injury to the police. He couldn't allow himself to be arrested now. He had to find Kelly. If he was in danger, so was she. He couldn't cool his heels in a jail cell while someone was out there after her.

He went straight to Bowie, into the new neighborhood and up the driveway of the Bartlett's. Kelly's car wasn't there, but he didn't really expect it to be. She was smarter than that.

He didn't ring the bell. He banged on the door. He could hear the footsteps approach the back side of the door, but the door didn't open. He knew he was being watched through the peep hole.

"John! Susan! Please open the door. Kelly's in danger."

"She's not here," John's voice sounded through the closed door.

"Come on John. At least let me relay a message to her."

"She's on vacation."

"Gawd dammit, John!" He began pounding on the door with all of his might and then the noise stopped.

John looked through the peep hole and saw no one, then turned around and shrugged his shoulders toward Susan. He motioned her to turn off the lights downstairs so they could see him if he came around the backside of the house. He then walked back to Susan and said, "He looked awful. Like he was out of control."

John then walked back up the hallway to the front of the house and peeked through the living room window toward the entrance foyer. There was Todd, sitting exhausted and expressionless with his bloody back to the side brick wall, with both legs extended out and limp.

"Shit! Susan! He's bleeding!"

"Oh God!" Kelly said from the top of the dark stairway.

"You stay up there, Kelly," said Susan in a controlled command.

John swung open the door and raced to Todd's side. "Todd. The hell happened?" he asked as Todd looked through him. Todd looked totally defeated.

"I'm cold," said Todd calmly.

"Shit. Shit. Let's get you inside. Susan, call nine one one."

"No! NO! I swear if you do that, he'll kill Kelly."

"Who?! Who will kill Kelly?!"

"Promise me. Swear you won't call anyone. You gotta swear!"

"O.K.," John replied with little sincerity.

"John," Todd said as he shivered and began to rise with John's help, "I'm in a spiraling descent. I'm gonna have to ask you to give me some trust here. This is gonna take some trust on your part. It's an uncontrolled descent. My whole life is crashing and I can't pull up."

"Don't worry, Todd," John said as he and Susan helped him walk down the hallway slowly as they alternately inspected the blood-soaked back of his shirt, afraid of having to both face the wound and face the facts of why the wound was inflicted.

"I'm thirsty."

"We'll get you something to drink. Wait. I don't know if that's a good idea or not. Are you shot?"

"Nope. Just a stab wound," he replied with no emotion.

"Susan. What do we do?"

Susan stood there in shock. Kelly trembled as she watched the pitiful threesome vanish down the hallway from her dark vantage point at the top of the staircase.

• • • •

"Hey! Stu Baby!"

"Yea. Who's this? James?" he asked into the phone as he fumbled around his night stand for the light switch.

"Yep, it's James."

"What time is it?"

"Eleven-twenty. Hey, what time did you go to bed tonight?"

"Me? I don't know, maybe nine, nine-thirty...."

"Well, at least you got a few hours of sleep. Listen, I just saw the Eleven O'clock News. You'll never believe it."

Stu sat up on the edge of his bed. His wife opened her eyes and squinted toward his back. "Try me."

"Better get dressed. This is gonna be a long night for you."

"Cut to the chase."

"I just saw a report on channel four where a young man named...."

Stu Varney chimed in to say the name in stereo: "Todd Grant!"

"...had gone on a rampage and attacked his wife with a knife. He's been charged with attempted murder and—get this—he is also charged with the murder of a lady that he had just confessed to his wife of sleeping with."

"Wo gee."

"Yea. Wo gee. I guess you don't have a motive yet for the plane crash, huh."

"Like the *bump off the guy who knew about the affair* motive or the *take down the airplane she was supposed to be on, but wasn't* motive."

"Sounds like our boy Todd's in a heap a' trouble!" James said in his best redneck white-boy voice.

Stu chuckled at James. "I'll get dressed. Where's he being held?"

"He's not. He got away and his wife is no where to be found either. They don't know if she's dead or alive."

"Well, it's now a criminal investigation. You might as well hit the sack. I'll be at your office tomorrow morning when you arrive and fill you in...."

"Are you kidding? Who can sleep with news like that? Let's meet at the Hoover Building at, say, one a.m. We'll gather our notes then drive to Anne Arundel County and talk to the county investigators."

FIFTEEN

AT TODD'S INSISTENCE, John quickly hosed the blood from the brick and concrete surrounding his front door. It had taken both John and Susan several minutes to carefully escort Todd into the living room. They sat him temporarily on the piano bench, then they set off on independent tasks while Kelly waited in darkness above. Susan grabbed a painter's tarpaulin from the garage and laid it over the carpet, followed by a set of old sheets. Todd now looked more exhausted and vanquished than injured. He had only smudges of blood on the front of his shirt but the back was a dark, dirty, multi-shaded red painting. Because of the stab wound in the right side of his upper back, he couldn't lift his right arm to remove his shirt. It took the two Bartletts working as a team to get the shirt off. The wound proved to be deep and clean. As Susan raced upstairs to grab some antiseptic and washcloths, she was met by a horrified Kelly.

Susan spoke quietly and matter-of-factly. "I think he'll be O.K. He's pretty bloody, though." She didn't slow as she passed Kelly towards the linen closet.

"I'm going downstairs."

Susan stopped, turned, then pointed a stern finger at her. "Not yet. We need to find out more, first."

"Why. Clearly someone's after him."

"Yea. Probably. But we don't know the whole story, yet. What if Todd got mixed up with that girl after all. What if it was her jealous husband? How would you handle that? 'You gonna stab his other shoulder?"

"It could've been that guy that he punched out three days ago."

"Well, let *us* find out. You just hang here for a while."

Downstairs, Todd was now lying prone and shirtless on the sheet and tarp-covered carpet. Todd had a mouse-eye view of the living room as he rested his chin on his left wrist. His feet were toward the hallway and his eyes were facing the bottom edge of the rear sliding glass door. He saw the reflection of Susan when she disappeared down the dark hallway toward the staircase by the front door. His right arm couldn't raise without a lot of pain and remained at his side. John sat erect in his chair near Todd's feet and tried his best to stay calm.

"Why is Kelly in danger? Why can't we call the police? Who stabbed you?" John asked.

Susan reentered the room and interjected. "You think it's O.K. to give him some water?"

John looked at her, then him. "Have you spit up any blood?"

"Nope. I think he just jabbed me through my muscle maybe down to my shoulder blade. I'd probably know it if I some massive internal hemorrhaging going on, wouldn't I?"

"Damn it Todd. You're not a doctor and neither am I. That's a no-shit stab wound right there and I tell you one thing—when you pass out, I'm calling an ambulance."

"Like hell you are."

"O.K. kids, calm down," said Susan.

"Listen, John," said Todd in a forced serene voice. "I would really relish a glass of water."

"Fine."

"John—and Susan, I know this is tough for y'all. But I've got to make sure that Kelly is kept in seclusion until I can get this guy who's after me. I need to talk to her. I need her involvement. He's going to try to put me in jail or worse."

"So you know who he is?" Susan asked as she leaned down and handed him a small glass of water. As she moved away, he noticed Kelly's reflection in the sliding glass door as she listened from the dark hallway.

"Kelly," Todd said softly. He tilted his head down toward the sheets and covered his eyes with his left thumb and index finger. "Dear God, you're O.K."

Kelly froze, not knowing what to say or expect next. He lifted his head and again looked at her reflection in the glass. She looked back at him through the glass. She decided to begin, her voice shaking: "Answer this. Was the fax you sent me yesterday true?"

"Fax?!"

"Did you sleep with Chris?" she asked with more confidence.

"Sleep with Chris, come on. What fax?!"

"Who knows about our nicknames?" She was now in control.

"Wait. Stop. Lemme see the fax."

"Where's the laptop?"

"It's in my flight bag, I think. Let me see the damned fax."

"I left it for you at the apartment."

"When did you leave the apartment?" "This morning."

After a long pause, Todd rose slowly and began talking to the threesome. "O.K. Here goes. First, the denials."

Todd continued to rise awkwardly and slowly. He then rolled over and sat, very gingerly, Indian style and finally faced her. A grimace was unmaskable as he accomplished the maneuver. Everyone in the room felt the pain.

Tom Sylvester

"First and foremost, I never slept with Chris. Don't ever doubt me. It's a fabrication. Period. Get it out of your mind. Point number two: I didn't send you a fax. I haven't even turned on the laptop."

Todd shifted. "Someone tried to kill me at the apartment tonight. I gotta admit, that spooked me."

He gave pause for her to counter him. However, when she saw the pitiful, injured man sitting low on a sheet-covered tarp, she couldn't. He continued. "If *you* had been at the apartment earlier tonight, you would probably be dead now. He was probably after you, not me."

"Why? What did *I* do?" Kelly moved, at a safe distance, but closer to him. She figured he was not in a position to do anything to her in his condition. Susan stood motionless with warm washcloths and antibiotics in hand.

"You found out that I slept with Chris, of course, and attacked me with a knife."

"What?!"

"Sure. Only I showed up at home first and screwed up his scheme. He's followed me all day. I bet he thought you'd be home first, where he could easily overpower you and take you out. He probably wanted it to look like we had an argument and when you attacked me with the knife, I ended up stabbing you with it. Then, bingo, he takes me out with a gun or something and puts it into your dead hand. The police then blame me *in absentia* for Chris's death and he's off scot-free."

"This ain't the movies, Todd. Sounds a little dramatic," said John abruptly.

"You want drama. Hey. Drama in real life...." Todd snapped back at John as he rotated his bloodied back towards him. Todd had a glare in his eyes that no one had seen before. John made no attempt to answer him. Susan, at last, moved in and began gently rinsing the skin around the wound with the washcloth.

He turned back towards Kelly. "Look," he continued. "All I know is I'm in deep shit and as long as that bastard is out there, so are you. And shame on you for thinking I slept with another woman."

"So this guy you punched at Dulles was having an affair with Chris?"

"Well, I don't know. He may very well have, but so did quite a few other guys. But he's not the one who stabbed me tonight."

"How can you be so sure?"

"Because I broke his finger just before I came home."

"You did what?" Kelly asked.

"Yea. I went to his house right after I informed the Chief Pilot that I had been pulled over for DUI."

"Oh no," Kelly said softly as the Bartletts remained motionless.

"Shall I start at the beginning of my day from hell?"

All nodded.

Todd was uncomfortable sitting upright but recognized that there was probably no better position. He then continued slowly. "I figured Gary had told you that I slept with Chris in retribution for the fight in the pilot lounge. I cut short my shift and went to Leesburg to file a complaint against him with the county police. It was there that I found out that they think Chris Thomas was murdered on Route 28 last Saturday night."

Kelly remembered that the fax that said "I didn't kill her, though. I swear."

Todd continued, "On the complaint form I described the fight I had with Gary in Chris's defense, and they then started pointing fingers at me. They made me mad and I stormed out. Just out of town, the police pulled me over and found a big Miller bottle behind my seat. I thought the police had staged it at first, since I had been so rude to them. But I figured out that it must have been Gary."

The three listeners were motionless—as was Todd after lowering his head to gaze down at his crossed legs. "After a trip to the hospital for a blood alcohol test, I went straight to the Chief Pilot to inform him."

He looked up at John. "The company requires immediate notification of any charges involving alcohol." He then looked down again. "Then I went to Gary's apartment and kicked him in the gut, broke his left pinkie, then told him to go to Leesburg and file a statement, explaining what he had done over the past three days to ruin my life."

Todd took a deep painful breath, then continued. "In retrospect, I shouldn't have whooped up on him, 'cuz it wasn't Gary who stabbed me tonight."

"So, you've ruled him out completely?"

"Well, I beat him up pretty bad. He would have either gone to Leesburg like I asked him to or he'd have gone to the hospital to fix his finger. He's also smart enough to know better than to come close to me with a knife in my frame of mind. And he's completely gutless to boot. And he's too tall. The guy that came after me tonight couldn't have been more than five six or five eight."

"How tall is Chris's husband?" John asked.

"You want me to take a guess? Probably no more than five six or five eight. You know, the guy that attacked me could have been a simple crook—but I doubt it. He wasn't there tonight to steal a TV. He was waiting there for the Grants. Look, I've got to figure out a way to trap that sum' bitch before either he gets me or before the police get me."

John twitched. "The police! Shit! As far as they're concerned, we're harboring a criminal! We can't do this!"

"Shut up, John!" Susan snapped. "You and I know he's not a criminal."

"How do we know that! How do we know this isn't just some elaborate scheme that Todd is making up to protect himself from blame?"

Todd erupted. "Blame! Blame for what? You think I've done something? You think I stabbed myself? How the hell could I have stabbed myself way back here?" Todd tried various stabbing motions, then ended up grimacing in pain as he continued. "I asked you to trust me, John! If you can't trust me now, you just call the police. But, dammit, you better trust me on this one. O.K.?" Todd glared at him. "O.K.?!"

John nodded slightly.

"Trust. That's all I'm asking of you..." Todd said more softly, then looked away from John and talked again to the group. "All right. Now, let's evaluate the situation. The police *are* probably interested in me, since Behlman saw me wielding the bloody knife around and others should have heard me when I pushed the bastard through the window. I *did* leave the scene of a crime."

"You pushed him through the window?" Susan asked. "But, you live on the second floor."

"Yep. He landed in the bushes, then scampered off."

Susan shook her head in amazement.

"Look guys. It's hard to believe or accept it myself, but my life changed forever today. I didn't want it to change, but it has. Now, unless I'm proactive and careful it will only get worse. I can't get that bastard alone. I'm gonna need your help."

John looked away.

"First, what time is it?" Todd looked at his watch. "Shoot. We've got twenty-two minutes to go until midnight. Susan. I need you to drive me south on Route 301 for ten or twenty miles."

"O.K., but why?"

John interrupted. "Hold on. I'll drive you. I don't want her arrested if you get pulled over."

"That's fine with me. Also, somewhere heading south along 301 I'm gonna have to ditch my car."

"Wait, why risk getting out on the road and being spotted. We have a perfect place to hide your car." Susan looked at John and smiled. John nodded.

"Great. The keys are in it. Please be careful."

As Todd ever so slowly rose, Kelly walked the few steps over to him. She stood toe to toe, then said softly, "Todd, I love you. I believe you—and I *trust* you."

She put her arms around his waist and hugged him. He embraced her and held her tightly. The pain from the embrace was almost unbearable but was also so welcomed.

••••

Midnight was quickly approaching as Todd and John pulled into Upper Marlboro, about ten miles south of Bowie. They located an automated teller machine, where Todd walked up to machine and withdrew two hundred dollars. Two hundred was the most the ATMs would allow him to take out in any calendar day. He made an overt effort to hide his face from the video camera, but managed to let the camera record a good look at him. After that they drove south on Route 301 to Waldorf and arrived at about twelve-twenty a.m. He stopped at another ATM and took out another $200, since it was a new day. Again, he acted like he was hiding his face. He figured that was the last money he would be able to get before the police would freeze the account. Todd Grant would be traced leaving town, heading south with at least four hundred dollars in his pocket. The seed was planted. They then turned around and drove back home to Bowie.

John drove in silence. Todd had rotated left in his seat because of his shoulder and slumped low to avoid being seen. He looked down at the seat cushion. After ten minutes of silence, John was hit with an anxiety flash. "Todd, the police are so much better suited to catching this guy than you are. They have the expertise, the manpower, and the equipment to get him when he screws up."

Todd spoke as if talking to himself. "That's the point. He won't screw up. This guy is sharp. I've never met him—don't even have a good feel for what he looks like—but I *do* know he's a calculating person that leaves nothing to chance. He thinks through his moves and leaves no footprints. The police *must* have talked to him after Chris's accident. I'm sure he had a concrete alibi, particularly since he and Chris were in the midst of a nasty divorce."

John looked down the dark road ahead. "So, you'll need to get the statements that he gave the police, as a minimum, to even begin to unravel his alibi."

"Yep."

"Why not let Kelly go to the police and prove that she wasn't attacked by you."

"I thought about that. But remember, he wants to have a ring of terror surrounding me. He wants all fingers pointing at me. If she surfaces, he'll just go after her again and I can't risk that. I think its better if she stays hidden for now. We can always have her surface at any time we choose and prove that I'm innocent of attacking her. By hiding her and keeping the heat on me, maybe he'll let down his guard."

"So how are you going to get the police to cooperate. And how long before they search our house?"

"Probably take a day or so but it'll definitely happen. We'll need to really clean up there and ya'll will probably have to leave town for a while to avoid having to make a statement to them."

"We can't just leave town and not tell anyone where we're going."

Tom Sylvester

"Well, just stay there until they show up and tell them either a big fat lie or that you aided and abetted a suspected felon! I say you dodge all of that and just disappear until I either get arrested or until I get Al Thomas trapped. Either way, the next couple of days are going to be a real lollapalooza—the kind of lollapalooza that you should definitely avoid."

SIXTEEN

THE SUN began to illuminate the promise of a nice late summer day. Todd slept well, given the injuries and anxieties of the day before. His eyes opened slowly, then the unfamiliar surroundings gave rise to the realization that yesterday's events had been real. He bolted up from the floor, and let out a muffled scream from the knife wound that he had all but forgotten about. He finished getting up, examined his bruised knee and lashed shin, then looked around. All was quiet. He walked slowly from the family room, carefully past the sliding glass door, and into the kitchen.

A note was on the kitchen counter, along with a large stack of twenty dollar bills sticking partially out of an unsealed envelope. The name "Marjorie" was printed on the outside of the envelope in large letters. Next to the envelope was a small, hand-held cellular phone with a *Post-It* attached to it. A smiley face was hand-drawn on the *Post-It*.

Todd smiled, removed the *Post-It* and tossed it in the trash. He quickly picked up the note and read it:

"Dear Marjorie:

You're probably reading this Thursday morning on your usual day to clean. We are away for a while due to an illness in the family. We took separate cars, since John can't stay away as long. If he is back next week, then he'll leave the cleaning instructions. We really don't need you to clean this morning. We're embarrassed to say, but we forgot your last name and couldn't locate your number. Since you obviously made the trip here, here's the thirty dollars anyway. Thanks. See you next Thursday.

- Susan.

P.S. Our new neighbors will be arriving on Sunday. Would you like us to recommend you to them?"

"Hi, R.C. How ya feel?"

Todd turned around and saw Kelly standing in the hallway. "Fine, I s'pose. What's today?"

"Wednesday, August the, uh..."

"Good. John and Susan left town last night. Please do me a favor and check the garage."

Kelly looked a little puzzled, then walked through the laundry room to the garage, then disappeared into the garage. In a moment, she returned. "Yep, the garage is still there."

"How many cars?"

"One. Found this smiley face in the driver's side window," she said as she held up another *Post-It*.

Todd smiled, then reached into the trash, uncrumpled a *Post-It* and held it up. "Like this one?"

"Yea," she replied with a puzzled expression.

"Found this one on a big lump of cash and another on the cellular phone."

"That's the firm's phone."

"Here, read this," said Todd as she walked over to him. "Find any hidden meanings in it?" he asked, smiling.

After reading it, Kelly said, "Boy are they slick. She didn't forget Marjorie's last name! It's Forbes! She once said to me that she knew she had 'arrived' when the last name of her cleaning lady was Forbes. She's letting us know that they've bolted, that we should use the cash, car, and phone, that Marjorie will be here tomorrow, and that we need to get our cars out of the neighbor's garage by Sunday."

"More importantly, they're now not in a position of having to lie to the authorities about our whereabouts. And *most* importantly, they trust me. That means a lot these days."

"Well, Todd. What's the plan?" asked Kelly as she reached into the fridge and pulled out some orange juice.

"It's time to make a courtesy call."

• • • •

The Bands Javelin aircraft descended from eight thousand feet down to its assigned altitude of five thousand, six hundred feet. The controller working the flight sat at station six in the large, dark radar room at the Washington Air Route Traffic Control Center in Leesburg, Virginia.

The aircraft was flying just above the cloud deck that covered the mountainous terrain of southwestern Virginia. Their destination was Shenandoah Valley Airport, with its single runway aligned parallel to the valley. Voice and radar communications were made via a remote transmissions facility atop Pollard's Hill, fifty-five miles northwest of Shenandoah Valley Airport.

The weather was generally good everywhere except for some pockets of dense morning fog and low clouds near their destination and a separate, rather large area of fog near Rocky Mount, North Carolina.

The controller on duty for that part of the FAA's Eastern Region had three areas, or sectors as they are called, that he controlled. Since it was only an hour after daybreak, the morning airborne "rush hour" was still about an hour away. The controller was finishing his "back side of the clock" shift and would be going home in about thirty minutes. He was controlling seventeen aircraft in the three sectors that covered eastern West Virginia, southwestern Virginia, and northern North Carolina. He was using three different frequencies—one for each sector—to talk to the aircraft. He was a seasoned controller and could handle it was ease. The new shift would have one controller for *each* sector, since the amount of traffic in each sector essentially quadrupled during "rush hour." If he put all seventeen aircraft on a common radio frequency, he would have to tag each one and change them back to their standard sector frequency once the new controller arrived. With so little time left on his shift and the relatively light workload it was less work just to—every so often—listen to two aircraft talk at the same time.

All major airports and many smaller airports have transmitters on the airport that allow aircraft to descend down through the clouds to the runway using special navigation receivers in the aircraft. These transmitters, along with runway approach lights and markings, are collectively called an Instrument Landing System or ILS. One transmitter is located at the far end of the runway in use and transmits directional position information, i.e. whether the aircraft is left or right of the runway. The other transmitter is located about a thousand feet down the side of the runway at about the spot where an aircraft would normally touch down. It transmits vertical position information, i.e. whether the aircraft is too high or too low from a standard glide slope. The ILS receivers in the airplane allow the pilot to fly down through the thickest of clouds to within a couple hundred feet above the ground. At that point, the pilot either sees the runway area and continues to land or he climbs back up into the clouds in a specific direction until he is safely above any hazardous terrain.

The Bands aircraft was eight miles from the airport when it leveled at five thousand, six hundred feet. That altitude was the minimum height to stay on the controller's radar screen and remain clear of the precipitous terrain that surrounded Shenandoah Airport. The crew would soon obtain the clearance to conduct an ILS approach down to the airport from the southwest. Both the pilots aboard and the controller in Leesburg knew that the controller would soon lose radar contact with the airplane when they intercepted the glide slope signal and descended from the minimum radar vectoring altitude. They knew, however, that they would still remain in voice contact with the controller. What the pilots *didn't* know was someone was about to send them into a mountainside.

"Bands Twenty-two Thirty-five, maintain five thousand six hundred feet until established, cleared for the ILS Runway Four approach," said the controller.

"Five point six till established, cleared for the approach," replied the Copilot.

"Bands Twenty-two Thirty-five, radar service is terminated. Cancel your flight plan on the ground with Flight Service or with me on this frequency."

"We'll talk to you again in a few," the Copilot again replied. They were about five miles away and their instruments showed them lined up with the runway when the glide slope indicator in the aircraft started to move from the top of the dial. They were just skimming the top of the cloud deck as the sun was rising into the pink sky off the right side of the aircraft. Both pilots were thrilled with the scenery, but knew that as soon as the indicator moved down to the middle of the dial they had to begin their descent into the solid clouds and fog below. As long as they kept the needles on their dials centered, they would be assured of being exactly where they were supposed to be when they reached the Decision Height. At DH, they would either see the runway and continue to land or they would immediately execute the ILS 4 Missed Approach Procedure. According to the printed missed approach instructions for that particular approach, they would first climb straight ahead to two thousand feet, then make a climbing *right* turn up to five thousand six hundred feet directly back to a navigation transmitter near where they made their initial descent. The missed approach procedure, if executed properly, would keep them safely away from the high terrain to the west.

The controller could not allow another airplane into the airspace around Shenandoah Airport until the TransGlobe Express airplane either landed or climbed back up and regained radar contact. The airspace was theirs exclusively.

"Gear down," the Captain stated as he intercepted the glide slope and began his descent.

The Copilot reached over and lowered the gear handle. After a few seconds he replied, "Three green." The three green lights beside the gear handle indicated that the three landing gear struts were fully down and locked.

"Three green," the Captain confirmed, then continued, "gimme flaps twenty-five and the Landing Checklist."

The Copilot lifted and dropped the flap control handle into a slot marked "25%", watched the flap indicator move to twenty-five percent, then began reading the final landing checklist items to the Captain. They completed the checklist and continued their descent. When they were one thousand feet above their DH, the Copilot double-checked the instruments and stated: "One thousand to go, cross-check: no flags."

At two hundred feet to go, a voice came over their headsets. "Bands Twenty-two Thirty-five, I'm gonna have to break you out of the approach. Someone's apparently departing Shenandoah to the south without an IFR clearance."

The transmission was made from the floor of the valley and the controller didn't hear it.

"Twenty-two Thirty-five, roger."

The controller said, "Bands Twenty-two Thirty-five, say again?" The experienced controller heard the Bands aircraft reply to some instruction that wasn't given by him. Unfortunately, the controller's transmitter, though much more powerful than the one used by the man in the valley just south of the airport, wasn't strong enough to get through without interference from the hand-held one that was only within a mile of the aircraft.

"Turn *left*, that's a *left* turn to heading two-four-zero and climb and maintain three thousand for now."

"Roger, left two-four-zero, three thousand," the Copilot rattled off as the Captain commanded: "Max power. Flaps fifteen."

The Copilot followed the captains right hand on the power levers as the engines revved to maximum levels and then the Copilot moved the flap handle to "15%." What was just moments before a calm descent in the clouds now was a scramble to get the aircraft configured for a climbing turn to the left.

"Positive rate!" the Copilot stated loudly.

"Gear up!" the pilot commanded. The Copilot turned a heading bug on the Captain's heading indicator showing the required direction of flight. The turn was complied with as though it were valid.

"Bands Twenty-two Thirty-five, say again?" The controller couldn't believe his ears. An aircraft on another frequency checked in with him. He pressed the button for transmitting on all frequencies: "All aircraft on frequency—stand by. Bands Twenty-two Thirty-five, say again?"

The controller's query was again stifled by another transmission from the man in the valley, who was now just below the aircraft as it turned southwest. The ridge that the man on the ground was trying to run the aircraft into was only a mile and a half away. The lowest point of the ridge was about three thousand four hundred feet above sea level.

"This ain't right," the Captain said to the Copilot. "Isn't there a ridge to the west of the airport?"

"You're right," the Copilot responded, then immediately transmitted to the controller: "Confirm you want Bands Twenty-two Thirty-five on a two-four-zero heading?"

The first part of the transmission was intentionally interfered with by the man on the ground. The controller, however, repeated himself several times: "Negative! Negative! Execute the *published* missed approach. I say again! Execute the *published* missed approach!" The controller's voice trembled with adrenaline. He couldn't see the aircraft on radar, since it was below the mountain ridges. He repeated the clearance no less than three more times. "Give me your best rate of climb up to five thousand six hundred!"

Just after the first ungarbled transmission of "Negative!" was received, the pilots figured out that they were being lured into a mountain obscured by thick clouds.

They immediately began barking commands at each other: "Gimme max power! Vee Final—Flaps Up!"

"Flaps up! Crank it over—give it more bank angle!"

"Come on, baby," the Captain said softly to the plane as he pulled it up and to the left.

"You got it, keep hanging it! Keep it on Vee Final!"

The aircraft lumbered around to a heading back to where the airport should have been, then they climbed at the best rate that they could muster until they broke out of the top of the clouds in a right turn back to the outer marker navigation beacon. They were safe. Both pilots were well aware of how close they and their passengers came to dying. They finished the *Go Around - Missed Approach* checklist, then gave each other a serious, *boy-are-we-lucky* glance.

"Bands Twenty-two Thirty-five."

"Go ahead."

"I've got you back on radar. Can you recognize my voice?"

"Yep. You're the good guy. I would imagine the bad guy is down near the airport somewhere."

"Well I've now closed Shenandoah to all IFR arrivals until we find out who made those illegal transmissions. I'm going to have to take you to your alternate."

"Ready to copy the clearance..."

The Copilot noticed that his hands were shaking as he wrote down the route of flight to take them back to Dulles—the airport listed on their flight plan as their alternate if they couldn't get into Shenandoah Valley Airport.

"Bands Twenty-two Thirty-five. Please write down the illegal transmissions that you heard while they are still fresh in your mind."

"Sure will. Incidentally, he was definitely either a pilot or controller. His instructions were very convincing."

"Unfortunately, his transmissions weren't picked up here at the center. All I heard were your acknowledgments to him. When you get on the ground, please give me a call at the ARTCC in Leesburg. My initials are Pee Bee—Papa Bravo."

The pilot wrote "PB-controller" next to his recollection of the illegal transmission on a yellow notepad.

The controller spoke again: "Bands Twenty-two Thirty-five, as we speak, the FBI is being notified of the occurrence. Good job staying out of the trees."

"Thanks for *keeping* us out of the trees. Must have been a close one. We could smell the pine needles."

The man in the valley turned off his hand-held transmitter and slowly faced his car. He peered at his reflection in the driver's side window. It showed the many small scratches on his face and neck from his fall from the window the night before. He needed a couple of days of healing before he could go back to work.

He wasn't disappointed that the plane didn't crash. He accomplished his objective. He knew Todd was in hiding from listening to his police radio. It's hard to have an alibi on your whereabouts when you're in hiding. He got into his car and drove back to Washington, where he would arrive by lunch time. He needed to get some sleep, but there was no time for that now. Among other things, he had negatives back home to develop.

SEVENTEEN

TODD AND KELLY sat at the Bartlett's breakfast table, each with a pad and pencil. Their breakfast plates and silverware completed a full load in the dishwasher, which had been switched on minutes before. Todd was moving slowly because of his injuries, but his mind was nonetheless quick and alert. The noisy dishwasher forced them to speak louder, which amplified their anxiety.

The sun caught a firm grip on the eastern sky, just above the horizon. The bright sunshine weaved its way through the numerous skinny pine trees in the Bartlett's backyard, darted through the kitchen window, and danced across their notepads. Todd was keenly aware of the limited time he had to uncover Al Thomas. The authorities would inevitably catch Todd. He just hoped he could get Al before they got *him*. In the hour and a half since sunrise, they each filled three pages of notes and facts surrounding the fax message, phone calls, and recollections of events from the past couple of days.

"O.K. K.W., here's what we have. Al knew the police would or were beginning to suspect foul play, so he tried to pin Chris's death on me. He must have known that I had been paired with her for a whole month of flying. He also knows a lot about *us*—not only where we live—but where you work, and also some very personal things. K.W. and R.C., for instance. We have to presume he knows what you and I look like."

"I remember when I came home night before last that the door was ajar. It spooked me. I gave the apartment a good once-over—thinking we might have been robbed. The only thing I noticed was that the computer was gone. After I discovered the fax, I figured you had it. Everything's on that computer—our bank accounts, letters, faxes, addresses. He could figure out a lot about us by just turning it on!"

"As far as I know, it never left my flight bag. He must have found some other source of information."

Kelly flinched as she remembered: "The drawer! The bottom drawer of the filing cabinet was opened, too. Did you get anything from it?"

"Nope," Todd answered, then looked up from his notes.

Kelly smiled. "Nothing's in there but some photos and some-of-your-old-love-letters-to-me, *R—C!*"

"Bingo. *K—W!*" Todd said as he smiled back. "So, here's the challenge: We need to prove he broke into our place, found out some personal stuff about us, then tried to use that knowledge to frame me."

Todd then shifted gears. "Actually, who cares? What we *need* to do is link him materially to Chris's death. Everything else should take care of itself."

"That's gonna be tough. The people that could help us the most are the very ones that are after us," Kelly said. "But, maybe you could negotiate a deal with the police that are investigating Chris's death to share their information with you."

Todd almost laughed. "'Fraid not. We're not exactly on speaking terms. Besides, all I have to offer the Loudoun police at this point is my surrender to the Anne Arundel police for last night's events."

"Well, I'm gonna see if the Bartletts have a paper out front. Maybe there's some news about a knife-wielding man who threw another man out of a window..." said Kelly as she walked toward the front of the house and peered through the living room curtain. "...You know—that standard everyday news stuff we get around these parts."

"Please don't let anyone see you."

"I won't. Besides, the neighbors wouldn't exactly expect a *dangerous criminal* to be staying here," Kelly mocked as she opened the door and walked out.

Todd continued compiling notes. A few seconds later, Kelly came back in and gave Todd a distressed stare and bit her lower lip before turning around and locking the deadbolt.

"Todd," she muttered softly. She took a few steps, then stopped. Her lower lip quivered as she held the paper out to him.

Todd raced out of the kitchen and down the hallway to her. He looked at her face, took a big sigh, then, then looked down at the paper. The cover of the *Washington Post*, upper half, bold lettering: "**Man Sought for Aircraft Accident**." Just beneath the bold title was a subtitle: "**Suspect Attacked Wife Last Night, Remains at Large**."

"Oh, Gawd! Kelly. This can't be!" Todd began reading the paper as they stammered back toward the kitchen. Tears were streaming down Kelly's face and onto the hand that covered her mouth.

"Todd Grant," he read aloud, "a pilot with TransGlobe Express, is being sought in connection with the crash two months ago of a TransGlobe Express commuter aircraft in Prince William County. The crash, which killed sixteen, was previously thought to be caused by pilot error and weather. The FBI, in cooperation with officials of the National Transportation Safety Board, this morning issued a warrant for the arrest of Mr. Grant, citing evidence found in the crash and discussions with him earlier this week.

Numerous other warrants have been issued, including last night's attempted murder of his wife. Also, an arrest warrant was issued by Virginia's Loudoun County Police for the murder of Ms. Chris Thomas, a female pilot also employed by TransGlobe Express. She was killed by a previously suspected hit and run accident near Centreville, Virginia late Saturday night.

Tom Sylvester

Last night, Mr. Grant was seen leaving his Severna Park, Maryland apartment holding a bloody knife, asking neighbors the whereabouts of his wife, Ms. Kelly Grant. Several neighbors reported hearing a scuffle, followed by breaking glass. Anne Arundel County police report that a facsimile was found in the apartment, allegedly sent by Mr. Grant to his wife, admitting that Mr. Grant had an affair with Ms. Thomas. A hand-written note across the fax that said 'Screw You!' was allegedly made by Ms. Grant.

The whereabouts and condition of Mrs. Grant are unknown.

Mr. Grant had flown with Ms. Thomas during the month of June, according to a source at Bands Airways, the company that is doing business as TransGlobe Express. According to the NTSB, Mr. Grant was a close friend of Scott Bradley, the Copilot who was at the controls of the aircraft when it crashed.

Earlier yesterday, Mr. Grant was arrested by the Loudoun County police and charged with having an open alcoholic beverage bottle in his possession while driving. He was later released. Just before yesterday's arrest, he had visited the Loudoun County police to file a harassment complaint against a fellow pilot with whom he recently had an altercation at the company's pilot lounge at Dulles Airport.

Blood samples from the apartment are being analyzed. A statement from the FBI is expected at a specially arranged press conference at 4:30 p.m. this afternoon."

Todd stared at the paper in disbelief. Kelly walked away in an effort to control herself.

"You O.K.?" he asked loudly.

She didn't answer.

"Want me to save the food section?"

She slowly reentered the kitchen and looked his way. "What are we going to do?"

"The first thing we need to do is have you surface. This is much bigger than a case of spousal abuse."

"No way, Todd. If I show up now, you'll have no one to help you. They'll be watching me like a hawk. I'll have no way to contact you."

"Then I'll just turn myself in. Surely, they have Al Thomas's fingerprints all over our apartment."

"Hey, you have three grave charges against you. It's not like you ran a stop sign. You'll be handicapping yourself against Thomas. He'll be free to continue trying to nail you while you sit in prison."

"Wait, I may have an ally. I went and visited the NTSB the day before yesterday. I hit it off with a guy named James Hatch. He's probably tied into all the goings on. His boss wasn't very friendly to me, though. He's all I have right now. Get dressed, we have to make a trip downtown."

"Are you crazy? We'll be caught for sure!"

"I'm not going to sit here and have more bad things happen to me. It's time that I go on the offensive."

• • • •

The phone rang at Keisha's desk. It was 9:00 a.m. and the entrance foyer was rather empty and quiet.

"L'Enfant Plaza Building, how may I help..."

"Kiesha?"

"Yea, who's this."

"Well hi, Kiesha. It's Todd Grant," he said happily.

"God! It's you!" she exclaimed with fright.

"Yea. It appears I've become quite a news story."

"Did you really attack your wife!"

"Of course not. But there's a guy that's trying to kill both her *and* me."

"You gonna turn yo' self in?"

"You bet. But I have to talk to James first. Is he around?"

"I'll see. Hang on." She punched the hold button, then nervously pressed James's extension.

After one ring, he picked up: "James Hatch."

"Hey, you'll never guess who's on the other line."

"Who?"

"Todd Grant."

"No way. Put him through!" James scrambled for a pad as he heard a clicking sound in his headset.

"Hello!?"

"Hello, James?"

"That you, Todd?"

"Yea. Hey, I need your help, James. I need you to help me nail the guy who's framing me."

"Where's your wife."

"She's fine. Sitting right here. Hang on..." He handed the phone to Kelly.

"Mr. Hatch? This is Kelly Grant."

"Call me James. Are you O.K.?"

"Oh, I'm fine, James. Not a scratch. I wasn't even at the apartment last night. Listen, please trust Todd on this. I love him and I don't want him hurt. You're the only one he can turn to for help. Trust your instincts."

"I'll see what I can do, Kelly," James said as he frantically wrote down notes of the conversation.

"James, it's me again. Kelly's going to turn herself in to the police a little later this morning. Please ensure that she gets full-time protection. I'm not gonna be able to protect her once she surfaces. He's gonna try again, I know it."

"Who's gonna try again?"

"I'll explain the whole thing to you in person in, uh, one hour and twenty minutes. Please meet me at the Air and Space Museum cafeteria at ten o'clock. Please bring with you copies of all the police reports you can muster from Loudoun and Anne Arundel, plus your own findings so I can study them. I know he must have slipped up somewhere."

"Todd, you're asking a lot of me."

"Please, James. And please don't let the police know about me until I've had a chance to see what the reports and depositions say. I promise, we'll nail this guy. You'll be a hero and I'll get my life back. But, I need your trust."

"Cafeteria at ten. I'll be there."

"Thanks, James."

James hung up, then quickly called the FBI. He could barely contain his excitement as he waited on hold while Stuart Varney finished another call. Finally, he picked up: "Stu Varney."

"Hey, Stu. Anything new on *your* end?" He began clearing his desk of the many police reports that, during the past eight hours, had almost doubled the size of the Bands 2235 accident file.

"You always have news when you start a conversation like that," said Stu.

"Just talked to Grant..."

"What?!"

"Yea. He wants me to meet him at ten at the Air and Space cafeteria."

"Holy shit. That's wonderful! Looks like you just caught a bad guy. I'll grab four or five agents and we'll be there."

"Wo! Wait. He says he's figured out who is trying to frame him."

"Sure he has."

"No, really. I talked to his wife. She didn't sound like she was talking under duress. He said she would surface later today, but *he* needed more time and information before he was ready to come forward."

"Sorry, James. But he'll just have to let us help him. We have to take him into custody."

"Tell you what. Let me talk to him. You can hide in the corner. If he becomes a threat, then you can step in. Otherwise, you fibbies can tail him back to wherever he's hiding. Maybe he'll incriminate himself even more if he *is* guilty."

"O.K., two things then. One, I want to approve the materiel that you plan to give him. Second, I'll give you a loose-leaf binder to use with a tracker in it, just in case he slips away."

"A tracker? You guys really have those kind of gadgets?!"

"You'd be amazed at what we have."

"Well, you better get here fast with it, 'cuz I'm meeting with him in a little over an hour."

••••

Todd looked great. He was wearing one of John's suits. Todd had the same broad shoulders that John had, but Todd's waist was much thinner. The pant's belt was buckled using the first hole, but it gave the pants a kind of comfortable, baggy appearance. He looked better in the suit than John ever would. The suit made him blend in quite well with the regular visitors.

Some high clouds had moved in as the clock approached ten, but he wore the Ray Bans nonetheless. Kelly had driven carefully from Bowie to downtown D.C. If they had been pulled over, the game would have been over. There was no traffic at mid-morning as they pulled off I-395 at the L'Enfant Promenade exit. They had all but finished discussing their plan of attack and alternatives if the plan failed.

Kelly pulled into a No Parking area just off 7th Street between NTSB headquarters and the Air & Space Museum. They had a couple of minutes to spare. He definitely did *not* want to be early. At 9:55, they repositioned the car one block south of Independence Avenue where they could see James walk across the street to the museum.

After about one minute, they saw James emerge from the building and cross the street. He made a motion, a kind of thumbs-up signal to another man that walked down the street, then crossed at another crosswalk.

"I knew James was punctual. Sure makes things go smoother. There's the FBI feller—see him?" Todd pointed to the slender, confident man a block away. Kelly nodded.

"Wish me luck."

"Luck," Kelly said with a plastic smile.

Todd got out and walked, briefcase in hand, around the corner to 490 L'Enfant Plaza. He entered the building and strolled right up to Kiesha. He swallowed hard and took a deep breath.

"Hi Kiesha. Boy, you look great!"

"Todd! What are you doing here?!"

"Got my ten o'clock with James," he said as he lifted up his briefcase.

"He ain't here. He just left with Stuart Varney, the FBI guy, to meet *you*."

"Where?!"

"I dunno."

"Shoot. Well, I'll just stand right here until he comes back." He crossed his legs awkwardly and immediately looked uncomfortable and disappointed. He lifted up his briefcase to the counter top. He flipped up the top, took out a pen, then added a note on the bottom of the single sheet of paper inside. She couldn't see what he was writing. As he wrote, he shook his head slowly and said softly, "I was supposed to meet him and Stu in James's office at ten." He looked up at her with an angelic frown.

"You can wait up there if you'd like."

"Well, uh, O.K. You want me to sign in?" He closed his briefcase and lowered it to his side.

"Already got ya. Just sign right here." She swiveled the register around to him.

He signed it, clipped the visitor's badge on his lapel, then turned and walked toward the elevators. "Thanks, Kiesha. Wish me luck."

She smiled and watched him suddenly race to beat a closing elevator door.

Moments later, he arrived at the fifth floor. He took another deep breath and stepped out of the elevator. The wide main hall was empty. He turned left and walked through the glass doors marked "Office of Research and Engineering" and through the maze of cubicles, passing a few unfamiliar faces along the way. He greeted them with a smile. Reaching James's office, he closed the door softly. He went straight to James's desk and opened the soon to be momentarily empty briefcase. He took out the handwritten note and placed it in the center of James desk. He then grabbed the huge manila envelope with "Bands 2234" written across the front from the edge of James's desk and placed it into his briefcase. James's organized nature had worked to Todd's advantage. The files could have been with James over at the Smithsonian, but that was unlikely. James was a perfectionist. If anything left his office, it would be copies—not originals. Todd was expecting to find it in James's filing cabinet, but was fortunate to have it all assembled on the desk top, ready for borrowing. He closed the now heavier briefcase, then turned and left. Done. Quick and easy.

He rounded a corner, walked casually up to the glass doors and ran right into Bernard Ruddman. His heart sank. There was no chance of escape. He had to think quickly.

"Hi, Barney. Todd Grant." He extended his hand to Barney and offered a smile.

"What the... What are you doing here...."

"I've got a ten fifteen with James and a guy named Stu Varney from the FBI. Are you joining us?"

"Uh, no. What's going on?"

"Well, we're trying to straighten out the frame-up before this afternoon's press conference. You know, restore my dignity and yet keep egg off the FBI's face for barking up the wrong tree."

"You mean that in addition to mixing metaphors, you say you're being *framed*?"

"Yep. The sucker tried to chop me up last night in my apartment. You got time to sit in on the meeting?"

"Uh, yea."

"It's in James's office in ten minutes. They're not there yet. I'm gonna run to the little boy's room right quick."

"O.K." Barney's expression hadn't changed much since the conversation began. Barney was an investigator—a seasoned one with a lot of horse sense. Todd was still caught. His story was quick and believable, but he realized it only gave him an extra minute or so.

Todd knocked his knees together and gave Barney an embarrassed smile. "Be right back. Too much coffee..."

Todd walked with a moderately fast pace down the long, wide hallway. Unfortunately, the elevators were in the other direction, but he had to make himself absent. Barney smelled a rat. Todd knew it and didn't care to prolong the intense eye contact as he weaved the lie. Walking away, he noticed a large red exit sign at the end of the hallway. He thought to himself that if he were to run full speed to the stairwell that he could make it out of the building by the time Barney could call down to the guard on duty. He didn't dare look back. He knew Barney was watching.

He opted instead to go into the bathroom as expected. He figured that Barney was going to watch him all the way. Once inside, he went right into a stall, dropped his briefcase, and rubbed his face. He was trapped. It was over. "Give up now" echoed off the stall walls.

If he darted right back out of the bathroom, Barney would know that something wasn't right. Yet, if he waited too long, Barney might go into James's office and discover the note. No, he assured himself. He would be patient and remain in the bathroom. Maybe Barney would not be in the hallway when he emerged.

After an eternal minute, he walked up to the bathroom door, grabbed it and paused for a moment, eyes closed. He then swung the door open, came out of the bathroom and made a turn towards James's office. He glanced and noticed that Barney was not there. He immediately turned and sprinted toward the stairwell. His bruised knee and sore shoulder slowed him down and changed a beautiful stride into a noisy gallop. He figured he only had a few seconds before he would be discovered. Barney walked back up to the glass doors right as Todd swung open the door to the exit stairwell. From sixty feet away, they made a very brief but solid eye contact. He was caught. Damn.

As Todd disappeared into the stairwell, Barney dashed across the large hallway toward the elevator, which proved to be the wrong move. Realizing that trying to beat him down by using the elevator was futile, he then turned and, in a very unathletic fashion, ran back to the first phone that was available. A man was sitting at a desk in the office closest to the glass doors. He had his phone propped up to his ear with his shoulder. With his head down facing a notepad, he didn't notice Barney approaching. In one motion, Barney ripped the phone away from the man with one hand and hung up the phone with the other. The man jumped back in his chair, shocked by the sudden event.

"What's the number for the lobby downstairs?! Shit!" He pressed the zero key, hoping for help. The man reached forward and pulled out a building directory from his center drawer as Barney yanked it from him.

Todd's tie flew back around his neck as he rounded the stairwell's first turn. He painfully leaped down three or four concrete steps at a time. The stairwell was seldom used and poorly lit. He could, however, make out the smooth cinder block walls, covered with enamel, as he rounded each corner. The black, round metal banister allowed him to swing around each one with considerable speed. On the last turn before reaching the lobby level, he missed the banister. The centrifugal force slammed his shoulder against the unforgiving wall, which made him cry out in pain. As he got to the bottom he slowed to stop, pulled his tie forward, and made one pass of his hand through his blown-back hair. He was in a lot of pain, but had to control it for about twenty yards. He opened the stairwell door and entered the lobby at a good clip.

He spun-tossed Kiesha the visitors badge and cheerfully yelled "Catch!" right as her phone rang. "They're all over at the Air and Space Museum!" He gave her a hurried smile and left the building right as she picked up the phone.

He sprinted around to the side of the building and leaped horizontally into the car. "Go, Kelly. Go!"

She made a right turn onto School Street and disappeared. Todd painfully spun around low in his seat to see if anyone saw the car they were in. No one emerged from the side of the building as it disappeared behind another.

He slumped hard into the passenger seat, facing away from Kelly. He was hurting and couldn't seem to catch his breath.

Kelly glanced down at him a few times, then waited for him to say something. To give her a clue. Anything at all would suffice.

Finally, since he didn't offer, she asked him in a southern tone, "Honey, didjew' have a bad day at the office?"

"Nope," he said, still panting and facing eye level with the passenger armrest. "Just a might hectic, that's all." He held up the briefcase with his left hand, then gravity pulled it back down.

EIGHTEEN

BERNARD RUDDMAN, A.K.A. BARNEY RUBBLE, sat in James's chair behind James's desk and stared at the doorway as he heard James and Stu approach. Barney constructed a serene pose with hands clasped as James and Stu quickly entered the office.

"Hey! Well if it isn't Starsky and Hutch. No-No-No. It's *Stuuu*-skee and *Hatch*!" They both stopped just inside the doorway. "So, what's, uh, new, boys?" said Barney slowly as he began rocking back and forth. The two watched him watch them squirm.

"Um, Kiesha said I had a visitor while I was out," James said finally.

"Yup."

"Young boy, 'bout twenty-four, blonde hair, handsome...."

"Yup."

No one was smiling.

"I guess he was on a mission."

"Guess so. He told me that the two of you were going to meet with him at ten fifteen. It's ten thirty. James, I thought you were more punctual than that. Did you have something more pressing somewhere else?"

"I thought I did, Barn."

"You said 'the two of you.' How did he know about me?" Stu asked.

"Beats me. He knew you were from the FBI and your name was Stu Varney. Says so right here." Barney lifted a lone piece of paper from James's desk and dangled it between two fingers as though it was contaminated. "I think you guys are dealing with one smart son of a bitch."

"What does it say?" Stu asked. Neither walked over to the desk to retrieve it. They just stood there, embarrassed.

"Have a seat, guys." Barney wasn't smiling but it was obvious he was kind of enjoying himself. "Stu, I bet we've known each other for, what, over ten years. As you know, I've always been impressed by your work in sabotage and air piracy. You could find out the facts and background information about anyone. But today, I realized that your skills in simple apprehension are less than admirable. James was just plain suckered. But Stu, you were professionally embarrassed."

"Shame on me, Barn. Now, what does the note say?"

"O.K. Yes, the note." He melodramatically flexed his elbows outward and positioned the note to a good orator's reading distance.

The handwriting was neat and legible, even though all but the P.S. had been written in a moving vehicle. Barney began reading it aloud:

"*Dear James:*

I'm sorry that I had to trick you in order to get the Bands 2234 files. I gave you no reason to trust me and I know it will be harder for you to trust me now. I also understand that you had no choice but to try and corner me at the museum. I promise that after I make copies of all of the relevant documents, that everything will be returned to you in the same condition that I got them.

I'm now prepared to start building some trust between us. Kelly will turn herself in to you later this afternoon. That will, as a minimum, dispel any accusations that I attempted to murder her. Please ensure that she gets round-the-clock protection. She's in a great deal of danger.

Once I get organized, I'll give you everything I know about the guy who's trying to frame me. I'll also give you all of the facts surrounding last night's attack at my apartment.

Please understand that I'm not—nor ever will be—a spectator. If I allowed myself to be arrested now, I would give up any chance of assisting in catching the guy that killed two of my closest friends.

I'm relieved that Scott will no longer be blamed for the accident. He was a gifted pilot and a fine person. Chris Thomas was, too. But just clearing Scott's name isn't enough. I'm not giving up until the guy that killed them gets 300,000 volts.

I left a message for you on CompuServe. It's the first set of facts for you and the authorities to start working with. You may also reach me there. My I.D. number is 72448, 2541.

Look forward to working with you.

Sincerely, Todd Grant

P.S. Please extend my apologies to Stu Varney. I'd like to win the FBI's trust and assistance, too."

Barney lowered the note carefully back to the desk top. Both Stu and James waited momentarily, then raced over to the computer. Stu turned around and grabbed a chair as Barney rose to let James have his chair back. Barney could have grabbed another chair, but chose to stand and look at the monitor from behind. No one spoke a word as James grabbed the computer's mouse and moved the screen cursor over to the icon labeled "CompuServe" and clicked the mouse's left button. After an anxious fifteen or so seconds, he was in.

The top of the screen filled with a host of options, one being "Mail." He highlighted that word, then pressed "G" to get the single message that was waiting for him. The screen went mostly blank. Then, line-by-line, Todd's message to James appeared:

<<MAIL DATE: 08/13 TIME: 10:18aEDT>>

Dear James: His name is Al Thomas. I'm sure the Loudoun County Police have interviewed him and he probably has a strong alibi regarding his whereabouts last Saturday night. I've never met him, but I know he had a grudge against Bands for not hiring him. And, according to Chris, he was a jealous man who had beaten her on at least a few occasions.

Al repairs VCRs at SunVisor Video in Alexandria and is also a part-time flight instructor at Hyde Field just south of Washington in Clinton, Maryland. Please check out his alibis closely.

I've made it clear to Kelly that she will not know where I'll be hiding once she surfaces. It's better that way. I'm sure she wants to help me, but I don't want her involved, less she be charged with aiding and abetting. We've talked at length this morning and she will have several pages of notes to give you.

James, I'm gonna get this guy. Somehow, Al must have screwed up and left something unchecked. I'm gonna find out what, then I'm gonna nail him. When you leave a message for me on CompuServe, beep me at (202) 555-7313 and I'll pick it right up. Look forward to hearing from you.

-Todd

P.S. "Truth, crushed to earth, shall rise again..." -William Cullen Bryant.
<<END OF MAIL.>>

"Can you print that message?" Stu asked.

"Sure." replied James as he pressed a couple of keys.

Stu turned and began a slow pace around the room. "Just who does that son-of-a-bitch think he is? And who does he think *we* are—shopping mall police?"

"Of course not. You're *Stu*sky and he's *Hatch,*" Barney said, pointing twice, reminding them of his witty-the-first-time pun.

Stu turned to James, who was removing the message from the laser printer. "Well, Hatch. What do you think? If the Loudoun County Police couldn't find probable cause with Al Thomas, then what makes him think that he can?" Stu uncharacteristically placed his hands under his jacket and into his front pants pockets.

"I kinda hope he's *not* guilty, *Stusky,*" said James, now mocking the pun. "I would hate to think that someone as crafty as him is the bad guy. You realize that CompuServe is a perfect way of communicating with us without allowing us to trace the call."

"I can have any call traced," Stu said indignantly.

"Think about it, Stu. Grant knows that thousands of calls go into that computer from all over the world every day. To try and trace the originating number would require that they have *Caller I.D.* on every node. Every channel. They're not set up for that! Even if they could, it would take time—and time is what he's after."

"Well, I'll see what I can do. Where's CompuServe's headquarters?"

"Columbus, I think."

"O.K."

"Do you think we should leave a message for ole' Todd?" Barney asked Stu.

"Definitely. We'll get him to talk—and talk often. The more the better. And I'm gonna have James's line tapped right away in case Todd gets lazy and calls James directly." He faced James. "Well, James. First, you convinced me that the accident was no accident. Now you've become a conduit to the criminal. I guess you need to stay in the game until time expires."

"All right," said James as he began an outgoing message for Todd on CompuServe.

"Wait! He doesn't belong to you, Stu! It's a criminal case now. James is an NTSB investigator, not an FBI agent. One: I'm backlogged with accident investigations and can't afford to give up one of my varsity to do fibbie work. And two: You're asking him to converse with a guy that killed his paramour and a planeload of people..."

"Allegedly..." James interjected.

"O.K. Fine. He *allegedly* killed twenty people. Call me stupid, but that seems somewhat dangerous."

James obviously didn't want to be pulled from the game. "Barn, when you gave me this case, you said I should always listen to as many people as I can. And when I *do* find the truth, I'll almost always be surprised who it was that finally led me to it. Well Barn, I'm just not convinced that I have the whole truth yet. We have more to learn from Todd. Let me stay in."

Barney turned towards the door and began walking. He looked at his watch, then peered straight ahead toward the open doorway. "It's not a good idea. I don't like it. Be careful, all right?" By the time he finished talking, he was already in the hallway.

"All right," James said, loud enough to be heard in the hallway.

"Was that a yes?"

"We refer to that around here as a *Pontious Pilot* yes."

After some discussion about their approach, James and Stu prepared a message for Todd, sent it, then dialed his beeper number to let him know that the following message was waiting:

<<MAIL DATE: 08/13 TIME: 11:22aEDT>>

Todd:

The best way for you to help us is to turn yourself in. I must also remind you that the documents you possess are official, confidential, and are the property of the U.S. Government. You must return them immediately. If, after their return, any document is missing or in any way altered, you will find yourself in jail for a long time, other charges notwithstanding.

-James

P.S. "Trust none; for oaths are straws, men's faiths are wafercakes..." -Shakespeare.

<<END OF MAIL.>>

• • • •

K.W. pulled into the Bartlett's garage and pressed the button attached to the car's visor, lowering the door behind them. Todd's shirt and jacket, borrowed from John Bartlett, were soaked with blood from reopening the stab wound as a result of slamming into the stairway wall. The pain, though present, wasn't felt. Todd had been consumed with the borrowed documents. He had scoured them out loud as Kelly had driven them back to the Bartlett's. The documents were divided into four sections.

The first section was the largest and contained all of the reports surrounding *the accident*. For the first time, Todd read about the plastic toy penguin with the wire attached to one of its wings and the aluminum foil placed in its path. He read about how it was used as a switch to electrically engage, then disengage the airplane's stall recovery system. How, like a metronome, it was timed to match—perfectly—with the reaction time of the pilot, thus amplifying the pilot's response and overstressing the airframe. He was intrigued by how much Al had obviously learned about the airplane's stall protection system. He realized that Al was both incredibly cunning and technically brilliant.

The first section also contained a memorandum about Todd's meeting with James and Barney. There was an attendance sheet from the NTSB press conference with Todd's name circled. A five page FBI background check on Todd was also included. The background check had numerous references to his engineering skills while in college, all highlighted. The last page of the section was the FBI's warrant for Todd's arrest. By the time he finished the first section, he found himself physically shaking. This was real. He was in deep trouble.

The second set of documents contained the Loudoun County Police files. The bulk of it regarded Chris Thomas's death. It described how Chris's oil tank drain was stuffed with a paper towel, allowing the car to fail on her way home. How she was first kicked in the cheek bone after she stopped along the side of the dark road. How she was then dragged and propped against her open car door, then rammed by a car—a light blue car, based on the paint chips found on Chris's car door. The pebble marks, the scrapes, the blood, the shoe polish. All the gory details. Todd lived the incident as he read it. He asked himself how anyone could do such a thing.

Enclosed was the Thomas' separation order: Irreconcilable Differences. One of the police reports included the text that described how they had not been able to contact Al until late Sunday night, a full day after her death. He had been out of town that weekend. He was in Charlotte. There it was—the alibi. Attached to the police report were gas receipts from his drive down and back from Charlotte.

Other documents included the complaint that Todd had filed against Gary. There was an internal memorandum describing how Todd angrily left the police station yesterday. There was a crewmember pairings sheet from Bands Airways showing the trips that Todd and Chris had flown together. Also included was a complaint filed just last night by Gary, saying he was attacked in his own apartment by Todd. Attached to Gary's report was a medical report that detailed the contusions and *two* broken fingers. Notably absent was the admission by Gary that he had harassed Kelly. There was yesterday's alcohol arrest citation and summons. The section was completed with last night's arrest warrant for Todd.

The third section was just a few pages and was read aloud as the car had entered the Bartlett's neighborhood. It included the Anne Arundel County Police report from last night's attack at Todd's apartment, including copies of Ted Behlman's statement and the fax. There it was, the fax. He read the fax three times. The fact that "Screw You" was shown on the copy in black and not the original red ink didn't diminish the impact that it had on Todd. His eyes welled-up as the garage door came down behind them. He sat up in his seat as she took the keys from the ignition.

"The words in this fax are quite believable," he managed.

"Yes. They are."

"I see the anger here...." he said as he moved his finger along the handwritten "Screw You."

"I was *very* angry—and *very* hurt."

"Gawd, he's smart. He has all of his bases covered. He's got me up to my ass in alligators."

They walked from the garage, through the laundry room where Kelly stopped to place the notebook computer and the cellular phone, still connected together with a short phone cord, on top of the dryer. They would need it again to send more CompuServe messages later. Todd continued through the kitchen and began to go upstairs, undressing as he walked. Todd's beeper sounded, which startled him. As he looked down at the beeper, clipped to his waist, Kelly suddenly exclaimed: "Todd! Someone's been here!"

Todd turned and glanced at the counter top. The note and envelope had been moved and there was an additional note beside them. "Cleaning lady—Forbes?" he asked hurriedly.

"No! Todd, it was the police!"

Todd hurried back into the kitchen as he said, "We were only gone for a couple of hours....what does it say?"

"It says: Dear Ms. Bartlett: An employee of yours, Kelly Grant, was believed to have been attacked by her husband last night. She fled from the scene and we thought she might have stayed with you last night. When you return, please give me a call at the above number. - Lt. Mike Bigston, AA County Police. 8/13, 10:45 a.m."

"Holy shit, they must have just left here!" he said.

A wave of panic hit Kelly. "We've got bloody clothes in the laundry room. Finger prints everywhere. What if they had decided to really check out the house?"

"Then I'd be in the pokey now," he said as he turned toward her and thought for a moment. "I guess we need to be more careful while we're here. We have to be smarter about this or we're gonna get nabbed. We must wipe everything down that we've touched. We have to hide the bloody clothes. Under no circumstances should we use their phone. The house must remain dark at night. The newspapers must stay in the driveway. Nobody's here. They could be watching."

"I think we should leave."

"Well, let's think about it for a minute. The heat is on now. Where would we go? The note apparently worked, for now. They probably called Susan's office, who reported that she would be gone for a couple of days. Let's plan on leaving no later than tomorrow night. I think we'll be safe here until then."

He gazed at his surroundings, then said, "K.W., I gotta admit, I'm scared. I'm up against a monster who's smart—and willing to do anything to get me convicted. He's got the FBI and two separate county police investigators after me. I just don't know if I can prove it was him."

"We'll get him. I know it. Why don't you get changed into something less bloody and we'll work on it."

"O.K. By the way, could you turn on the laptop and see what message we got back from James. He just beeped me."

"Sure."

NINETEEN

A SQUEAKY, SOUTHERN VOICE answered the phone: "Charlotte Hyatt. May I help you?" The voice was cheerful and by the tone of it, Kelly knew it would be fairly easy to get the information she needed, even before she asked.

"Hi. I was wondering if you might be able to help me...." Kelly asked as she raised her eyebrows to Todd. He was pacing between the Bartlett's kitchen and family room. The window shades and curtains in those two rooms were closed to allow them some movement inside. The rest of the house, as seen from the front, remained undisturbed. The two rooms were no longer bright and open. The shades were so light-tight that the only illumination came from the light down the long hallway from the front of the house. Though it was 2:00 p.m. on a fairly bright day, a light over the kitchen table had to be turned on for Kelly to see her note pad without straining. They would have preferred to stage their investigation from the basement of the house, but they found the cellular phone's reception to be severely degraded below ground level. Any computer communications via the cell phone would be riddled with transmission errors. However, they would nonetheless be forced to turn out the lights and move to the basement when dusk neared, thus ending any outside communications for the day.

"I'll try," the lady from Charlotte said even more cheerfully.

"I understand that there was a video technician's conference held at your hotel last weekend. Could you tell me who sponsored it, please?"

"Sure. If you can hang on for a second, I'll check," she said.

Even before Kelly could say thank you, she began hearing elevator music through her earpiece. Kelly had her pencil positioned with the lead touching the seventh page of a yellow pad of paper. The first six were pulled over the top of the page and creased to stay behind the pad. She put her left elbow on the kitchen table and balanced the mobile phone on her left shoulder as she rubbed her temples and looked down at the pad.

After a couple of seconds, the music clicked off and the woman's voice spoke: "Ma'am, that conference was sponsored by Sierra Enterprises out of Reno, Nevada. I don't have their phone number. If you could call back after lunch, our events scheduler will be in and could find it for you."

Kelly graciously thanked the lady, then hung up. She grabbed a phone book from the kitchen cabinet and found the area code for Reno. After a couple minutes of rerouted calls, she was talking with the conference director.

"Hi. My name is Sarah Jenkins with the Loudoun County Police Department in Leesburg, Virginia," Kelly said.

"This involve that Thomas fellow again?"

"Yes, as a matter of fact, it does," she said politely.

"Listen, lady, you got my statement. When are you gonna quit pestering me?" he asked with an angry tone.

"I know, and we won't be bothering you any more. But, we need a copy of the sign-in sheets for both Saturday's and Sunday's presentations."

"Hold on," he said, then immediately punched the hold button on his phone. She rubbed her temples a little harder as she questioned whether she was handling the call well.

He clicked himself off hold after about half a minute. "Yep. He signed in at...you there?"

"Yes, go ahead." She could hear papers being shuffled.

"He signed in at 8:30 a.m. on Saturday, then again after the lunch break at 1:00 p.m. Let's see. And...on...Sunday, he signed in again at 8:30, and again at one. Yep, he was here for all four sessions."

"Is there any chance that he could have signed in, then left—or signed in late, but filled in the normal sign-in time."

He lectured a response. "Lady, we give out completion certificates. We don't give them an exam at the end of the seminar. How much they want to actually learn is up to each attendee. The *only* thing we require of them to get their certificate is to physically sit through all of the presentations. Yep. He was there through all of them, I guarantee it. Now, you need anything else?" he asked abruptly.

"No, sir. I'd like to thank you for your coopera..."

"Good. So long," he said as he slammed down the phone.

She pushed the END CALL button on her cellular phone as she looked up toward Todd, who was now sitting across the dimly lit table from her, eating a jelly sandwich and typing something into the laptop. A thick book lay open on the table to the right of the laptop. The glow from the computer screen made his face appear gray and cold.

"Well, he was definitely in Charlotte last Saturday," she announced.

Todd spoke with food in his mouth. "You don't think he would have hired someone to kill her, do you?" Todd reached over, grabbed the cellular phone and plugged a phone cord into it from the computer.

"Whomever it was that did it, sure had it planned down to the smallest detail."

Todd looked back at his computer screen as he talked to Kelly. "You're right. If he *had* a hired gun, I don't..." Todd stopped mid-sentence to swallow, then continued. "...think he would have gone to all the trouble—he would probably have just killed her in her apartment and made it look like it was done by a burglar or somethin'." He pushed the rest of his sandwich into his mouth. "Too many things could have gone wrong with the hit and run scenario for him to trust someone else to do it," he said slovenly. Todd overtly tapped the ENTER key which sent a single line message to James, then closed the book of quotations he had earlier found on the Bartlett's bookcase. The message was:

<<MAIL DATE: 08/13 TIME: 1:57pEDT>>
"We must try to trust one another. Stay and cooperate." -Jomo Kenyatta. First President of Kenya, to the white settlers.
<<END OF MAIL>>

Todd turned off the computer, tilted the screen down until it latched, unplugged the phone cord between the laptop and the cellular phone, then pushed them and the book off to his right.

"So how did he get up here? We know he drove his car to Charlotte. We've seen the fuel receipts. His Saturday afternoon session concluded at...." She flipped through the police files. "Uh, five p.m. That means he only had about seven hours to get back to Washington."

"He could have taken a flight back," Todd said as continued to chew.

"You're right, but how could he have been back by 8:30 a.m. the next morning. There aren't any flights that leave Washington in time for him to sign back in by then."

Todd suddenly quit chewing, bolus halted, as a thought came to mind. "Yep, he could have flown back here," Todd said, frozen in thought.

"Todd, you're not listening. There are no three or four a.m. departures to Charlotte."

Todd *wasn't* listening. "Yep, he flew up here, I bet."

She stared at him, waiting for him to finish chewing and finish his thought. He lowered his head and ran his hands rearward through his now-oily, blonde hair. His fingers stayed in back and massaged his upper neck just below the sagital crest of his skull as his elbows landed gingerly on the tabletop. Kelly had seen this posture before. Todd was reconstructing facts and she wasn't going to interrupt his train of thought now. She, like the partially chewed jelly sandwich, would have to wait.

After a few seconds, his hands dropped and crossed in front of him as he raised his head, which now exhibited a sly smile. He finished chewing. He had a serene, check-mate smirk on his face.

"What?!" she asked enthusiastically.

"I've got to make some phone calls. Do you feel like hunting down a car for me?"

"Yea. Of course. Just tell me what I'm looking for and where I should begin looking."

"It's a blue car and it's submerged in the Chesapeake Bay," Todd said as he rubbed his mouth vigorously with a paper napkin, indicating he was getting ready to bolt into action.

She chuckled out loud. "Oh, I see. And how am I supposed to get to the bottom of the Chesapeake?"

"The car's probably just below the surface, right along the shoreline. I just want you to spot its tracks through those tall weeds leading to the water at the end of Bay Bridge Airport, then call that Officer Bigston fellow over at the Arundel County Police to have his boys fish it out." Todd was now grinning broadly.

"You sly dog, you," said Kelly as she tilted her head to the side in a sultry-smiling fashion. "What do you know?"

Todd stood up and mocked a pompous attorney, adjusting his imaginary tie. "Counselor, counselor. Do you deny that Suspect Al Thomas was, himself, a licensed pilot?"

"No. And objection—your vague and overbroad assertion reeks of being both arbitrary and capricious." She played along with his mock courtroom examination.

"Objection overruled."

"Wait. Who are you role-playing here, the prosecutor or the judge?"

"I AM THE PURVEYOR OF THE TRUTH!" he announced with his right index finger raised skyward and his left hand behind his back. "And counselor, do you recall being witness to the recollection of a conversation between a fellow model airplane enthusiast and the Bay Bridge Airport manager last Sunday afternoon?" Todd paced back and forth in the shadow beyond the kitchen table.

"Yes. And that's hearsay."

"Please describe the elements of that hearsay to the court."

"He said that he was thinking about charging the radio-controlled modelers a fee for use of the airport while it was shut down."

"While-it-was-shut-down. Hmmm. What else happened at the airport that had the airport manager upset?—And I must remind you that you are under oath," he said, dramatically pointing his finger at her.

"Todd! He said someone took the airport car without signing it out!"

"In legaleze, we refer to that as *swiping a car*. Please continue, Madam Counselor!"

"Uh...Uh...." she said as she struggled to remember the events last Sunday.

Todd continued his opprobrious interrogation. "Did he not say that someone had departed the aerodrome in an aerospace flying vehicle in direct violation of the CABBA court order that prohibits all departures except one-way departures over the water?"

"Huh?"

"Did someone sneak out of the airport in an airplane late Saturday night?"

"Yea. Yea. He said that, didn't he!"

"Prosecution rests." He sat down and ceased his feigning.

"How long does it take to fly from Charlotte to Bay Bridge in a light plane?" she asked.

"I imagine about three hours."

"So he would have had plenty of time after five o'clock on Saturday to rent—or steal—a plane, fly it to Bay Bridge Airport, steal the airport car, drive to Dulles, rig Chris's car, then follow her till she pulled over, ram her with the airport car, drive back to Bay Bridge, ditch the car in the bay, hop back in his airplane, and fly back in time for the eight thirty sign-in Sunday morning? All without being seen? Sounds simple to me," she said in an acerbic tone.

"It is, when you think about the information that he had available to him to plan this event. Every licensed pilot in the Washington area received a letter from the FAA, reminding them of the Notice to Airmen that placed the flight restrictions on Bay Bridge Airport. I got mine, and I don't even fly the small planes anymore."

"Yea..."

"So, he knew that he could probably get in and out of there unnoticed. And he knows that most small airports have a courtesy car available to transient pilots. Hell, as a flight instructor at Hyde Field, he probably took students over to Bay Bridge all the time. I don't doubt that he checked it all out completely ahead of time."

"Yea..."

"So, all he had to do was get a plane and fly up here. That's where I come in. I'm gonna find out who rented him the airplane in Charlotte while you go find that car."

"Color me gone." She stood up as he did, offered him a high-five, which he returned with a smile. After she left, he felt around to see if the high-five reopened up his aching shoulder wound.

• • • •

Sergeant John Cripp walked by Dwight Conners's office as Dwight frantically waved his arms at him. The chief homicide investigator, standing behind his desk, had the phone up to his ear and motioned for the Sergeant to pick up the corner phone.

"Hang on just a second, Mr. Thomas. I'm gonna have Sergeant John Cripp pick up."

A click was heard as John lifted the receiver, but John lacked some basic social skills and said nothing. Al Thomas knew John was now listening. But, since he said nothing, it made Al feel quite defensive. Dwight was much more cordial and said "Al, Sergeant Cripp is on the line. He helps me out a lot with cases around here."

"Hello, Sergeant."

"Hello," he replied. By the tone of John's voice, Al knew he would be merely an eavesdropper on the conversation.

"Al, we've been by your place a few times in the last couple of days and left messages on your machine. Glad you finally got back with us."

"I've been shipping Chris's stuff back to her parents and getting her things in order over at her place."

"How are you holding out?"

"I'm doing better now, thanks."

"Listen Al, can you come out and talk to us sometime today?"

Al walked the few steps over to his bathroom with the cordless phone and looked in the mirror at his scratched face. "Does it have to do with the article in this morning's *Post*?" He dampened a washcloth with warm water as he spoke, then dabbed it at one of the larger scratches.

"We're not really sure about anything at this time. And we know it hasn't been a week yet since your wife passed away, but we've got to ask you some, well, personal questions, if you don't mind."

Al continued talking. "It's a long way out to Leesburg and I've got a lot left to do. Can you just ask me the questions over the phone?"

"I guess so, but I'm gonna have to record the conversation. Is that O.K. with you?"

"Sure, I guess."

"Hang on while I hook it up."

Al continued to clean and dress his wounds and think about the upcoming questions.

"O.K. Al, we're now recording. Did the two of you have any enemies? What I mean is, is there anyone that you know of that was upset with you or your wife?"

"No. Why?" Al maintained his quiet, almost deliberate tone.

"Did you or Chris owe any money to anyone?"

"Just the car loan, that's all. Why?"

"Well, these hit and run accidents always have to be looked at from every angle. We wouldn't want anyone to get away with murder if there was the slightest chance of it."

"Do you really think she was murdered?" Al asked, still solemnly.

"People in this quiet county have been murdered for things such as insulting someone else's hairdo and stepping ahead of someone in line at a movie theater. I'm just amazed at how crazy things have gotten around here. So when someone dies in Loudoun County, I always take a peek at the circumstances, however insignificant. You understand, don't you?"

"Yes, sir. But, not Chris. Everyone loved her. I loved her, too. I mean, we were separated and all, but we weren't divorced and we still cared for each other. We disagreed on stuff such as children and home life, but we always shared a certain closeness."

"Have you heard of a man by the name of Todd Grant?"

"Sure have. I read the *Post* article twice this morning. She did fly with him a few months back, as I recall. But, I don't believe for a second that she slept with him. I don't know what his motive was for in admitting that to his wife. Chris wouldn't do that. She's still married to me. As a matter of fact, we weren't even separated when they flew together. I'm not trying to defend that Grant guy—he sounds like a real wacko—but I know Chris. She wouldn't do that. Then or now."

"Have you ever met him?"

"No."

"Did Chris ever say anything to you about him?"

"Come to think of it, she did say he was—well—kind of moody."

"In what way?"

"I don't remember the details, but he must have flown off the handle over something really minor, which kinda shocked her a little."

"Did Grant mention his home life to Chris?"

"I don't know. Who knows. But, they flew together for a whole month. You sit together in a tiny cockpit for a month and you get to know the other person fairly well. As to whether he mentioned his home life to her or not, I couldn't tell you."

Dwight shrugged his shoulders at John, who returned the shrug. "O.K. Well, Al, the investigation on the circumstances surrounding her death will continue. We'll be sure to keep you informed."

"Thank you, sir."

"Oh, and Al. Please check back with your answering machine every couple of hours. We may need to get in touch with you rather quickly."

"I will. And thank you for your persistence. I'm going to continue to believe that she was killed by a hit and run and that the guy that did it will turn himself in soon. The idea that she was murdered makes me ill."

"Don't worry. We're working hard on it."

After hanging up, John spoke first. "I hope I find Grant first. I'll hang him by his nuts."

Dwight stared out into the hallway for a moment, then said. "I wonder if it really is Grant."

• • • •

Todd glanced at his watch: 3:00 p.m. He and Kelly had spent a solid hour inventing, then rehearsing her story if she were caught snooping around the water's edge at Bay Bridge. She grabbed her purse, then he rose and kissed her good-bye. She walked into the garage as he sat back down and picked up the cellular phone.

The garage door opened as the Bartlett's car started up. Kelly looked in the rearview mirror and began to back up. When the car was almost out of the garage, three loud bangs erupted. Kelly screamed out loud and she slammed the gas pedal to the floor. The car leaped backwards, sending her toward the steering wheel. She stomped hard on the brake and the car stopped. She instinctively slouched in the seat and assessed the situation. No broken glass, no blood.

A man holding gardening gloves tapped on the passenger's window. She looked up, shaken. He gave her a long puzzled look. He must have banged on her trunk. She put the car in park, then reached over and rolled down the window.

"You're not Susan," he said with a surprised, yet serious tone.

Her mind raced. She was not prepared for this and was not a good liar. "No. I'm not."

"You're in her car," he stated in a *you better start explaining* tone.

"Yes. I am. Uh, she's in Ohio. I'm driving her car out to her. I'm her niece, Kelly." She extended her hand. He shook her hand but didn't offer his name in return.

"I noticed a police car here earlier. Do you know anything about it?"

"Uh, yea...." She gave him an embarrassed smile. "I set off the alarm in the house when I arrived here a few hours ago. She forgot to tell me about it. I guess her mother is really ill and will be in Ohio for a while. I put her briefcase and clothes in the trunk and was just leaving now. Would you mind picking up the paper for John and Susan while they're gone?"

"Not at all. It's three o'clock. What time are you going get there?"

"Not until tomorrow. I'm gonna spend the night somewhere along the way tonight."

"Well, be careful. Tell the Bartletts the Grahams are thinking of them."

"I sure will, Mr. Graham." She smiled and rolled up the window, then punched the button to lower the garage door. She waved, then turned away from him to watch behind her as she backed out of the driveway. Her hands were shaking as she shifted into drive.

Inside, Todd was on the phone and unaware of what just happened in the driveway. He found out that there were several flight schools and aeroclubs at the four airports that surrounded the Charlotte area. He focused on the three at Charlotte International Airport, since the airport was right across the street from Al Thomas's hotel. He called one and asked if anyone had been checked out last Saturday in an airplane, then rented it for an overnight trip. No, he was told.

The second one said yes, there was a man in his early twenties that needed to go to eastern Tennessee to visit his mother, who had just been diagnosed with breast cancer. He showed up at 5:30 p.m. on Saturday, was checked out by one of the flight instructors, then topped off the tanks and took off.

"What was the guy's name?" Todd Grant *of the Loudoun County Sheriff's Office* asked the lady.

"The schedule book says Cal Thompson," she replied.

"Are you sure it doesn't say Al Thomas?"

"Nope. Says Cal Thompson right here."

"How did he pay for the flight?"

"Just a second..." After a few moments she said, "He paid cash, four hundred and twelve dollars. Hmm, I think he paid us too much. Lemme just add this up..."

Todd got the impression that it was a casually run business. "Did he leave a deposit for the airplane on a credit card?"

"Just a second..." Todd heard, then he anxiously scratched his head. She continued, "No Sir, I don't see one."

"So, y'all rented him a fifty thousand dollar airplane with his promise to pay when he got back?"

"Our pilots are generally honest people down here."

"I'm sure they are, ma'am. Listen, did he sign his name on anything?"

"Yea, here in the schedule book."

"Can you fax that page to me? I'd really appreciate it."

"What did this guy do?"

"We can't say just yet. I *can* tell you he didn't fly to Tennessee."

"Oh, my!" she said. "Yes, right away. I'll get it to you right away."

Todd gave her the fax number, which was actually his cellular phone number. By the time she copied the page from the schedule, then placed the copy into the fax machine and dialed the number, he would have his computer hooked up and ready to receive the fax.

Soon, he had the fax in his computer. After a few more minutes, he had the fax number for James Hatch. He passed along the fax to him, then left a message for him on CompuServe:

<<MAIL DATE: 08/13 TIME: 3:42pEDT>>

James,

A man by the name of Cal Thompson rented an airplane at Charlotte Int'l last Saturday night. Please check the FAA records and see if a Cal Thompson really exists. I just faxed you the schedule sheet from the flying club down there.

"Do not trust all men, but trust men of worth; the former course is silly, the latter a mark of prudence." -Democritus.

<<END OF MAIL>>

TWENTY

THE FBI'S FOUR O'CLOCK PRESS CONFERENCE interrupted every show on every channel. The public had become fascinated by this particular commuter plane crash since it was a local event and some prominent people had been killed. Then, when they found the pilot had questionable experience, they became more interested. Now, it was sabotage that brought the plane down. Add the confession of a torrid affair and attempted murder of the saboteur's wife and it was the kind of story that news people dream about.

A hush came over the large crowd of reporters, just outside of the camera's range, as Stu began to speak. "Ladies and Gentlemen, we've assembled this press conference to shed some light on recent events that have unfolded regarding the Bands Twenty-two Thirty-four accident. First of all, I am Agent Stuart Varney, Chief of the Air Piracy and Sabotage Division, Directorate of National Operations, Federal Bureau of Investigation...."

Stuart looked immaculate, given that he only had two hours of sleep the night before. Todd studied Stuart's face on the television. He wasn't very different than he had imagined. He looked like a man he would enjoy having as a neighbor. He quickly surmised that Stuart was intelligent, honest, and clean-cut.

"...Recent news reports in the past eighteen hours have described various stories surrounding the events over the past couple of days. I am here to give you as many of the facts and charges as we can, without impeding our investigation.

First of all, the FBI has charged Mr. Todd Grant with sixteen counts of first degree murder for the sabotage and subsequent downing of Bands Flight Twenty-Two Thirty-four. He has also been charged by the Loudoun County, Virginia Police with the first degree murder of Ms. Chris Thomas, a female pilot with Bands Airways. He has also been charged by the Anne Arundel County, Maryland Police with the attempted murder of his wife, Ms. Kelly Grant, although that charge is currently being reviewed for possible rescission. He has a number of other charges from various jurisdictions including the malicious wounding of another pilot, possession of an open alcoholic beverage in a motor vehicle, assault, leaving the scene of a crime, concealing evidence, and the list goes on and on...."

Todd listened intensely. Each time he read or listened to the gravity of the charges levied against him, he shuddered. It seemed as if they were talking about another man. He thought about the number of people that must have been assigned to the case by now. He thought about the magnitude and cost of such an investigation. He also thought that with everyone out to get him, nobody was left behind to evaluate other possibilities—that someone else just might have committed those crimes.

Stu finished his opening remarks, then presented James Hatch as though he were a hero, to describe the details of the sabotage. James, as always, had come prepared. He held up a small penguin, complete with a tiny wire glued to its wing, some aluminum foil on a balsa wood base, and tiny wires sticking out. The media ate it up. He then walked over to an easel, lifted the cover page over the top, and described, in broad terms, how the penguin was hooked into the aircraft's electronic boxes. The enlarged black and white photos of Station 110 gave a sinister aura to the presentation. He talked about the stall warning system that included a stick pusher. How the penguin tricked that stick pusher into thinking the aircraft was flying too slow and about to fall out of the sky. How the stick pusher was instructed to pitch the nose down, then disengage. Pitch it down, then disengage. Pitch it down, then disengage. He talked about how the pilot's reaction time actually aggravated his ability to control the aircraft. How the pilot must have been jerking at the controls trying to calm the bucking bronco. How it ultimately broke apart and fluttered to the ground.

He then played the cockpit voice recorder tape. The rhythmic sound of the stall warning horn was tapped out by James with his chart pointer. Todd, glued to the T.V., shut his eyes and listened to his friend Scott die once again. Just after the "Oh shit, we're dead" comment, James turned off the tape player. The conference room was deadly still.

James wound up the penguin, then held it very close to the microphone without saying anything. Tap, tap, tap, tap, tap, tap. The rhythm correlated perfectly. He lowered the penguin, walked backwards without expression and allowed Stu to continue speaking.

"We consider Mr. Grant to be quite dangerous," Stu continued. Todd kept waiting for him to mention that they had been in contact with him earlier. Then he recognized that it wouldn't be in the best interest of the FBI to let everyone know how they had been fooled by him. "...We are closing in on him and should have him in custody quite soon. Now, I'll be happy to answer any questions you may have...." Even before he finished, a rush of loud voices crescendoed. He stepped back, then pointed at a short, balding man in a cheap jacket.

"Do you have a picture of him that we could use?"

"Well, you guys always seem to be one step ahead of us," he said with a smile. "We had a college picture available from his apartment, but one of you guys just showed up with this..." He reached down to the floor into his leather notebook, ran his fingers through some papers, then lifted an eight and a half by eleven black and white print of Todd Grant and Chris Thomas, holding hands in a restaurant!

Todd bolted toward the TV to get a better look.

"Apparently, Mr. Grant and Ms. Thomas were enjoying dinner together in a restaurant in Richmond earlier this summer at the same time Governor Chaldren was also dining there. One of you took this picture when covering the Governor. I smell Pulitzer *all over* this picture!" Everyone in the room laughed.

Todd stared intently at it when the cameras zoomed in on the photo. There was no doubt—it was him and Chris! Todd thought hard, and finally *"...Gripus scrotum and yankum"* came to mind. It was the night when Chris told Todd about Al's beatings. Al was there that night! Al had this planned for months, Todd concluded. What will Kelly say when she sees it?!

Todd lowered his head and mentally surrendered. There was no use—he was up against too mighty an opponent.

Stu answered about five or six more questions, then broke off the conference with a smile. The T.V. screen leaped midway into a Magnum P.I. rerun. Todd sat motionless on the floor.

••••

Kelly heard the press conference on the radio as she drove eastbound on Route 50 beyond Annapolis and over the Bay Bridge into the eastern shore. She imagined what the photo must have looked like. She asked herself why a photojournalist would have photographed them in the first place, let alone recognized Todd? It never dawned on her that Al could have taken the picture.

••••

About thirty minutes after the press conference, Todd was busy reconstructing the timelines of last Saturday night. He had turned his notepad sideways, and labeled each hour from 5:00 p.m. on Saturday to 8:00 a.m. on Sunday across the top. Down a column on the left side of the page, he labeled "Chris", then below it he wrote "Al." He thought for a moment, clicking the pencil against his forehead, then wrote "Todd" below "Al."

Along a line adjacent to Chris, he noted on the graph when she landed at Dulles and the time when she finished her paperwork went off duty. The next entry was the police's estimate of when her murder occurred: 12:45 a.m.

The next line down, Al's, began at 5:00 p.m. when he ended the day's conference in Charlotte. Todd drew a line between 5:15 and 6:15 as an estimate of how long it would have taken him to get checked out in the Cessna 172. He then gave Al forty-five minutes for flight planning and refueling for the trip to Washington. The line on the paper ended at 7:00. He drew a line from 7:00 to 10:00, Todd's estimate of the flight time to Bay Bridge Airport. That gave him two and a half hours to steal the airport car, drive to Dulles—about an hour's driving time—and rig Chris's car so it would lose its oil. Plenty of time, Todd thought.

If Al murdered Chris at about 12:45 a.m., Al would have arrived back at Bay Bridge Airport and dumped the car not later than 2:45 a.m. Then Todd tapped the notepad as he thought to himself, "Where did he get the gas to make it back to Charlotte?" He finally concluded that he must have stopped at a large "open 24 hours" airport on the way back. Another alternative would have been for him to simply siphon the fuel from a nearby airplane.

In any case, topping his tanks would have taken time, possibly as much as an hour. So Todd drew a line across the pad and marked it "refueling." That made it 3:45 a.m. Three hours of flying back to Charlotte meant a 6:45 a.m. arrival—a full hour and forty-five minutes to go back to the hotel, shave, shower, and sign in for the morning session.

Todd then dropped down a line and played the devil's advocate on himself. He noted the time that night that he had spent in the simulator. He penciled a line from 8:00 p.m. to 12:15 a.m. After the sim session, he stopped at the doughnut shop at about 12:30 a.m. and was home by 2:00 a.m. The only reliable witness would have been the jerk he flew with in the simulator and the training pilot, but that meant he left the simulator facility—located about ten minutes north of Dulles Airport, about thirty minutes before she was murdered. Todd knew that the FBI would soon be getting subpoenas from anyone who saw Todd last Saturday night. They would conclude that he had plenty of time to murder Chris. Todd sat motionless in his chair and stared at the graphed timelines.

Suddenly, Todd's beeper pierced the solitude. Todd looked down at the beeper, clipped to his waist, then pressed a white button on it, revealing "1111111" across the top. Todd knew that a message was waiting for him on CompuServe and quickly plugged the phone cord from the laptop into the cellular phone. Within a minute was reading the message from James:

<<MAIL DATE: 08/13 TIME: 4:53pEDT>>

Todd,

You're right, there is no licensed pilot by the name of Cal Thompson, according to the FAA's current files. Tell me what you know, and I'll have it investigated. As an act of good faith on your part, how about sending back those documents you stole from me?

- James

P.S. He who trusteth not is not deceived. - Thomas Fuller.

<<END OF MAIL>>

Todd smiled, both at the news that there is no Cal Thompson and at the rapport he was building with James by playing the quote game.

• • • •

Kelly arrived at the Bay Bridge Airport and glanced around as she slowly drove past the empty parking lot adjacent to the tiny, house-shaped building that served as the flying school, fuel sales counter, pilot lounge, and airport manager's office. The clouds had gathered and lowered considerably throughout the day. The thick, dark clouds acted like a blanket and kept the virtually still air warm and damp. She felt like she could reach up and touch them. She glanced over towards the huge Bay Bridge and noticed that the twin pillars that supported the suspension lines high above the traffic lanes were hidden by the low clouds.

She stopped at the edge of the asphalt, looked back behind her, and saw no one. Two old, large hangars housed the maintenance shop and provided shelter for a few of the larger, twin engined airplanes on the field. The rest of the aircraft were parked in the grass, wing tip to wing tip, facing the runway and extending all the way to the overgrown grassy area next to the water. There was room for a second and third row of aircraft behind the single row, but many of the pilots had given up the fight and flown their aircraft to other small airports in the area. She drove the Bartlett's car off the pavement and along a path etched out by other cars behind the tails of the airplanes and towards the water's edge. Beyond the last airplane, she turned right and tucked the car behind the fuselage of the last airplane.

She got out of the car and stretched her legs. She had been in rush hour traffic all the way from Bowie to Annapolis, as Route 50 was the primary route for Annapolis residents to get home from their D.C. jobs.

She walked about thirty yards to the edge of the tall grass and looked for evidence that a car had been driven into the water. She then walked to the right where the edge of the tall grass made a turn and followed the taxiway to a tiny peninsula where the end of the runway butted right up to the water's edge.

As she completed the turn, she notice a twin line of damaged weeds and tall grass leading right to the water.

"Yes!" she yelled to herself and began running toward them. She chose the left line and walked along it, right up to the water. The car was there. It was really in the water! It was plainly visible about two feet below the surface. And it was a blue car!

She jumped up and down with excitement, then turned around to run back to her car when another car barreled around the taxiway and sped right towards her at about forty-miles per hour.

She was trapped at the water's edge with no where to go. It must be Al, she thought! What an idiot she was! Now she was dead for sure. She started running perpendicular to the car, and it turned towards her.

She screamed, then she tried to sidestep again , but was no match for the car. He had her. Her knees gave way and she fell to the ground, gripped with panic.

The car decelerated quickly, and an older man got out and marched towards her. He yelled, "What the hell are you doing here!"

She was so petrified that her shivers more resembled convulsions. She realized it wasn't Al, but she couldn't control her shaking. She didn't even notice that she peed in her pants. "You stay back!" she managed.

The man stopped about five feet from her, just as she scooted back away from him. *"Stop shaking and calm down!"* she thought to herself. The man moved slightly towards her.

"I said *stay back, gawdammit!*" she yelled as she moved backwards along the ground.

"Calm down, lady," he said firmly.

"*What are you doing* driving like that—don't you know you can't have a car out here on a taxiway!" she said indignantly.

"This is my fuckin' airport and I can drive anywhere on it that I want. Now. You are trespassing. I'll ask you again. What are you doing here?"

"Are you Jake McFadden?" she asked in angst.

He seemed to flinch when she mentioned his name. Kelly remembered Jeff Caldwell's advice and used it: "Answer me! I said are you Jake McFadden?" she asked forcefully as she stood up and faced him. Her face was bright red and her body continued to tremble.

"Yes, I am. And I want you to tell..."

"Shut up and listen!" she said in the most raging voice she could convoke. She faced him directly and pointed to the weeds and water behind her. "I am an attorney. Your airport car is submerged in the bay right back there. It was used to commit a crime. You touch it and I'll personally rip your fuckin' lips off!"

He stood there and took it as she shoved a finger right up to his face. "I am going back to my car to call the county police and report that it has been found. You stay here until they arrive. And another thing—if you ever fuckin' drive a car at someone like that again, I'll hang you by your nuts in a court of law!"

She darted toward him, her forearm poised for deflecting him. He jerked himself sideways to let her through. She headed back to her car at a brisk pace, leaving him there to let it all sink in. She was now sweating heavily in the thick, damp air. She hopped in her car, backed it up, then headed up the grassy trail back towards the asphalt parking lot.

She looked in her rearview mirror and saw him barreling towards her in his car. She sped up, made a left out of the airport without stopping and floored it until she was safely out of sight and heading westbound on Route 50 towards the Bay Bridge. He didn't follow her.

TWENTY ONE

JOHN BRIGGS answered the phone after the first ring. "Crew scheduling. This is John."

Todd wasn't sure if he would help him after all that had occurred in the past twenty-four hours, but he thought it couldn't hurt. "Hi John, it's Todd Grant."

"Jesus, Todd! What the hell is going on?"

"Long story, John. Listen, I've been framed for not only Chris's murder, but also for *the accident*. The guy that really did it is Chris's husband."

"Husband? She wasn't married."

"Yea. She was. And this guy is smart. What I wanna know is how come he picked me as the framee and how come he chose Bands Twenty-two Thirty-four as the one to bring down. I thought I might get some answers from you."

"Me? *No oblo* accident stuff, Todd."

"John, I've seen the company's reports that went into the NTSB files, but they don't tell me everything. Could you please check and see if there was an unplanned airplane swap at the last minute, or a last minute crew change? You know, anything out of the ordinary."

"I dunno, Todd. I mean, I want to help you out. But, look what you're asking me to do. You're kinda like a fugitive. I'd be—like—an accessory or something."

"I know, John. Hey, tell you what. You call Agent Stuart Varney at FBI Headquarters and tell him that I contacted you and that I wanted some info. If he agrees that it's O.K., then help me out, all right?"

"Uh, O.K. Todd. 'You sure you're being straight with me?"

"Of course I am, John."

"Well, I'll see what I can do."

"Thanks John. Just leave a message on CompuServe for me with whatever you find, then beep me when it's there. My CompuServe address is seven two four four zero comma two five four one."

"Will do, buddy. Good luck!" John said as he finished scribbling, then hung up. He moved some papers off the seldom-used *Caller I.D.* box at the back corner of his desk. The phone number of Todd's cellular phone was illuminated on the gray LCD display. John scribbled it just below Todd's CompuServe address, then called directory information for the FBI.

Minutes later, John was talking to Stuart Varney, who was just about to leave and grab some dinner before coming back to the office. Stuart's days were usually long, but starting work at midnight the night before made today particularly excruciating. "Can you tell me what he wanted, specifically?" Stuart asked.

"He wanted to know if there were any unscheduled airplane or crewmember changes on the day of the accident. He said he read the company's reports given to the NTSB and thought there might be more information that I could find for him."

"During the conversation, did you hear any noises in the background like cars, planes, TVs, lawnmowers, whatever?" Stuart asked, rubbing his eyes.

"No. Why?"

"Well, we need to get him into custody—fast. It'll be safer for the general public if he's guilty and safer for him if he's innocent."

John stared at the paper that had Todd's phone number on it. "He sounded as though he was really being framed." He circled the number with his pencil, then nervously tapped the pencil on the desktop.

"How was he going to get the information from you that he wanted. Was he going to call you back?"

"No, sir. He gave me his CompuServe address. Should I check on what he was asking for and let him know what I found?"

"Sure. All I ask is that I get a chance to review whatever is being sent to him before it goes out."

"O.K."

"Mr. Briggs, I know you've probably known Mr. Grant for some time. I'm going to ask you to treat this man as he is charged—a murderer. You know the extent of the charges filed against this man. You cannot, on your on, decide that he's either guilty or not guilty. It's in everyone's best interest to help out the FBI in every way. Do you understand?"

"Yes, sir. Listen, we, uh,..." John hesitated as he continued to doodle around Todd's phone number with the pencil.

"Yes?"

"Uh, we have *Caller I.D.* in the office here and...."

"You're shitting me! You've got the number! I'll be damned! Lemme have it!" Stuart was tired and, in his excitement, didn't realize his breach of professionalism.

"Uh, I, Uh, its, well..."

"Come on, Mr. Briggs."

"I don't want him hurt, Agent Varney...."

"Don't let me sing my Obstruction of Justice tune to you, Mr. Briggs...."

"It's, um, area code four ten, and the number is triple five, eight eight two two." John said it quickly so it wouldn't hurt as much. He gripped the pencil with his fist and pounded it right into the center of the paper, breaking the lead.

"Thanks, Mr. Briggs. Whether you realize it or not now, you've actually helped Todd."

"Please be careful, sir. I tend to believe him that he's been framed."

After John hung up, he got up from his desk and immediately began gathering everything he could for Todd.

• • • •

Another agent walked into Stuart's Office. Stuart hadn't gone to grab some dinner after all. The agent slung a small piece of paper onto Stuart's desk and said, "He's a smart guy, that Grant fellow."

"What now?!" Stuart asked in a *here it comes again* tone as he read the note.

"The number is a phone registered to a law firm in Bowie, Maryland."

"Yea. So?"

"It's a, uh, cellular phone."

"Damnation." Stuart stood up, stuffed the note into his pocket, and started pacing. "Remind me to hire him to come work for us when he get's paroled."

"I don't think the Bureau can hire convicted felons," he answered seriously.

Stuart stopped dead in his tracks and stared at the other agent. "Go home. Get some rest."

The agent smiled and shook his head slightly. "Sorry Stu. You'd think I'd have been around here long enough to recognize your sarcasm."

"Yea." Stuart was thinking and pacing.

"If it's any consolation, the folks down in the Operations Center think the Anne Arundel County Police may be tracking Mrs. Grant."

"What! Where?"

"She was heading west on Route 50 just coming into Annapolis."

"Great!" Stuart reached over to his desk and grabbed the phone. He pressed a four digit extension, then began talking: "Ops, this is Stu Varney. Relay to Anne Arundel County Police that they are to follow, but not stop—do not stop—Mrs. Grant. We want her to lead us to her husband." Stuart listened for a second, nodded, then said, "Good, I'll be right down."

Stu grabbed his pen from atop his desk and walked out of the door, forgetting to say good bye to the other agent. Moments later, he was greeted at the FBI Operations Center entrance by Agent Doug Berry, the Ops Manager.

"Stu. How are you. Hey, the airport manager at Bay Bridge Airport gave the county police a description of a lady that matched that of Mrs. Grant. She was driving a car registered to Mr. and Mrs. John

Bartlett of Bowie. The Anne Arundel County Police said Mrs. Grant works for Mrs. Bartlett at a law firm."

"A law firm!" Stu reached into his pocket and pulled out the paper given to him by the other agent. "What's the name of the firm, Doug?"

Doug reached over to his desk and grabbed a piece of paper. He scanned it for a while, then said, "It is Banks,...."

Stu chimed in: "...Yang, and Costello!"

"Wo! Have you been calling the Psychic Hotline again?"

"All right. So, the two are in on this together. Bonnie and Clyde. I want their line of communications cut—right now! Call the phone company and have them immediately disconnect their cellular phone service. And find out what pager service has his beeper with and stop it, too. We won't be able to talk with him anymore. But, they won't be able to talk to each other, either."

"We're on it. Oh, by the way, the Director wants to meet with you tomorrow at 2:00 p.m. Your press conference today was apparently a big hit." The ops manager held up a piece of official-looking correspondence.

"Big whoop. Listen, send a battery of police cars to the, uh..." He looked down at his paper, then continued: "...Bartlett's home. I bet we'll find Todd Grant there."

"We're way ahead of you, Stu. Now, do you want to know what this is?" He held it up again and smiled.

"I don't have time for any of that public affairs horse shit, if that's what it is."

"It's from the White House."

"Let's see," said Stu, bothered by the obvious sidetrack. He read the memorandum slowly, then threw it on the desk and rubbed his tired eyes. "Fucking politicians."

"So *you* get to go with the Director to the White House tomorrow night and sit in the back while the President assures the nation that our air transportation system is safe."

"Doesn't the President of the United States have anything more pressing to do than to waste his time and ours by getting involved in this?"

"Hey, people think he's not paying enough attention to domestic affairs. I see this as low risk for him, with a good chance for improving his domestic report card. He'll take credit for keeping the skies safe for democracy. It'll make him look more presidential."

"What a load of crap. Look at this. He's invited the FAA Administrator, the Secretary of Transportation, the Chairman of the NTSB, and the presidents of American, Delta, United, TransGlobe, Southwest, Northwest, and TWA to join him when he addresses the nation. Count me out."

"Count you out? You can't just decline an invitation like that!"

"If I catch the bastard by tomorrow night, then I'll think about it. I am not here to help reelect the President."

• • • •

As Kelly had turned onto Route 50 just east of the Bay Bridge, the airport manager had already contacted the Queen Anne County Police. They, in turn, immediately contacted the Anne Arundel County Police, who had jurisdiction on the western side of the Bay Bridge. By the time she was halfway across the bridge, an officer in an unmarked police car was waiting at the western toll plaza. Route 50, the six-line artery that connects Maryland's eastern shore region with Baltimore and Washington, makes a large arc around the northern side of Annapolis, with Severna Park on the northern side of the road.

The exit for the central part of Annapolis is some four miles west of the Bay Bridge. Kelly's intent was to take an exit onto a side street as soon as she arrived on the western shore of the Chesapeake. That way, she could get to a phone and let Todd know the good and bad news: 1) the car was found and 2) the police would, by now, have a description of both her and the Bartlett's car. He would need to leave the house.

Once she passed the bridge toll plaza, however, she knew her plan would have to be modified. She noticed an unmarked police car accelerate into a lane adjacent to hers. She didn't think they could have reacted so quickly! Damn! She was caught and she needed to somehow alert Todd that if he didn't leave the Bartlett's house quickly that he too would be caught!

The cruiser got fairly close to her car, then slowly backed into the moderately heavy traffic. *"He just checked the license plate number,"* she thought to herself. She had to lose him and get to a phone!

The exit to the Naval Academy was about a quarter of a mile up the road. She checked all around, then put on her left turn signal and transitioned to the far left lane, which was clear of traffic. The officer in the cruiser took the bait and also moved over to the left lane right as the down sloping Naval Academy exit passed by on the far right.

Kelly positioned herself where she wanted to be in traffic, then floored it. The back of the car dropped and a faint trail of black smoke came out of her exhaust pipe as she accelerated. As expected, the cruiser also accelerated.

Kelly took one last glance, held her breath, then wildly swerved directly across all lanes. She then slammed on the brakes and the back of her car fishtailed clockwise, perfectly into the right shoulder, where she accelerated quickly in the reverse direction of traffic back towards the off ramp. It happened so quickly that the cruiser had no time to safely react. He found himself boxed between other cars that were swerving to avoid hitting the cars in front of them, who had braked hard to avoid an accident with Kelly.

She flung the car onto the off ramp, then floored it until she was down at the bottom of the ramp. She pulled around to the back side of a Shell station, parked between two pickup trucks, got out, and ran to the intersection.

She thumbed at a few passing cars, then jogged along the street that went under the overpass to get away from the Bartlett's car. Her eyes scanned every car coming off the ramp. She was prepared to dive into heavy underbrush just beyond the side of the road the moment she saw a police car. At last, a couple of short haired men slowed down for her.

"Can I get a ride?" she asked as the passenger rolled down the window. He looked clean cut enough, but it really didn't matter to her at this point.

"Sure!" the passenger said excitedly.

No sooner than the door opened, she flung herself into the back seat. She could smell a faint odor of sweat and urine on her. Her hair was a disaster. Her pants had mud and grass stains on them. Yet, there was no disguising the fact that she was a beautiful woman. She sat low in the middle of the back seat, out of breath.

"Um..." the driver of the car said as he looked at her in the rearview mirror. She looked back at him in the mirror. He finished the sentence, "Are you O.K.?"

"Yea. I guess."

"You look like you've been in a football game." The two men in front gave each other a bewildered glance at each other, which Kelly saw. The passenger added, "Where are you heading?"

She took a deep breath, then said, "Naval Academy. Actually, Annapolis Harbor right next to the Academy."

"Really?! We're middies—midshipmen. This is Sam and I'm Randall," the driver said.

Kelly looked around as much as she could without looking too suspicious. "I'm, uh, Kelly Smith."

"You live around here, Kelly?" Sam asked.

Kelly wasn't in any mood for small talk. She had to get to a phone, which was still a few minutes away. She raised her left hand and ran her hand through her hair, exposing her diamond wedding ring. "Yea. We live in Severna Park. I work in a restaurant down on the Harbor." She paused to think, then continued. "My husband is Lieutenant Commander Scott Smith. He's the, uh, an electrical engineering instructor at the Academy. Do you know him?"

"Uh, the name sounds familiar," said Randall.

"Yea. Right." she thought to herself. "Well, we just arrived here two months ago. Hey, how come you two are off campus on a weekday night?"

"Well, ma'am, we're not really supposed to be. But, sometimes the pull of a Whopper and a large fries is simply overwhelming."

Kelly chuckled nervously. "I'm a mess. I was at a horse show and lost track of time. Then my car broke down. Now, looks like I'll be late. And I still have a phone call to make. If you see a phone booth, could you let me off, please?" She found that it was actually becoming quite easy to make up a story.

As they turned past the Navy football stadium, they all spotted a phone booth. They pulled over and stopped. She leaped out and said, "Thanks Randall and Sam. You middies sure are polite—and handsome!"

Flattered by the compliment, they said good-bye and drove off. Kelly quickly pulled out a quarter, jammed it into the slot and frantically dialed the cellular phone's number. After one ring, she got three tones, followed by the following recorded woman's voice: "We're sorry. The number you dialed is no longer in service. Please try again, or call an operator."

She hung up. "Shit," she mumbled to herself as she grabbed the quarter from the coin return, placed it in the slot again, and redialed the number. The same tone and message was heard. She grabbed the quarter once again and dialed the Bartlett's home number. It rang three times, six times, ten times. She hung up. She knew he was there, but wouldn't answer that phone. She called it again. After about ten rings, it was answered, but nobody said hello.

"Todd?! Todd?! It's Kelly. It's me." She spoke, but no one responded. A million thoughts went through her mind. The police were there and had already arrested him. Al Thomas tracked him down and shot him. His stab wound was actually more serious than previously thought and he was on the verge of passing out.

"Damn it, Todd. They're on to us! Get out of there, now! Todd?! Answer me!" The phone clicked and the line went dead.

"Shit. Shit," she mumbled again as she slammed the phone down.

• • • •

After Todd hung up the phone on the kitchen wall, he grabbed the cellular phone and pressed the ON button. No dial tone was heard. In one motion, he shoved all of his notes into a gym bag, then crammed both the phone and the laptop on top of the papers. He threw in his airport I.D. badge, then zipped up the bag as he ran toward the front door. Midway, he stopped, looked through the front windows as he thought for a couple of seconds. He ran back to the table, grabbed the book of quotes and opened it to the page mark. He tore out about three pages, shoved them into his pocket, bolted toward the sliding glass door, and peeked through the curtain into the backyard. Seeing no one, he slid the door open, walked out onto the deck, and closed it behind him. After one more good glance, he sprinted across the grass and into the grove of thin pine trees that provided the neighborhood some noise suppression from the busy Route 301 thoroughfare.

Tom Sylvester

He jogged straight ahead until he reached a point where he could see the traffic on 301, but stayed well tucked away in the trees and began walking parallel to the southbound traffic. He saw a police car zip by with his lights on, but no siren. Then there was another. Then another. He counted six in all. He couldn't tell how many approached from the north, but there was no doubt—they were after him. Jogging quickly through the woods, he remained clear of all inhabited areas. It would be dark soon, and he could move about more freely. His mind raced with questions of where to go and how to get back in contact with Kelly.

TWENTY TWO

THE ANNAPOLIS HARBOR was bustling with activity when Kelly arrived after a six-block jog from the phone booth. The transition from daylight to nightfall had been subtle, because of the heavy cloud cover, but nonetheless reminded her how quickly the time was passing. Was he caught? Was it the police that answered the phone?

Kelly walked right up to the water's edge and looked at the myriad of boats in the harbor. The large part of the harbor was egg shaped, with boat dealers, slips, condos, and restaurants along the perimeter. At the inner-most part of the harbor was a much smaller harbor-within-a-harbor. This area had tie-downs for people to anchor their boats while they went grocery shopping or went out to eat. A small brick and concrete park separated the edge of the smaller harbor from the busy cross streets. She sat down on a cast iron bench and nervously crossed her arms. She gazed at an approaching boat coming into the smaller part of the harbor and thought about her next move.

No rain was in the forecast and the Annapolis locals were taking advantage of the comfortable yet humid weather. The park where she was sitting at the edge of the smaller harbor was the eye of the hustle and bustle hurricane. Everywhere she glanced, people were shopping, eating, talking, walking, and generally enjoying the late summer evening. Kelly remembered earlier this summer when she and Todd had joined Jeff Caldwell and his family on his boat here and reflected on how utterly pleasant life on the Bay was. Tonight, though, was anything but pleasant for her. The sky would soon be jet black, starless, and still. She had no time to waste—but she couldn't make a move unless she first gave it a lot of thought. She couldn't afford a mistake.

She had to presume that Todd didn't answer her because he was afraid of using that phone—a dead giveaway to his location. She had to also assume that he was able to get safely away from the house. She leaned forward, put her head in her hands, and stared down at her dirty shoes. All of their plans were made with the idea that she would be able to contact him via the cellular phone. All he had left was his beeper. The beeper! She got up, turned left, and hustled down the wooden and concrete pier toward a rest room facility at the end of the smaller part of the harbor. She walked up to a group of pay phones just outside of the rest rooms, put in the same quarter she had used before, then dialed his beeper number. Her chest tightened as she heard the same recording as before: "The number you have called is no longer in service. Please check the number and try again."

As she retrieved her quarter from the change slot, a thought came to mind. She nervously scratched her gritty scalp for a moment, checked her watch, then called her law office and left a message on her own voice mail: "Todd, I hope you're O.K. Please meet me at ten tonight at the place where we had our anniversary dinner. If I'm not there, please wait for me. You were right! The car was ditched in the bay! I love you, hun'. Please be careful."

Kelly had no confidence that Todd would think to use her law office's voice mail. She had given him the retrieval code once to check her messages when they went camping for a weekend last spring. Even if he thought to call it, she didn't know if he would remember the code: two four one. It was her only hope.

She went into the rest room, washed her face, and generally tried to clean up. Feeling better, she double checked her purse and looked around with a broader, slower view. She had plenty of cash—four hundred forty dollars. Todd had eighty with him, since he was staying put.

She could take a taxi or rent a car. But, there was some risk of getting caught associated with either of those options. She could hitchhike again, but the personal safety risk was much more of a factor now that she had more time to think about it. She needed time to think, but had none to spare.

She decided that, for now, it was probably better to move off to a side street and think rather than to try blending in with the masses of people in the harbor area. She walked back along the water's edge, hoping an idea would come to mind.

She crossed over the busy road and walked away from the harbor, down a side street towards a corner market about two blocks away. She nervously kept her eye on every car that came down the quiet road.

That's where she spotted it: an old Chevy Caprice in front of a tiny wooden frame house. The car had a "For Sale - $500" sign on it's dashboard. She jogged across the poorly lit street, up the badly cracked concrete walkway, onto the creaking wooden porch, and knocked on the door.

She heard slow, heavy footsteps that creaked the wooden floor behind the door. She quickly reached into her pocket and pulled out the wad of cash. She grabbed a twenty from it and stuck it in her back pocket, then put the remaining wad back in her front pocket. The deadbolt twisted firmly, then the door opened slowly as Kelly shifted her weight from foot to foot.

• • • •

Todd sat in what he thought was dirt with his lower back against the rear wall of a tire shop located at the end of a small strip mall along Route 301. He could tell by the way his shirt was sticking to him that his back was bleeding again.

The rear wall faced the now completely dark woods from where he had emerged. The only way he could even tell where the woods started was to look up and see the top of the trees, illuminated by the parking lot lights in the front of the building. He searched with his hands through the gym bag for the phone, then pulled it out. He felt for the ON button, then pressed it. A green LED lit up like a laser, making him squint. He brought the phone up to his ear, but again heard no dial tone. He lowered it, moved his finger to the right of the green light and felt for the OFF button, which he pressed.

He put the phone back in the bag after pulling out the laptop computer and turning it on. Moments later, the gray hue from the screen lit up the area where he was sitting, giving him his first view of the area around him. Trash and shin-high weeds, complete with crickets and other bugs scampering about—a place worse than he had imagined.

He reached into his pocket and produced the ripped-out pages from the book of quotes. Holding them up to the glare of the screen, he scanned them for something appropriate. He then prepared a quick message for James and saved it on his hard drive until he could get to a phone to send it:

<<MAIL DATE: 08/13 TIME: 8:06pEDT>>

```
The only way to make a man trustworthy is to
trust him.
  -Henry L. Stimson
Please turn my cellular phone and beeper back
on.
  -Todd Grant
```

<<END OF MAIL>>

He turned the computer off and placed it awkwardly back in the gym bag. Having been blinded by the computer screen, he now had to feel his way around the bag until he found the zipper. He secured it, then sat in the total darkness while he thought about his next move.

• • • •

"Yes?" the elderly woman's voice produced. From behind the back of the door emerged a short, stocky lady of about seventy years. Kelly sighed as the porch light came on, but continued her nervous back and forth motion.

"Ma'am, I'd like to buy your car."

"Come on in, please," she said politely as she backed up, exposing the house's stark interior.

"Thank you," Kelly replied as she entered. The room had a stillness, a kind of lifelessness, about it. The room had a couple of old recliners on either side of an old coffee table. Seven or eight framed pictures sat atop the table. A large black and white picture of a handsome man in a nineteen fifties-era pose was the central photo. Her late husband, Kelly thought. The others, based on the hair and clothing styles, were pictures that dated from the seventies to the present.

"It's my grandson's car. He's overseas. Philippines. He's a Marine. Lance Corporal. Right here is his picture," she said methodically. She reached slowly towards the coffee table and lifted a picture of a very young man with a large nose. His pimples were the same hue as his maroon football jacket.

"He's very handsome," Kelly said as honestly as she could.

The lady looked at the picture herself for an eternity, then said, "Yes. Yes, he is." She then returned it respectfully back to its spot.

Kelly changed the subject back to the car. "Ma'am, I'd like to give you five hundred for it, but I only have, let's see...." She pulled out the wad of cash from her front pocket and started counting. The lady stared at the money as if she had never seen that much all gathered together in one fist before.

"...three eighty, four hundred, four twenty. I've only got four hundred and twenty and I really need that car."

"He said for me to try and sell it for five hundred."

"Ma'am, you may have trouble selling it for five hundred. I'll give you four-twenty now—in cash. O.K.?" She looked her straight in the eye.

"It *has* been sitting out there for a month...."

"And a month from now it may still be out there."

"O.K. Four hundred and twenty it is..." she said effortlessly. "...I'll go get the pink slip."

Kelly, with a courteous poker face, controlled her urge to leap skyward. "Thank you, ma'am. That's a good price for that car."

Kelly's momentary joy was instantly replaced with thoughts of arriving at the Sante Fe West restaurant and not finding Todd there. The chance of him escaping and working his way three miles south along Route 301 without being caught were slim, notwithstanding the chance of him even thinking to call her office voice mail. That realization nullified any momentary joy of winning a car haggle with an old, indifferent woman.

The lady returned slowly with the title and the keys. Kelly handed her the cash. The lady put the keys and the title down on the coffee table, rather than exchanging them for the cash. She then slowly stacked each twenty atop another, next to those keys. Counting out loud, she almost seemed surprised when her own count matched Kelly's.

Kelly shifted and fidgeted as time kept forging ahead. She needed to be on the road.

• • • •

"He was here all right!" Lieutenant Mike Bigston of the Anne Arundel County Police said over the FBI Operations Center's speaker phone. Numerous plain-clothed and uniformed officers moved through the Bartlett's house like ants as he talked to Stu Varney on the other end of the line. "He must have just left within a few hours of our arrival. We found several shirts and bandages soaked with blood—lots of blood—wrapped in plastic garbage bags and stuffed behind some blankets in the upstairs guest bedroom closet. He knew we'd show up eventually and hid the stuff fairly well. But, listen Stu, he's been damaged. With the amount of blood he's lost, he won't be running any marathons or even thinking clearly now. I bet he's lost three or four pints."

"You sure it's his blood?" Stu asked in the direction of the speaker phone as he jotted some notes. Three other agents in the FBI Operations Center were listening intently as others mulled about.

"I'd say so. The shirts are all stained in the same spot, the back side, right upper shoulder. One of them, Jeez...," he said disgustingly as he held it up to examine it again, "...is *so* caked with dried blood that I could stand it up in the corner."

"What do you have on Mrs. Grant?"

"Hang on," he replied then yelled out, "HEY ANDREW!" He didn't move the phone far enough away before yelling across the room. Everyone in Ops froze and looked in the direction of the speaker phone. Some agents smiled.

"Just a second, Stu," he said, then thoughtlessly dropped the Bartlett's wall phone onto the countertop.

An agent standing next to Stu, waiting for such a break in the telecon, said, "I've got two calls here. She called the Bartlett's home phone there in Bowie forty five minutes ago from a pay phone in Annapolis." He then handed him a fax from the phone company that transcribed the conversation.

Stu read it slowly:

"Todd. Todd. It's Kelly. It's me. Damn it, Todd. They're on to us. Get out of there, now. Todd. Answer me. <END CALL>"

"So he didn't say anything back to her?" Stu asked.

"Nope. And it's unclear if she hung up or he did."

"So, we don't know for sure that it was Todd who answered the call."

"Well, no."

"Where did the call originate?"

"Phone booth outside the Seven Eleven around the corner from the Naval Academy Football Stadium. They think she's still in the Bartlett's car, 'cuz she made another call from the Annapolis Harbor about fifteen minutes later. Here's that call," said the agent as he handed Stu another fax. "We got it off the wire tap of her office's voice mail. Obviously, they had a backup plan in case the cellular phone service was disconnected."

Stu studied it as slowly as the first:

"Todd, I hope you're O.K. Please meet me at ten tonight at the place where we had our anniversary dinner. If I'm not there, please wait for me. Todd, you were right. The car's in the Bay. I love you, hun'. Please be careful. <END CALL>"

Stu laid the faxes on the large operations center desk and rubbed his face with his palms.

A voice came over the speaker phone, "Stu, you still there?"

"Yea. Go."

"She swerved off Route 50 and disappeared down a side street. We've got every cruiser out there looking for her. We know she's still in Annapolis, 'cuz she made a phone call to this house."

"Yep, from the Seven Eleven by the stadium. She also made one from the Annapolis Harbor."

"How'd you..."

"Listen Mike!" Stu announced in the direction of the speaker phone as he made a note on a pad. "Don't touch the car that was found in the bay next to Bay Bridge Airport. We'll take care of that. I want YOU to find the car that Mrs. Grant is driving. I also want YOU to locate the Bartlett's and bring them in for questioning. Mr. Grant is probably on foot and left there no earlier than forty-five minutes ago, so make a FOUR-MILE-CIRCLE around that house with every cop, K-9, cruiser, and 'copter you can find. I want that sucker CAUGHT! YOU GOT IT?!"

"Yes, sir."

"If your choppers don't have night infrared, call the Maryland State Police helos. Hell, call them anyway. I also want YOU to find out the date of their anniversary, then check reservations on that date with every restaurant in the county. You've got an hour and a half. I'm on my way out there."

"Stu, we're stepping all over each other here. There's no need for you to come out."

"I'll be at Bay Bridge Airport, checking out the car. Listen, Mike, I don't want to tell you how to do your job, but you can't make a four mile circle of cops around that house with every cop STILL IN IT! GET 'EM OUT OF THERE AND START HUNTING HIM DOWN!"

Stu punched the button on the speaker phone, grabbed his pad and papers with both hands, and turned towards the five people surrounding him. He muttered, "I must be getting tired." He then raised his index fingers up from the papers and said, "Gentlemen, the quote of the night: 'Todd, you were right. The car's in the bay.'" He shifted the papers to his left hand, grabbed his wallet with his right, and continued, "Why was she out there snooping around? Jack, call Pizza Hut on New York Avenue. Medium Veggie lover's, for pickup. Who's going to Bay Bridge with me?"

"I'll go if you'll share your pizza," said Jack.

"Then make it a large. Order up some cokes, too. Here." Stu spun a coupon his way. "Tell 'em we get two bucks off."

TWENTY THREE

THE SMELL OF STALE BEER AND MILDEW was inescapable. Kelly rolled down all of the windows, then looked behind and under the seats for the source of the smell. The old lady, standing on her porch, waited anxiously for the engine to turn over. She'd have to wait a few minutes while Kelly gathered the four or five mostly empty beer bottles from the back seat and placed them into a McDonald's bag. The car hadn't moved in at least a month. Given a hot, summer month of fermentation inside an airtight vehicle, the car smelled like a waste bin aback a brewery. Rather than booze and burgers, the lady's son probably should have spent his money on acne medicine.

Kelly tossed the bag of bottles into the front passenger floorboard, then put the keys in the ignition. When she turned the key, the car started right up, surprising both her and the old lady. After some searching, Kelly turned on the headlights, exchanged a wave and a smile, then backed out of the yard. She checked her watch: 8:50 p.m. It would take thirty-five minutes to get to the Sante Fe West restaurant in Bowie. She had some extra time to make lodging arrangements.

••••

"Stu? Where are you?" the voice asked from the earpiece on the hand held two-way radio. The call was being relayed from the NTSB offices to Stu via the FBI's Operations Center.

"East on Route 50 almost into Annapolis. What's up, James?" Stu looked over at Jack, who was driving, then he picked up another piece of pizza and took a big bite.

"I sent another note to Todd on CompuServe and beeped him twice, but he hasn't picked up the message." James sat with his elbows on his desk in the now silent office, balancing the phone with his shoulder and rocking his eyeglasses with his fingers.

"We wurned wis—wold on." Stu mumbled to hold on as he finished chewing. "We turned his beeper and his cellular phone off."

"Why!?"

"Because he and the misses have been using it to communicate to each other. We felt it was more important to sever their communication link than to keep our link with him."

"I guess. Listen, Stu. Think back to the press conference today and the picture of Todd and Chris that surfaced."

"Yea."

"Has anyone yet claimed it?"

"Don't know, James."

"What are the odds that such a picture would have been taken of them? Beyond that, what are the odds that the photographer would have matched their faces with the faces on the photo?"

"I call it a combination of dumb luck and good photojournalism. Listen, Mrs. Grant may have led us to the car that was used to kill Chris Thomas."

"How or why is *she* involved?" The voice transmission was becoming faint and garbled.

"Don't know. But she tipped him off that the police were on there way to the house in Bowie where he was hiding."

"So he lurked off?" James asked, crackling badly on the other end.

"Huh? Say again?" Stu held the radio closer to his ear and quit chewing.

"So he got away?"

"For now. They're close, though. They'll probably get him sometime tonight."

"Well, Stu. With the phones off, I'm out of the loop now. But, I still want to help out. Stu? Stu?"

The connection faded, then an unfamiliar voice came on. "Mr. Hatch, Agent Varney's radio must be weak. If you'd like, I can get you the number for his cellular phone, but it's not a secure line."

"Don't Bother," he said, since he probably had the number nearby, anyway.

"No bother at all."

"That's O.K. I'll talk to him later. By the way, for my records, what was the number for the cellular phone that Stu had disconnected? I've got the guy's beeper number, but not the phone."

"Uh, just a second."

James was convinced that his request for the phone number was futile. The FBI, as a rule, keeps all of its information closely held, since any information given out could potentially help a felon. James knew this, but he also sensed that the guy working the phones in the operations center was being overly helpful.

"Triple five, eight eight two two," the voice said.

"Thanks. Uh, what area code is that?"

"Four Ten"

"Thanks. If Stu calls back, tell him I've left my home number on my voice mail here at the Safety Board."

"O.K. Good night, Mr. Hatch."

"Good night."

James walked around to the next office and sat at someone else's desk, since his own phone was still bugged by the FBI. Barney Rubble's quote kept ringing through his ears: "You should always listen to as many people as you can. And when you *do* find the truth, you'll almost always be surprised who it was that finally led you to it." He stared at the phone as he thought about all of the quotes he had seen and written back and forth to Todd about trusting people. He thought about the ramifications of the action he was about to take. And he thought about how badly he wanted back in the action. He picked up the receiver and called information. He then called the cellular phone company that serviced the phone that Todd had.

"Operator. May I help you?"

"This is the FBI operations center again," said James hurriedly.

"The operations center?" the operator asked.

"Yes, please bring up the account for area code four one oh, five five five, eight eight two two. We need to quickly reconnect the service."

The operator was heard tapping away at a keyboard. "Uh, sir we're showing the service was disconnected by your agency's request at six ten p.m. earlier this evening."

"That's right. And I need it reconnected again—Now!"

"What's your name, sir?"

With a momentary pause, James said, "Stu Varney. Stuart Varney. I'm chief of the Air Piracy and Sabotage Division." He recovered from the near slip nicely and finished the sentence as though he was pressed for time.

"And your number?"

"Right there on your screen ma'am!" he said tersely.

"Is it two oh two, triple five, one eight two two?"

He thought the operator might be testing him—giving him a fake number. "No. The last four are seven three one three." *"Might as well give her the correct extension,"* James thought.

"Are you going to need the wiretap continued?"

"Uh. Um. Yes, but I'll first need another court approval for that. That'll take a couple of hours. For now, we cannot."

"O.K., I'll give this to my supervisor, and he'll take care of it."

"No madam. There's no time for that. You'll reconnect the phone NOW, then tell your supervisor of your actions. Have him call me if he has a problem with it!"

"Yes, sir."

"Thank you. When will it be back up?"

The operator tapped some more keys. "It's up right now."

"Good. Thank you. Good night."

"Good night, sir."

James sat back in his chair and thought about the trouble he had just gotten himself into. *"Trust,"* he kept reminding himself.

• • • •

"I can't see anything. *They* can't possibly see anything. Can you see anything?"

"Nope. But I know I'm being eaten alive by bugs!" Jack said as he slapped the back of his neck.

"Here we are trying to work with one floodlight from the cab of a tow truck. We're gonna screw up the evidence. Let's can this and come back at daybreak."

"Great idea. There's a hotel right down the road from the bridge."

Stu and the other agent told the guy operating the winch in the front of the tow truck to call it quits for the night. An officer in a wet suit sloshed up moments later after he, too, was informed. Stu asked two of the uniformed Anne Arundel County Police Officers to stay around and guard the still submerged car until morning. He told them that two investigators from the Loudoun County Police were en route and should be told to report at daybreak.

"The car has been in the water for five days now. Any fingerprints are now gone. But the paint damage will remain for quite a while. We'll get what we need tomorrow," Stu said, then spoke into his hand held radio, "Ops, Varney."

After a moment, they answered, "Go ahead, Stu."

"I've called off the recovery until daybreak. Do us a favor and call the Comfort Inn in Stevensville, Maryland and get us a couple of rooms."

A voice crackled over the radio, "All right."

"Also, Dwight Conners of the Loudoun County Homicide Division is on his way out here, too. Please get word to him that we're to meet at first sun here at Bay Bridge Airport."

"O.K. Will do."

"Thanks, call me there if they get Grant or his wife."

• • • •

Kelly pulled into the parking lot of Mohney's Marina and stopped. She grabbed the bag of beer bottles and placed them quietly into a waste bin as she walked towards the marina's office. The marina office was new, but had a old-fashioned screen door. The manager heard her approach and was looking at her as she pulled back the flimsy, creaking door.

"Hi. May I use your phone, please?"

"Local call?" the handsome, yet tackily dressed man behind the counter asked.

"No, but I'll use my calling card."

"Sure, go ahead."

"Thanks," she said with a smile. She picked up the phone book and looked up the area code for Orlando. Then she called directory assistance, using her law firm's calling card, and got the number for the Vacation Inn, which was actually in Kissimmee. She wrote it down, then called it.

"Vacation Inn. May I help you?"

"Jeff Caldwell's room, please."

"One moment."

She was placed on hold, then it rang twice and was answered, "Hello."

"Jeff?"

"Yea. Who's this?" he asked cheerfully.

She turned away from the marina manager and said somewhat softly, "Jeff, it's Kelly..."

She turned back toward the manager as Jeff replied, "Kelly, where are you? Are you O.K.?"

She spoke loud enough now that if the marina manager wanted to listen in, which he did, he could, "Yea. I'm in Annapolis at the marina. I've got a big favor to ask you."

"I read the paper here this morning. Is it true? What's going on?"

"It's a long story and everything's fine, but I need to kinda get a way from it all for a day or two."

"Sure, Kelly. I was shocked when I read that Todd was wanted for, what, sabotage and murder?"

The marina manager moved closer, but could only hear her side of it. He acted like he was straightening up a shelf, but was clearly trying to eavesdrop. She continued, "It'll be a completely different story in a few days with a happy ending. I'd just like a little time on the water."

"Sounds like you can't talk."

"Thanks! You're absolutely right!"

"Sure, who's the manager there tonight—Randy?"

"Just a second," she said, then spoke in the direction of the manager. "Randy?"

He turned around and said "Yea?"

"Yes, it's Randy," she said back into the phone as she raised here eyebrows toward Randy.

"Tell Randy that the release name is 'Dismissed.' He's got the spare set of keys."

"Thanks, Jeff. I've been really following the advise you gave me right before you left."

"So you're being assertive?" he asked with a chuckle.

"Yep. Downright demanding! You'd be proud!"

"I am proud. Take the boat for as long as you need it. You take care, Kelly."

"Thanks, Jeff."

She hung up the phone, then said, "Randy, Jeff Caldwell is going to let me take out his boat later tonight. I'm gonna need the spare key and the gate code."

"What's the boat name and the release code?" he asked as he disappeared under the counter, presumably to get the key.

"The boat is 'Billable Ours' and the release code is 'Dismissed,'" she said to him, though he was no longer visible.

Randy didn't immediately reappear nor did he say anything. Kelly heard nothing. No rummaging noises, no unlocking of safes, no pulling open drawers. What was he doing behind that counter? Had Jeff given him a coded word that meant 'Call the Police?' Kelly felt a wave of panic go through her. Kelly knew Jeff was a straight arrow. Maybe he, too, had been contacted by the FBI today and was told to turn her in if she contacted him. She began walking backwards toward the door. She screwed up, she knew it now. Run, she thought. Get out of there!

He popped back up and said, "To get through the gate, press two and four at the same time, then press three." He handed her the spare key to the boat.

She accepted the keys and managed a smile. Her heart was pounding. She was at her limit of how much more of this could she stand.

"Thank you. I'll be back later to take it out."

"Hey. I close at ten. You'll have to back it out of the slip by yourself. Can you manage it?"

"Sure can, Randy. Thanks."

She smiled, turned, and left.

• • • •

Todd heard the helicopter approaching and by the sound of it immediately recognized it as a threat. He stood up from filthy ground and brushed himself off in the dark. Todd, facing west with his back to the tire shop wall, could tell that the chopper was coming up from his left, the south. Within thirty seconds it was right above the building and moving slowly northbound. He had not yet seen it and dared not try to.

At once, its powerful searchlight ripped through the trees just to his right about fifty yards from where he was standing. He quickly scurried around the south side of the building, under an unlit, rusted awning. The light on the helicopter went back out, yet it hovered loudly about seven hundred feet above the parking lot of the tire shop.

Todd, of course, recognized its unique sound. It was one of the Maryland State Police's new French-built choppers. It was larger than a common Huey or Jet Ranger helicopter, and its enclosed rear rotor made a very distinct and menacing howl as it moved slowly across the black sky. He knew if he got in the field of view of its infrared camera, he would be seen.

A couple of months ago, Todd had sat in a Maryland State Police helicopter at an air show and was told, first hand, of their capabilities in tracking people in heavy underbrush. The infrared signatures left by people and animals stood out like flares on their amber CRT located in the center console between the pilots. He remembered listening to the pilots boasting about how they located a lost hunter in western Maryland and how they caught a convenience store robbery suspect who ran into the woods and thought he was safe hiding in a tree. He remembered being told of how, in the winter when the heat contrast was at its highest, even warm footprints would show up as eerie fading marks on the ground. Fortunately it wasn't wintertime, but he would still become a glowing beacon if their camera pointed his way.

They must have spotted something on their night camera and shined their million candlepower floodlight down on it. But, they turned it back off now and continued their infrared search northbound along the western side of Route 301. He walked along the south side of the tire shop and peeked around the front.

He saw a run down, half empty parking lot, moderately lit by yellow mercury vapor street lamps, with five or six stores lining each side. The tire shop that he stood against was the largest store and covered the entire back end of the parking lot. The far end of the lot was the entrance to the twenty year old, three-cornered strip mall on the southbound lanes of Route 301. A laundry mat, a barber shop, a hobby card shop, and a photographers office lined the right side. The left side, obstructed by the side wall of the tire shop from where he was standing, had three vacant storefronts, followed by an insurance company and a cheap-looking Italian Restaurant at the far end. Most of the cars in the lot were in front of the restaurant. A lone pay phone was attached to a rusted awning pole at the far end of the right side storefronts. When he saw the phone, he remembered Kelly's voice mail.

By the sound, Todd could tell that the helicopter had moved slowly northward toward the Bartlett's house. There was no doubt in his mind that the chopper was searching for him. He looked, then dashed behind the photographer's office and along the back side of the south side row of stores. He had one quarter in his pocket. He had to make it count. Leaving his bag in the darkness behind the building, he slowly moved up the most vulnerable side of the building—the side facing Route 301 and the entrance to the strip mall. The brightness of the area made him squint.

He put in the quarter and dialed the number for her office, then pressed two three one for Kelly's extension. When her voice recording started playing, he pressed two four one. He remembered the code to retrieve messages from her because it was ten higher than her extension, which he used all the time.

Two lights illuminated the telephone. One was a powerful floodlight bracketed to the end of the metal awning that spanned the five storefronts. The other was the light above the phone itself. Either was bright enough to expose him to capture by any passing police car. He stared up Route 301, looking at headlights and hoping he'd get enough warning to bolt back into the darkness before being spotted. The playback of the messages seemed to take forever:

"<BEEP> Ms. Grant, Hal Nogrady. The affidavits are here. I'll courier them to you this afternoon. Thanks. <BEEP> Hi Kelly, its me. The title searches for Alphonse Properties have been completed. You can now schedule the negotiations for as early as next Monday.

Talk to you soon. <BEEP> Honey, its mom. Please call me. I watched the national news tonight. My God, I just don't believe it! Please just come home until they catch Todd. We've bought a ticket for you to Memphis, leaving out of BWI. All you have to do is pick it up there at the ticket counter. We're worried sick, honey. Please call us to let us know you're all right.. We love you. <BEEP> ..."

The sound of the helicopter became louder as it turned back southbound for another pass. Todd had been exposed long enough. He started to fidget while watching some bugs crawl in a complex pattern along the Plexiglas shell of the phone's wind screen. He needed to be safely back behind the building and was about to give up and hang up, when he heard the last message. It was Kelly's voice! *"...Todd, I hope you're O.K. Please meet me at ten tonight at the place where we had our anniversary dinner. If I'm not there, please wait for me. Todd, you were right. The car's in the Bay. I love you, hun'. Please be careful."*

Todd checked his watch: 9:37 p.m.

"Crap," he mumbled to himself, then hung up the phone and sprinted back into the darkness behind the building. The helicopter, approaching from the north, came close then turned back northbound.

Todd, unaccustomed to the darkness now, couldn't find his gym bag. He left it right next to the building, he thought, but he couldn't find it! "No. No!" he said as he frantically stepped around the area where his bag was supposed to be. He had a good mile to go through dense woods in only twenty three minutes. He couldn't afford the time to hunt for it now. He made the decision to leave it there and begin running south. He could find it later when things cooled down and he could be driven in and out of there quickly.

As he just entered the woods, he heard a phone ring. He stopped. It rang again. It was his cell phone! He ran back to the rear wall and listened. On the fourth ring, he reached down and felt along the ground until he touched the bag. He ripped into it and felt for the ON button on the phone. The green LED lit up.

"HELLO!" he said, thinking it was Kelly.

"Todd?"

Todd paused, then asked, "Who's this?"

"It's James. James Hatch."

"James! Hey, I have messages to send you! I found the car used to kill Chris. I'd have told you right away, but y'all turned off my phone." Todd was now jogging, phone in one hand, gym bag in the other.

James leaned forward and grabbed a pen from the far corner of the borrowed desk.

"It was the FBI who turned it off. I just turned it back on. They don't know I did it. The fibbies are fishing the car out of the bay as we speak. Listen, Todd. I'm really sticking my neck out for you. Don't lie to me now. We're you near Shenandoah Valley Airport yesterday morning?"

"Yesterday morning? No! I was stealing your files, remember?"

"That's right!" James got angry at himself for forgetting the time sequence for such an important event. "Listen, Todd. I'm gonna try out some of that *trust* stuff with you. Don't screw me over."

"I won't. I swear, James. What happened at Shenandoah Valley?"

"Someone using a hand-held transmitter tried to guide one of your Javelins into a mountainside. Close call."

"Lucky for me that I was up to no good elsewhere. Somehow I knew you'd start second guessing my guilt. I believe it was Winston Churchill that said: 'True genius resides in the capacity for evaluation of uncertain, hazardous, and conflicting information.'"

Todd had seen that quote earlier in the day while flipping through the Bartlett's quote book. He thought to himself how awkward he would look to a passerby right at that moment. He was still noticeably injured, yet managed a quick trudge through a dark forest while carrying a gym bag and talking on a cellular phone.

"Well, if you and I don't perform like a couple of geniuses with this, we're both screwed. Todd, my second guessing started when I concluded that the picture they showed of you and Chris in the restaurant was bogus."

"Nope. That was us all right. She had just confided with me about how Al had been beaten her and how miserable she was. Take a guess at who I think took the picture!"

"Probably someone that could care less about winning a Pulitzer!"

"Bet your ass! James, thanks for trusting me. I won't let you down. But, I've got to go. I'll call you back when I have a chance to talk, O.K.?"

"O.K., but don't call my office. It's wired. Call me at home. The number is...." Todd memorized James number as it was told to him. He repeated it back, hung up, put the phone in the bag, and began to jog faster.

• • • •

"Operations Center, this is Charles."

"This is Officer Mike Bigston over in Anne Arundel County. I have a message for Stu Varney."

"Go ahead, sir."

"We logged another call about fifteen minutes ago into the law firm where Mrs. Grant works. Someone picked up the messages from her voice mail. We'll get the location of that caller in a couple of minutes and send our troops there. We should have him nailed soon."

"Thank you, sir. I'll get the message right to him."

"Thanks."

• • • •

The old Capri pulled into the parking lot of the restaurant before Todd arrived. The Sante Fe West restaurant was located in its own building near the entrance to a new, million square foot mall that was mostly still under construction. The upscale, stand-alone restaurant building faced south near the entrance of the huge, new mall's parking lot. The woods surrounding the mall had been cleared to within about seventy five yards north of the building. Kelly scanned the lot and concluded that Todd wasn't there. It would be ten o'clock in a few more minutes. She was completely deflated, having come this far and failed. He was probably in custody. Her eyes began to water as hope faded. She parked in a space where she could see, then turned off the car and waited for a miracle.

Suddenly, a police car pulled quickly from Route 301 into the lot, then slowed to a crawl. She spotted it right away and darted down onto the filthy, sticky floorboard and prayed he wouldn't check car to car. She lay facing up and could see a vehicle move, based on the lights and shadows reflecting off the stained canvas car top. It became so quiet in her car that she could hear herself breathe, yet the solitude was anything but comforting.

She waited for a good five minutes before raising her head to peek over the dashboard. The squad car was still there, but no one was in it! Shaken, her eyes shifted left, in a three hundred and sixty-degree scan, her body twisting horizontally as she looked around frantically. No one was there.

She jerked her head back at the squad car which was double parked in front of the restaurant. They must have either gone in the restaurant or were around the backside of the building. Immediately thereafter she saw a head glance from around the back-right corner of the restaurant—it was TODD! From his angle, he couldn't see that there was a police car in front of the restaurant. He was walking right into their custody!

She started the car, slammed it into gear and sped right toward him. He saw the car approaching and froze, halfway down the side of the building. Kelly flashed her bright lights at him as she neared. She stopped at the edge of the pavement, reached over and flung open the passenger door. He smiled as he recognized her and dashed her way.

As he entered the car, she yelled, "Get down! Get down!"

No sooner had he ducked down, she made a one-eighty and back out to Route 301. The big wooden doors to the restaurant opened and two officers walked out right as she finished the U-turn. She watched them walk, in opposite directions, around to the back of the building.

"Take the first exit and get us on a back road somewhere," Todd said.

They looked at each other as she drove. They did it!

Both smiling now, Kelly wiped her eyes and said, "Woof! Look at you! You need a shower!"

He smiled. "No. I think its either you or this car!"

"Or all of the above..."

"Well, why don't we just roll down all the windows and drive through a car wash!"

Todd reached over and squeezed her hand.

TWENTY FOUR

THE DRAPES moved back and forth, following the lead of the boat's gentle rocking. The morning sun hit them and reflected the rays in every direction. The freshness of the morning was all around the Grants as they lay together.

Last night, they had talked all the way back to Annapolis and were clearly tired when they arrived at the harbor. They took the boat out of its slip and anchored it in the middle of the harbor, some thirty yards away from the closest of the ten or twelve other boats moored out there. Two quick showers, a light midnight snack, and the soporific swaying of the boat quickly lulled them to sleep in each other's arms and left the Grants fully charged for the important day ahead.

Todd woke first. He lay there for a few minutes as he watched the drapes slowly move back and forth and thought about the day ahead. She woke shortly thereafter. He was first out of the cabin, banana in hand, wearing a bathing suit and an Ocean Pacific T-shirt that he found in the cabin. He stood up, looked at the big, crisp, blue sky all around him and stretched—as much as his injuries would allow. After a follow-up phone call to James the night before, he knew the FBI was probably just beginning to pull the car out of the water on the other side of the bay. He was told the recovery and investigation would take several hours.

A half hour later, Todd was steering the large boat into the small part of the Annapolis Harbor. He moored the boat with remarkable grace, tied it, then gave Kelly a big hug and kiss before sending her ashore.

Today was the day. Time to go on the offensive. They both realized that Todd was really no match for the massive manhunt and he was on borrowed time anyway. The earlier conversation with James gave Todd no assurance that the FBI nor the two county police units were entertaining any thoughts that the guilty person might be someone other than he. They could sit around for days and accomplish nothing or they could get out and search out clues.

They didn't really have a plan, just separate tasks that might bring about some facts that might just point the authorities toward Al Thomas. They did, however, work out a couple of communications contingencies, if needed.

• • • •

They were standing behind the left side of the tow truck, next to the water. Stu and Jack were both wearing their FBI windbreakers, but with the sun firmly in the eastern sky it was already too hot for them. They, like the others, were focused on the car as it slowly emerged from the water. Although there were almost a dozen people around the investigation site, no one spoke a word. The only sound came from the grinding winch in the back of the tow truck. There was no bickering over who had jurisdiction. Though it was Stu who gave the order the night before to call off the recovery until dawn, he probably had the least to gain from being there. Anne Arundel Police had the tow truck and were more than capable of examining the vehicle. Their main interest was in obtaining evidence to determine who stole the car from the airport. Loudoun County Police had the murder of Chris Thomas to solve and had the most to gain from the evidence. The FBI was there simply because the suspect was also being sought in connection with *the accident*.

"Uh oh! There's a boo boo!" Jack suddenly said to Stu, pointing to the car's right front bumper as it was pulled backwards out of the water and past them.

James had his hands on his hips and a satisfied look on his face. "Oh, yea. Looks like the old boy must have hit something before he ditched it."

They walked along side the car as it inched closer to the tow truck. Their shoes became soaked from the water that gushed from the car as it rolled slowly through the weeds.

• • • •

Kelly arrived in Alexandria, Virginia, fifty-five minutes after she left the dock in Annapolis, including a quick stop in the Annapolis Mall to buy a cheap pair of jeans and a T-shirt. The clothes she wore when she left the boat, they both agreed, were too soiled and smelly to be worn another day. There was no way to stay anonymous in those dirty clothes. Unfortunately, buying new clothes exposed her, took up valuable time, and cost them precious cash.

Cash was a big consideration. Cash gave them flexibility; it gave them options. The car had cost them four hundred twenty, plus another fifteen for a couple of sandwiches and some fruit from a supermarket last night. Now, thirty bucks for the clothes. Between the two of them, they only had about fifty dollars—and no way of getting more. Their credit and debit cards were not only useless, they were downright dangerous and would not be used for any reason.

Money was on Kelly's mind as she pulled into a gas station for fuel and directions. Knowing she would probably not be driving that car much further—for reasons good or bad, she decided to put in only ten dollar's worth of the cheap stuff.

"Pump two. Ten bucks," said an ugly, middle aged woman from behind the glass at the cashier's booth.

Kelly gave the lady a twenty, then asked loudly through the glass, "How do I get to South Telegraph Road?"

The ugly lady never looked up; she just slid a ten back under the glass to Kelly and said while pointing, "Get on the Beltway westbound, about two miles."

"Thank you," Kelly said.

She was looking for the Towne Centre apartments on South Telegraph, the address listed by the Loudoun County Police as the address for Al Thomas. It was also Chris Thomas's address until they separated. She got back on the Beltway and exited, as instructed, a couple of miles west. Once she got about a mile south of the Beltway on Telegraph, she spotted the apartments. It was a host of individual, three-story buildings, each comprising some eight or ten apartments. He lived in apartment J-102. After driving down a couple of side streets littered with parked cars, she saw both Building J and apartment 102. The apartment was, by the architecture, more than twenty years old, but was in reasonably good shape. Two large, manicured shrubs hid all but the very top of the sliding glass door from her view from the street. A muted orange wooden door was next to the glass door and in clear view. She continued past the apartment to a place to turn around, then returned to a parking spot about fifty yards away from his door on the other side of the street, and pulled in. The apartment complex seemed very peaceful, though the buildings, which lined each side of the street, were crammed close to each other and the lots were so full of cars.

She felt safe in the car, too, since she was in a great position to see him emerge from the apartment and had plenty of time to get away if the need arose. She flung her legs up on the passenger seat and leaned low against the driver's door and waited.

After about five minutes of waiting for someone who was probably not even home, she pulled out her notes and started reviewing them. She reread her understanding of how the plastic penguin was wired into the airplane that subsequently broke apart with Scott at the controls. She was reminded of just how crafty and guileful Al was. She remembered the details of the deliberate act of murder by Al Thomas of his wife. He was a man without a soul, without sentiment.

The review of her notes made her, again, nervous. Al was an angry, vengeful man who, so far, only made one mistake: he wasn't able to talk the Javelin crew into flying into a mountainside.

She reflected on what the circumstances must have been to set him off: Bands Airways would never hire him, yet his wife continued to move up through the pilot ranks there. He was brilliant, yet because of his demeanor the only job he could hold down was a repairman at a video store. When she left him, *her* life was set to improve. He couldn't stand for that. Then, when he found out she was gaining a reputation for sleeping around, he must have snapped. He downs an airplane, then later kills his wife—and successfully guides the authorities toward Todd. Why he chose that particular aircraft and why he chose Todd remained unclear. But, clearly he was an angry neuropath with the capability and intent for inflicting more misery.

••••

The boat was anchored in light seas under brilliant sunshine. Todd had maneuvered it to within five hundred yards of the shoreline, directly in front of Runway 28 at Bay Bridge Airport. The wind was from the east, which was fortunate, because it made the bow of the boat shift directly towards the investigation teams. Even if they noticed the boat, they couldn't make out the name, since its name was painted on the stern. Todd could watch their activities for hours and could hide below the windscreen, if necessary. If anyone *were* to look at his boat from shore, Todd would have had ample time to duck down. It was a perfect vantage point.

The phone was being recharged through an adapter connected to the boat's cigarette lighter, but was still available for use. He had already talked to James once this morning during his four mile trip from the opposite shore of the Chesapeake. Todd gave James every fact and supposition that he collected over the past day. James told Todd everything he knew also, but felt he was no longer in the midst of the investigation. He said the FBI did visit Al's apartment, but found no soldering irons, no aircraft schematics, no sketches, no store receipts for toy penguins—nothing to link him to the plastic penguin. James said he thought the FBI was there primarily to ask Al what he knew about Todd. Al told them the same thing that he told the Loudoun County police. James said it was a *fill-the-square* search.

••••

The man that came out of Al Thomas's apartment was wearing a uniform under a light blue windbreaker. She noticed the straight-legged, almost shiny polyester trousers from a hundred and fifty feet away. He was in a hurry and had trouble zipping up his jacket. Otherwise, she wouldn't have seen the embroidered emblem on his right chest. It was clearly a uniform, but she was too far away to make out the logo.

It must be Al, she thought, but the uniform threw her. Then she reasoned that he repaired video equipment for SunVisor videos. It was a repairman's uniform, she concluded.

She watched him get into an old, brown Ford Thunderbird. He backed it out, then drove down the narrow apartment complex street towards Telegraph Road. She waited a moment before moving. It wasn't that she was trying to stay far behind and out of sight—it was her indecisiveness on whether she should try and sneak into his apartment while he was gone or whether she should follow him.

The Thunderbird made a left turn towards the Beltway. She missed an opportunity to squeeze into the median lane and had to wait. After nervously tapping her steering wheel with both hands for what seemed an eternity, a hole opened up in the traffic flow and she bolted ahead and left. Just as the Beltway came into view, she noticed his car entering the Beltway westbound. She wasn't expecting this, since she knew that SunVisor Video was on Duke Street, which would have been east of Telegraph Road! She went underneath the overpass, then made a two hundred-seventy degree turn to the right to the on-ramp of the eight-lane Beltway.

Staying at least a half mile back, she followed him for more than twenty minutes. He was doing the speed limit while everyone else was doing at least ten above. If he was in such a hurry to get out of the apartment, why was he being so cautious now? She stayed hidden back in the far right lane, but almost lost him when he took the Interstate 66 exit from the far *left* lane. She followed him for another ten or so miles into the closet community of Centreville, south of Washington Dulles Airport. He exited I-66 and entered a neighborhood of town homes and apartment complexes. She sped up and exited so she wouldn't lose him. Each turn he made through the neighborhood made it more difficult for her to keep up.

After about three turns, she lost him. He turned a corner and was gone. She was mad at herself for being so cautious and sped up in a desperate attempt to find him. Then, when she wheeled around a corner, she saw his car stopped in front of a mailbox about halfway down a tiny street. She panicked, stomped hard on the brakes, then wheeled left into a numbered parking space in front of a row of small, older town homes. The narrow street was virtually void of cars, since it was now after nine a.m. and most were away at work. She left herself wide open to being recognized if he looked around behind him.

She was much too close. After putting the car in park, she dipped her head down and acted as though she were gathering up her things. She even opened the door and put her left foot on the ground to act as if she were getting out. She didn't want him to get any hint that she followed him. Certainly, he would recognize her if he saw her face.

She didn't see him close the mailbox, but started to breathe again as she heard the car pull away. She continued to hold her head down, but glanced up with her eyes. His car made a left at a stop sign, then drove off. She considered following him again, but this time chose not to.

After a moment to let her blood pressure drop, she put the car into reverse and backed out of the driveway. She drove slowly down the street which was lined on both sides with old town homes, and noted both the street and the number on the mailbox. She looked for the town home that matched the number on the box and spotted it. Brown brick with pale white trim. Old and ugly. Long curtains were pulled closed in the front bay window just adjacent to the wooden front door. Leaves had piled up in the small patch of weed-infested grass in his front yard. The two homes bordering his had immaculate yards and a kind of cheerfulness about them. His needed work.

• • • •

If only he was there under different circumstances. The day was truly magnificent. The roasting sea air emitted a fragrance filled with happiness and contentment. Todd smiled, as he knew they were zeroing in on Al. It was becoming breezy up top, but Todd still heard the phone's electronic ring from below the deck. He reached down for it and pressed ON.

"Boiler Room!" he mocked.

"R.C.?" Kelly asked from the pay phone just inside the glass doors of a mall called Sully Plaza.

"Yea. Call me skipper. *Wassup*?"

"I followed Al out to Centreville. He stopped and got some mail from a box in front of a town house out here."

"Any name on the mailbox?" he asked, much more seriously now.

"Not that I could see. Got a pencil?"

Todd reached down to his gym bag and pulled out a pen and his notes. "Yea. Ready to copy..."

"Thirty three thirty two Crescent Creek Drive, Centreville."

"Got it. Listen, K.W. It scares me that you got that close to him. Why don't you come on back here to the boat, and we'll work out a better plan."

"O.K. I'll call with a rendezvous time a little later."

"Great. Hey, what does he look like?" he asked curiously.

"Kinda plain looking with brown hair. He was wearing a navy blue uniform, probably his video repairman's git up."

"Hmm. Hey, you stay alert. Love you, hun."

"You, too, skip'." Kelly hung up the phone, walked over to her car and drove back toward the town house.

Todd pressed STANDBY, then ON again. He dialed a number, then within a few seconds he was talking with James. He grabbed a towel and put it around his hot neck as he explained Kelly's finding.

"Wait. What was that address again?" James asked, grabbing for his pen.

"Thirty three thirty two Crescent Creek Drive, Centreville, Virginia."

"O.K., Todd, I'll call Stu Varney. He can find out really quick. I'll call you back when I get something."

"Thanks, James." Todd pressed the STANDBY key, then placed the phone back below deck and again grabbed the binoculars.

"Varney," Stu said, after retrieving his cellular phone from his jacket pocket. Todd focused the binoculars squarely on him as he answered.

"Hey, Stu Baby! How are you!?" James asked in a familiar tone.

"Uh oh. I smell a rat. You're onto something again."

With his binoculars, Todd could see Stu smile as he leaned against a police cruiser and talked with James. Other people had been going over the retrieved car. Stu, on the other hand, had been standing around with really nothing to do but observe. He was probably happy to get the call.

"Maybe. But I need your help."

"Go ahead."

"I need to know everything you can find out about who's living at thirty-three thirty-two Crescent Creek Drive, in Centreville. Call me back at my home. I'll wait here until you call."

From five hundred yards away, Todd saw Stu pull out a pad and pen. Then he saw him hang up, then dial another number and speak for about a minute or so. During that time, Stu glanced out over the water and noticed the boat.

After hanging up, Stu walked over to another car and grabbed a pair of binoculars. When he raised them towards the boat, Todd ducked down—and stayed down for at least ten minutes.

• • • •

After checking for Al's car, Kelly parked in the street, down a couple of town homes from where Al had taken the mail. She walked up the sidewalk to the concrete step and onto a thatched doormat, then knocked firmly on the flimsy wooden door. A large, mean sounding dog began barking immediately from a room away from the front door, and quickly came forward. The barking resonated within the town home, and as the sound of heavy hoofs moved closer to the door, Kelly pictured the inside of the town home to be bare, with a wooden floor throughout.

Kelly also pictured the size of the beast inside. From all indications it was a full grown—probably fully trained—guard dog. Images of Dobermans and Rottweilers came to mind. She looked around the entranceway, then glanced around the neighborhood. All was quiet, except for the dog. She lifted up the doormat, then let it drop. She ran her hand along the top of the door frame. No key there, either. About that time, she saw a huge nose move the curtain back from behind the adjacent bay window and two black eyes glared right at her. The dog showed his teeth slightly, then began barking again, this time with more conviction. At that moment, she remembered hearing that bark from the first anonymous phone call.

She stared at the German Shepherd with amazement but little fear. The dog wanted her, but couldn't get to her. Kelly looked at the entranceway's overhang and saw no place to stow a spare key. She looked to the right. A water faucet, behind some tall shrubs was covered by a sprinkler timer box. The timer had a black, plastic, flip-top lid. She took a few steps over to it and flipped it up. There, taped to the inside top, was a key. She bent down on one knee and examined it closely. "TuffLock" was inscribed on it. She stood up, brushed off her knee, then went back to the door and gave the knob a close-up look. The same "TuffLock" emblem was on it, inscribed around the keyhole. She couldn't just go right in—she'd be dog food. Then, she got an idea. She exchanged one more glance with the dog, went back to her car and drove away.

••••

Todd answered the phone cheerfully after the first ring. "Poop deck."

"Uh, Todd?" James asked as he wrote *poop deck* onto a pad.

"Oh. Hi James. I thought it was Kelly checking in." Todd screwed up and he knew it.

"Nope. Where is she, anyway?"

"On her way back here."

"Back to the boat?"

"Boat?" Todd mentally kicked himself for answering the phone so glibly. The game was far from over, yet he dropped his guard once again.

"Yea. The boat you've been hiding on since you left the Bartlett's."

"James. I'm not good at evasion. I was always the first one caught at hide and seek. I'm just lucky. Let me use up what little luck I have left before you tell Stu where I am."

"I'm gonna let *you* tell Stu where you are when the time comes. I'm just your conduit to him. Now, here's what he found out about the town home..." Todd grabbed a pen and listened intensely.

"...The guy that owns it is a Mr. Brad Roe. That ring a bell?"

"No. Sorry, it doesn't."

"Damn. How about Ben Robertson? Mr. Roe rented the place to a Mr. Ben Robertson about three months ago."

"Ben Robertson. Seems like..."

Todd looked up at the high cirrus clouds near the hot sun and thought hard. Suddenly, he remembered. "James! That sum' bitch is a ramper, a baggage handler for us. Jesus, James. Game over!"

"What about Al Thomas?"

"Oh, Al is still very much in the picture. The thing I couldn't figure out is how he had access to the planes. A ramper. That's how he got into Scott's airplane. I've got two theories on Ben Robertson. I need to think on this."

"Let me give Stu a call. They'll get right on it."

"Thanks, James. You might ask him to obtain the background check on Robertson from his employee record."

TWENTY FIVE

THE FLIMSY PLASTIC SEVEN ELEVEN BAG was unraveled and opened from its perch on the passenger seat. Kelly pulled out a package of hot dogs and opened one of the two plastic bags that contained four dogs each. She pulled out a single one and laid it on top of the others. She looked around the town homes to see if anyone was watching, then reached into the Seven Eleven bag again and pulled out some non-prescription sleeping capsules. Six bucks for the two items. Her cash was dwindling.

She slit open the hot dog longitudinally with several short swipes of a paper clip. Carefully, she pulled apart two capsules and distributed their powdery contents into the hot dog. She walked quietly up the concrete step, then went straight for the key hidden in the water timer behind the shrubbery. She every so slowly put the key into the lock and turned it. No barking. She pushed open the door about an inch, holding it in a position where she could slam it if the beast turned out to be right behind the door. She held the door with her left hand and listened. Still no barking or movement. A car whizzed by and startled her. She turned around and saw it continue on. She then tossed the hot dog onto the wooden floor and closed the door again. She waited a couple of seconds. Then, hearing nothing, she banged on the door. The huge dog immediately began barking and the scampering of heavy paws was heard coming into the front room. She turned back to her car without waiting to see the dog's black eyes peer from between the window drapes.

• • • •

"James, it's Todd. What have you found out?" The blistering sun was now directly overhead. Todd wanted to do something. Anything. He was tired of watching.

Some of the inspectors had left the airport, leaving only four or five people. Stu was still there, but was now in his car. It was hard to see what he was doing inside the car, because the strong sun reflected off the windshield.

"The FBI will shortly be on their way to Ben Robertson's apartment. Listen Todd. Stu is getting very suspicious of me. He wants to know how I came across the address of that town house. When he finds out I reconnected your phone and I've corroborating with you then it's jail for me. You tell me why I shouldn't call Stu right now and confess."

"You're right. I'm fairly confident that I have him nailed—maybe I should turn myself in. I can see that Stu's still at the airport."

"Damn, you *are* on a boat! You've been watching him all along!"

"Didn't you announce that finding in an earlier conversation?"

"Yea. But I didn't think you'd be stupid enough to clue me in as you did."

"I told you James. I'm not as devious as you think I am."

"So you're gonna turn yourself in?"

"Yep."

"You want me to call him and let him know you're coming?"

"No. Better not James. I think it'll be safer if I just walk up to him unannounced."

"Can I turn your phone back off?"

"Gimme thirty minutes, James—Kelly's supposed to check in with me soon. I need to let her know what I'm doing."

"O.K. Todd."

• • • •

A car pulled up the street, but stopped short of the town house when the driver noticed Kelly walk up the sidewalk and slowly sneak through the front door.

When she opened the door, two small wires touched together near the baseboard, just as he had hoped. These minuscule wires led along the baseboard, around the corner to the bedroom. The wires climbed the leg of a card table and connected into a circuit board. The board had two relays attached to wires that connected to the board. One held down the earpiece to a telephone. The other was braced above an autodial button on the phone labeled "Beeper."

The relatively simple burglar alarm that he constructed worked as planned. The opening of the front door started a timer circuit. The first action instructed an electric relay to mechanically release the earpiece switch, which produced a dial tone. The timer then waited two seconds, then started another electromechanical relay, which tapped one of the autodial buttons on the phone. After ten seconds, the timer circuit reenergized the first relay, which hung up the phone. It would have won a blue ribbon at a junior high science fair.

Kelly stood close to the still-opened door, and stared at the dog lying in the corner of the room. He was motionless on the floor. It had only been twenty-five minutes. Her scheme could have concluded in a number of ways. The laced hot dog could have not been eaten. It could have been ineffective. It could have put the dog to sleep. Or it could have killed the dog. At this point, either of the last two options would have been acceptable. She was relieved, however, when she noticed the shiny black fur above his chest move slowly up and down.

She stomped hard on the floor, but the dog didn't budge.

Closing the door, she looked around. It was bare all right. There was no furniture in the room. No pictures on the wall. She walked back towards the bedroom. The sound of her steps echoed loudly in the emptiness.

The bedroom was a mess. There was some electrical test equipment and big binders on a card table in one corner and an unmade bed beside it. The far corner of the room had two old wooden tables with film developing and camera equipment stacked high. A big pile of black and white photos caught her eye. She walked over some empty potato chip bags on the wooden floor for a closer look. She saw a TransGlobe Airlines schedule booklet on the table, with paper clips attached. She also saw crewmember trip pairing sheets, aircraft route schedules, and aircraft maintenance schedules. She could feel herself getting tense as she took it all in.

A spiral binder was to the right of the stack of schedules and had several pages of schedule iterations scribbled and scratched out. Two handwritten notes stood out: "Aug 24—#2252—Shenandoah Valley—05:30 a.m." The other was "Aug 26—#2236—Raleigh— 12:40 p.m." Both were circled, but the first one was crossed out.

Kelly checked her watch, then ran to the far corner of the room and grabbed the phone. Dialing frantically, she squeezed her temples with her left hand and prayed for Todd to answer.

"Hello," Todd said, much more cautiously this time.

"Todd. Thank God. Write this down..."

"Are you O.K.?"

"Write this down, then call James or the FBI. Flight Twenty-two Thirty-six, today at twelve forty. He's gonna take it down."

"Gotcha. Where are you?"

The phone went dead. The cord was ripped from the wall. Kelly wheeled around and saw a huge, double barreled shotgun an inch from her nose. She let out an indecipherable groan and dropped the phone. She swayed slightly but the gun's barrel stayed right with her nose.

"What did you do to the dog?" a man with a deep voice asked slowly.

Kelly's eyes rolled back and she fainted, hitting the floor hard.

TWENTY SIX

THE BEEPER, attached to his belt, sounded. He was startled by it, and dropped an attachment screw onto the airplane's carpeted floor, just aft of the cockpit. The plastic penguin was in place and all of the wires were properly connected to both the stall warning system's Signal Summing Device and the relay box to the engine boost pump. He checked for a call-back number on his beeper, even though he knew there would be none: Yes, someone had definitely entered his apartment. He lowered the cover panel at Station 110 in order to pick up the dropped screw. He had to finish his work quickly, get out of the airplane, and disappear.

There was plenty of risk involved with being caught by another ramper, a pilot, or a maintenance technician. Now, he had to concern himself with the person that just opened his front door back at the town home. It could be the owner of the town home—after all, he insisted on keeping a key. It could be a burglar, or it simply could have been an erroneous beep or a malfunctioning alarm. He was concerned, but reminded himself that he could still down the plane and escape before they could piece it all together.

• • • •

Following ten seconds of silence, a dial tone sounded in the earpiece of Todd's cellular phone. Todd knew something was terribly wrong as he listened to the dial tone for a second or two, then dialed Bands Airways' operations office at Dulles. As the phone began ringing, he quickly pulled up the anchor and thought to himself who should be called next: The FBI, the Loudoun County Police, or James Hatch. It rang four times before it was answered. The person he was hoping to hear spoke: "Hello, this is Charlie Brooks."

"Charlie, this is Todd Grant."

"Todd, what are..."

"Charlie, you've got a flight Twenty-two Thirty-six to Raleigh leaving at twelve forty."

"Uh..."

"Don't let it go—there's reason to believe that one of the rampers has rigged it to fall out of the sky."

"What?!"

"Call airport security and have them round up a ramper by the name of Ben Robertson," Todd spoke as he started the boat's twin inboard engines. The vessel rocked lightly from the foot-high waves. With the anchor retrieved, the boat began to drift counterclockwise away from the shoreline.

"Wait. You say Ben Robertson?"

"Yea. He's there. I know it. Have 'em lock down the airport if they have to, but they must get this guy."

"I want to believe you, Todd, but..."

"Listen, Charlie, you have no choice. Procedurally, treat this just like a bomb threat. The only difference is, it's not a threat—it's gonna happen if you don't act."

"O.K. Todd."

"I'll explain it all to you later," Todd said, then he pressed STANDBY on the phone, then ON again. Moments later, a female voice came over his earpiece as he raced for the shoreline. The deep drone of the engines and the wind in his face made it difficult for Todd to hear her.

"Directory Assistance. What city please?"

"Not sure, but the last name is Ness, first name Paul."

"One moment...."

Todd balanced the cellular phone between his ear and his shoulder as he grabbed his pen from a cup holder and clicked it.

The lady said, "Checking Paul Ness.... Oh, here it is, please hold for the number."

The operator punched a function key on her computer to have it automatically read aloud the number. The female sounding, computer generated voice spoke as Todd wrote it on his forearm. The boat was bouncing rhythmically as he sped towards Charlene's Crab House, next to the airport.

He spotted a vacant slip right next to the restaurant and decelerated the boat to a fast drift. He was by no means an expert boatsman, but brought it in and tied it without incident. He loaded his gym bag with his computer, his notes, and a couple of bananas. He gave the boat keys to the dock boy and told him he'd be back in a couple of hours. As he dashed down the gravel road that circumnavigated the runway he pressed the ON button and dialed the number on his forearm.

"Hello."

"Paul, this is Todd, the R.C. modeler at Bay Bridge Airport."

"I'm sorry, who?" the man on the other end asked. Todd was unsure if he would remember him, when Paul said, "...Oh, yea. How are you, Todd!"

Todd sensed that the man was unaware of the news blitz surrounding him over the past few days. "Paul, I have a big favor to ask of you. I'm over at Bay Bridge Airport and I need to get to Dulles fast. May I please borrow your plane for a few hours?"

"Uh, yea. It hasn't flown in a couple of months, so you'll need to give it a good pre-flight."

"I sure will, Paul."

"Wait. What am I thinking. You can't fly it outta there, 'cuz the feds won't let it back in. The airport's still closed to inbound traffic."

"I'll have a fed with me. I'll get it back." Todd looked over his right shoulder towards the western end of the runway where the police cars and tow truck were parked. His shoulder began aching from carrying the heavy gym bag as he jogged along, so he switched the phone to his right hand and grabbed the gym back with his left.

"Well, O.K. The spare key is with the airport manager, Jake McFadden."

"Thank you, Paul. I really appreciate it. I'll top the tanks off when I get back."

"Just be careful, Todd."

"I will. Thanks again."

••••

Kelly woke up to a room filled with people and activity. A towel was underneath her head as she lay extended and upright on the wooden floor. One man, kneeling beside her announced: "She's back."

An older, well groomed man turned, smiled, and said, "Good day, Mrs. Grant."

She felt clammy and groggy, but managed, "Why don't you introduce yourselves..."

"Oh, I'm terribly sorry. I'm Agent Russ Mitchell, FBI. These are my colleagues. We saw you sneak in here, and were unsure of your intentions. Sorry if we startled you."

She raised up to her elbows and glared back. "I normally don't get alarmed when I see a shot gun inches from my face, but I've been under some stress lately," she said angrily.

"Ma'am, please understand that we put ourselves at risk every time we approach a suspect."

"What time is it. There's a flight to Raleigh leaving at twelve forty...."

"We know. We just got a call from the airline operations office. They've canceled the flight. Also, the airport police are looking for the man that rents this apartment as we speak."

"I have to call my husband."

"We can't let you do that, just yet."

"And why not?! Look, you know now who's responsible!"

"We have some evidence to support that claim. However, you and your husband are not exactly cleared of all suspicions yet. If you've been innocent all along, why have you been running?"

"Who was it that found this place? We did! You think we could've done that from jail? And who could have assured me of my safety? This guy is a wacko."

"Look, we'll have Mr. Robertson in custody within minutes. Just sit tight for a while we sort through everything."

"Sit tight? You want me to sit tight?! I want you to drive me to Dulles—now!"

"Why Dulles?"

"Because I know what he looks like."

••••

"Paul, there's a guy here who wants the keys to your plane...." Jake said into the phone.

Todd was out of breath and sweating heavily as he stood in the airport office awaiting the verification.

"All right. Well, I don't just hand keys out to anyone who walks in here, you know."

Todd smiled at the grumpy manager, who then turned away from him as he said good bye to the man on the phone and hung up. Todd withdrew his smile.

"I need to see your pilot certificate and a current medical certificate," he said, condescendingly, while retrieving the keys.

Todd was startled. He didn't want to know who he was. "Are you with the FAA?"

"No. I'm the manager of..."

"–Well, I'm *not* with the Fish and Wildlife Service, but I'm gonna need to see your hunting license," Todd replied abruptly and angrily. Todd was right. The manager wasn't renting him the plane. The manager had no right to ask him for those documents.

The manager turned around and looked at him. Todd stared him in the eye, completely serious. The manager turned back to the key box, then asked, "Where are you going, son?"

Todd remembered the last time he was called son and raised his index finger. "I'm not your son..." The adjacent finger then came up. "...and I'm afraid that's none of your business!"

"You're kind of a smart ass."

"Thank you for that observation. Look, I'm in a hurry."

The manager slammed the keys down on the counter top. Todd scooped them up and said, "Thank you." The tone was deliberate yet conciliatory.

Todd sprinted the couple of hundred yards towards the blue and white Cessna. He quickly untied it, unlocked it, checked the fuel for contamination, checked the oil level, and checked for bird nests in all of the plane's cavities. He pulled the chocks away from the nose tire, then hopped in. The easterly breeze had provided some relief from the noon-time heat, but the inside of the airplane was an oven. He pulled down his shorts as far as he could, so the hot vinyl seat cushions wouldn't scald the back of his legs.

"Clear!" he yelled loudly, then turned the ignition key to the right. After a few slow rotations of the propeller, the engine sputtered to life. He immediately began to taxi straight ahead, and picked up the cellular phone from the gym bag. He placed the bag in the back seat, then quickly dialed James.

"James. It's Todd. I'm taxiing toward Stu Varney in a Cessna. Call him up and tell him he needs to fly to Dulles with me. We're gonna nab a bad guy."

"Will do..."

"And James..."

"Yea?"

"I need you to also call Inspector Dwight Conners at the Loudoun County Sheriff's Office and have him go to Bands Airways Operations, near Gate 10, to identify the bad guy once he's nabbed."

"Will do. I'm ten minutes from Dulles. I'm gonna head out there, too."

"Good. And James..."

"Yea?"

"Please tell Stu not to shoot me."

"O.K."

Todd taxied left, out of the grassy parking area and onto the asphalt taxiway toward the investigation team. He checked the magnetos and flight instruments as he neared them.

The four or five investigators turned around when the heard the advancing aircraft. He stopped the plane about fifty feet from Stu's car, his left wing pointing directly towards it. After half a minute, Stu stepped out, overtly unlatched the safety strap on his revolver, and walked toward the plane.

When he got within ten feet of the left wing, he stopped. Then he looked at Todd, pointed to the engine, then motioned him to kill it.

Todd shook his head vigorously, then motioned Stu to come around and hop in.

Stu stood there as other investigators joined him. He spoke to them over the noise of the Cessna.

Todd looked at them for a few moments, then reached across and opened the passenger door.

It was an old-fashioned standoff.

Todd gave him a *come-on-we-gotta-get-going* look, then raised his left wrist and tapped his watch anxiously in his direction.

Stu just stood there, pondering. After a long thirty seconds, he said something to the other men, then he began walking around the back of the airplane. The other men spread out, drew their weapons, and pointed them squarely at Todd. He shook his head slowly, raised his hands, and placed them atop the hot glareshield.

Stu walked awkwardly up to the passenger door, his tie fluttering around his neck from the wind off the propeller. He opened it fully, shielding him from the propeller wash but not the noise.

"I want you to stop that engine and get out!" he yelled.

"I'm going to Dulles, Stu. Now, do you want a ride there or not?"

"No! Now get out!"

"Stu, you gotta just trust me. I could've just left without you. Why would I offer you a ride if I was guilty of anything? James trusts me. You should too. Come on. We need to get going!"

Stu stared at Todd. Todd stared back with an equal intensity. Stu looked into the back seat, noticed the gym bag, and also noticed how very small and noisy the airplane was. He then glared back at Todd.

"You know how to fly this?" he yelled.

"It's kinda what I do for a living."

"Hang on," Stu shouted, then mumbled to himself, "...the Director is gonna have my ass for this...." as he disappeared from the door. He stood tall behind the wing and held up his cell phone so the other agent could see it. He pointed at it, then pointed in the direction of Washington. The agent gave him a thumbs up, then Stu hopped into the plane and closed the door. The airplane now seemed smaller than ever, albeit a little quieter. Sweat beads appeared on Stu's head, probably in part because of the heat, as he struggled with his seat belts.

"I hate small planes," Stu said as he adjusted his seat and stared at the instrument panel in front of him.

••••

Charlie Brooks walked briskly down the long hallway connecting the pilot lounge with the operations office. As he entered the pilot lounge, he looked around, then announced, "Has anyone seen a ramper by the name of Ben Robertson?"

The ten or so people looked up. No one spoke. A few people shook their heads. A middle aged ramper, slouched in a chair, dropped his walkie-talkie onto his fat belly, stuck his right leg out horizontally and let it drop on the cushion of another couch. Now properly positioned, he reached into his right front pants pocket. He retrieved and unfolded a worn piece of paper. "He's here today. He's scheduled to work, uh, gates twelve through fifteen."

Just then, the electric door lock leading to the passenger gates clicked, the door opened, and two uniformed officers came in, looked around, and walked towards the hallway. Charlie backed up, extended his right arm, and corralled them as he spoke to the people in the room. "If you see him, don't approach him. Just point him out to one of these guys. O.K.?"

Most of the room nodded, now much more attentively.

Charlie escorted the officers down the hall and explained the situation to them.

••••

"Baltimore Approach, Cessna Echo Sierra Sierra," said Todd into the plane's microphone. He was climbing over the Chesapeake and hadn't yet spoken with Stu. Stu was looking out the window at the cars passing over the huge Bay Bridge, but his stiff posture gave away his nervousness.

"Cessna Echo Sierra Sierra, Baltimore Approach, go ahead," came over the speaker.

Todd keyed the mike and said, "Echo Sierra Sierra is a Cessna One Seventy Two, just departed Bay Bridge, climbing westbound out of one thousand for two thousand five hundred. Request clearance to enter the Class B airspace, destination Dulles."

"Cessna Echo Sierra Sierra, squawk five one two six."

Todd repeated, "Five one two six," then dialed the four numbers into his transponder, the device that makes him identifiable on the controller's radar screen.

Shortly thereafter, the controller's voice came over the speaker again, "Cessna Echo Sierra Sierra, radar contact. You are cleared to enter the Washington Tri-Area Class B Airspace. Fly heading three-three-zero for now. I'll have direct Dulles for you in about thirty miles."

"Cleared to enter, heading three-three-zero, Echo Sierra Sierra."

It became clear to Stu that Todd was indeed going to Dulles, that Todd was tired, injured, and on a mission. Stu was just about to say something to him when an alarm rang out.

"What's that?!" Stu clamored as he scoured the instrument panel.

Todd smiled. "Sounds like your phone. Don't talk long though, 'cuz you're not supposed to use those things in the air."

Somewhat embarrassed by his nervous reaction, he smiled, pulled the phone out of his jacket, and flipped down the mouthpiece on the tiny phone. "Stu Varney," he said into the phone.

Stu listened to the caller, looked at Todd and said, "No, I haven't shot him yet."

Todd smiled straight ahead as Stu continued, "Listen, James. You told me to trust you on this. Here I am, three thousand feet above the Chesapeake in a noisy aluminum bug smasher with a suspected murderer at the controls. I need details. Level with me."

After listening for a moment, he said, "Fine. I'll do that," then he hung up and called another number. Moments later, he said, "Ops, Stu Varney. What's current?"

Todd couldn't hear the voice coming over the earpiece: "Stu, the agents in Centreville have Mrs. Grant in custody and found a jackpot of evidence relating to the aircraft accident at the Ben Robertson address."

"Good, I, uh, have Mr. Grant in custody as well," Stu said, looking at Todd and raising an eyebrow.

"We understand that you are no longer at the airport."

Stu hesitated, then said, "That's right. I'm escorting Mr. Grant to Dulles. We'll need agents dispatched there ASAP. I'll check back with you after while."

He hung up the phone and looked at Todd, who was tuning in a navigation facility on the instrument panel. "This is completely out of the norm. I'm allowing you, a guy who's wanted for numerous federal and state crimes, to fly me to arrest a guy who, ten minutes ago, didn't exist on our list of suspects. What kind of investigation is this?"

"It's one that's now on track. Did they arrest Al Thomas?" Todd asked.

"No, they arrested your wife."

"Shoot. Well, at least she's safe. Did you have breakfast this morning?"

"No. Wait. What do you mean: Al Thomas? The agents just said the man they're after is a Ben Robertson. Enlighten me."

"O.K. Here, steer for a second," Todd said as he reached back to his gym bag.

"No. Hold it! I can't fly this thing!" Stu gripped the wheel and froze.

"Thanks. Here." He produced two bananas, tore them apart at the stem, and dropped one in his lap. He offered one to Stu as he lightly grasped the yoke with his left hand.

Todd let go of the yoke in order to peel open the banana. The air was smooth and the airplane was perfectly trimmed. He continued, "Although I've actually never met him, Ben Robertson is probably five-six, a hundred and fifty pounds, with brown hair. He'll be all scratched up from being thrown out of my two-story window into some shrubs a couple of days ago. And he'll be tired looking like me. But, the best way to find him is to yell 'Al!' as loud as you can, then see who turns around."

"Ben Robertson is Al Thomas?"

"Sure. Robertson is a quiet, recluse, part-time ramper that no one really knows. He started working for us just before *the accident*. I saw him once earlier this week and sensed he was avoiding me. He must have seen the fight I had with Gary in the pilot lounge."

Todd was thinking out loud: "You see, I decked a guy when he made a lewd comment about Chris right after I had been told that she was dead—that's why he picked me! Sure. That's it. I—a married man—cream a guy in defense of her—a woman with a bad reputation—in front of twenty-five people. Two days later, I'm her prime murder suspect. The phone calls to Kelly, the fax, the beer bottle in my car—it all makes sense now."

Stu listened intently as Todd looked at the horizon and continued his introspective rambling. "Yep. All he needed was a real person's social security number and a corresponding driver's license number. Make a fake license with his picture on it and—shazam!—he's a new person! My guess is he gave our airline his new address in Centreville. Hell, he's a part-time ramper. They probably just checked with the police to see if a Ben Robertson had any criminal convictions, then they put him right to work. The only one that would recognize him would be the chief pilot, and his office is at corporate headquarters. Amazing. He knew when airplanes were down for maintenance. He knew what flights were going where and when."

Todd flew an assigned heading that took him north of Washington, then approach control allowed the aircraft to head southeast toward Dulles Airport. Along the way, Todd explained everything to Stu from the start.

When he got in range, he called ahead on his other aircraft radio on the Bands Ramp Control frequency and advised them that he and a Federal Agent would be arriving at their gates in about ten minutes and to pass the word onto Charlie Brooks, the station manager, to meet them. They said they'd have a parking spot for him and that they would get word right to Charlie.

• • • •

Two airport policeman walked toward the plane that was supposed to be on it's way to Raleigh. They approached it with caution and stopped altogether when they got within about thirty feet of it. Al had left that airplane ten minutes before but couldn't make his way off the ramp. Minutes before, he clearly saw that the police were also guarding the entrances to the pilot lounge and operations, as well as the passenger gates and the baggage claim throughway. They checked the I.D. badge of every person that entered or left the ramp. Twenty minutes ago it would have been much easier to slip away unnoticed. The ramp had been full of aircraft and activity. Now, over two thirds of the aircraft had departed, leaving only a dozen or so aircraft on the ramp. Soon, only a couple would remain. He was trapped in a high security area and needed to find a place to wait it out until the police were convinced that he wasn't there.

Baggage trains normally made their way back and forth across the ramp to the Midfield Terminal from the commuter ramp. He thought that might be a way to get out of the immediate area. But since it was nearing the end of the noon arrival and departure bank, there were very few trains making runs back and forth and, hence, little opportunity existed. He'd probably be spotted, anyway.

He thought about hitching a ride on a fuel truck away from the area. But there were only two left on the ramp and they were too far away.

He studied the area immediately around him. He was leaning against a large garbage bin just next to a de-ice truck, some spare power carts, and a lavatory service cart. Everything but a couple of Javelin aircraft were to his left as he faced the ramp. The passenger gates, the pilot lounge and operations office entrances, and the aircraft maintenance shack were too far away and too risky.

From his right, he saw two fluorescent green fire trucks pull up to the Raleigh-bound aircraft—the one he had attached the plastic penguin to. A white Ford Bronco pulled up from the left and stopped directly in front of the plane. The policemen walked around to talk with the man in the Bronco.

Al thought about hiding in the garbage bin, but decided that if and when the police began a detailed search, the bin would be one of the first places that they'd look.

Because of the heat on the ramp, the rear passenger door and cockpit windows on both Javelins were open. The closest aircraft was no more than forty feet away. The other was lined up to it on the other side. Neither aircraft appeared to be going anywhere soon. There were no bags outside it, waiting to be loaded. There were no pilots preflighting it. There were no detailers cleaning the cabin, arranging the magazines, safety cards, and barf bags. The planes were just sitting there. It wasn't a great place to hide, but it was certainly safer than standing around and waiting to be noticed.

He grabbed a computer printout from the trash bin and folded it. Al looked in the direction of the Bronco. The policemen were chatting with its driver. Al lifted his baseball cap, wiped his sweaty brow with the sleeve of his dark blue short sleeve shirt, and readjusted his cap. He took a deep breath, then walked slowly toward the more distant Javelin. A ground power unit, hooked up to the aircraft's rear fuselage via a long rubber cable, was not running. He walked straight to the GPU and pressed the START button. The gasoline engine that ran the generator in the cart was quite noisy, but another Javelin had its turboprop engines revving about sixty yards away and easily masked the sound of the starting GPU. Once the engine RPM stabilized, he pressed the SYNC button, followed by the CLOSE button. A needle on the panel swung to the right side of the dial, indicating that electrical power was now available for use by the aircraft.

He dared not turn around, which would have made him look suspicious. So he looked down at his computer printout as though he was checking something. He then walked around the wing to the back of the airplane, up the five airplane steps and into the cabin. All of the plastic window shades had been pulled down to reflect the sun's heat away. The window in the emergency exit door had no shade, so he trotted up the aisle and peeked through the one on the left side. He relaxed when he concluded that he had not been seen. He walked back near the open door and waited until he felt it was safe. Then, he pulled up the rear passenger door and latched it shut.

He walked to the cockpit, knelt between the two pilot seats, and grabbed the laminated checklist. He had watched some maintenance technicians test run the engines once on a Javelin and generally knew how to start them, if the need arose. He could probably get it airborne, too, though he knew it wouldn't be pretty. He turned on the electrical circuits and ran down the checklist. He turned on the air conditioner and the gasper fans. Soon, cool air was working it's way up front, where he knelt.

Even during the day, the aircraft's navigation lights are normally turned on as a reminder to nearby workers that the aircraft was powered up. Just prior to starting the engines, pilots always turn on the aircraft's bright red rotating beacon, to warn everyone of an engine start.

He left all of the lights off.

Slowly, he went through the Aircraft Acceptance Checklist and the Before Start Checklist all the way to the point where he'd next flip on the fuel boost pumps and press the START button on the overhead panel. He could have one engine going and be rolling in less than thirty seconds. That might just be enough time.

• • • •

The phone in Stu's jacket pocket rang again. He had to reach to the rear seat of the plane to get to it. The unrelenting heat inside the cockpit forced him to take off the jacket and toss it back there.

"Please don't jabber, Stu," Todd said. They were beginning their descent towards Dulles Airport at a time when the airport was still fairly busy. Dulles Approach gave Todd radar vectors towards the airport, but in a different direction and altitude than he was used to. He reasoned that it was because the top speed of his Cessna was slower than the approach and landing speeds of most of the aircraft that use the airport. Hence, they were going to merge him onto the final approach course from an odd angle.

"Varney," said into the small phone.

Right as the person on the other end was speaking, a voice came over the aircraft speaker: "Cessna November One Sierra Sierra, due to the number of arrivals and departures, we'll be unable to land you at Dulles for at least twenty minutes. I can get you into Manassas, if you prefer. Say your intentions."

"Negative. I request priority handling and immediate vectors for landing."

"State the nature of your urgency."

Todd thought for a moment. "I am transporting a federal agent to Dulles. There is a possible crime in progress at the field."

"Roger, One Sierra Sierra. You'll soon see a Boeing Seven Thirty-seven at your one to two o'clock position. Tell me when you got him."

"One Sierra Sierra has the traffic in sight," Todd spoke into the microphone.

"Cessna One Sierra Sierra, follow that traffic for Runway One Nine Left."

"Follow him to Nineteen Left, One Sierra Sierra," Todd repeated back.

A moment later, the controller spoke again, "Cessna One Sierra Sierra, you can contact the Dulles Tower now on One Two Zero Point One. Good Day."

"Twenty Point One. Good day, sir," Todd acknowledged. He twisted the knob on the radio until the frequency on the dial read "120.1" and he transmitted, "Dulles Tower, Cessna One Sierra Sierra is number two for Nineteen Left."

"Cessna One Sierra Sierra, Dulles Tower. You are cleared to land, Runway One Nine Left. Where are you parking?"

"One Sierra Sierra's cleared to land, nineteen left and we're going to need to go to Bands Ramp, gate Alpha Twelve. If you need an authentication, contact Bands Ramp Control on One Three Three Point Four."

"Roger. We'll do that. Plan on Gate Alpha Twelve and we'll confirm it."

"Thanks."

Two minutes later, the Cessna that Todd was piloting glided smoothly over a light blue sedan that was occupied by Kelly and two FBI agents as it also arrived at Dulles Airport.

• • • •

Al bit his fingernails as he studied the flurry of activity beyond his exit row window. The longer Al sat there watching the host of policemen and people in ties wearing badges and swarming throughout the ramp, the more nervous he became. He could see the shadows of people walking around the aircraft that had been destined for Raleigh. It was dreadfully obvious now that they were inspecting the aircraft for sabotage, because a second Bronco and an unmarked police car joined the other Bronco and the two fire trucks.

The Raleigh-bound aircraft was about thirty yards away. But Al didn't have a very good view because of the other Javelin aircraft between them. He could tell that people were in it, however, because the top of the tail moved slightly when people stepped up on the aircraft's rear steps.

He looked around the rest of the ramp. Six aircraft now remained: The one he was in, the one next to him, the Raleigh plane which was another wingspan away from the one adjacent to him, and three others at the far end of the ramp. Those three were being loaded with passengers and would soon be gone. He wiped his forehead again.

• • • •

Todd landed and contacted Dulles Ground Control after leaving the runway. They gave him approval to taxi to the Bands Ramp, Gate Alpha Twelve. As he slowly moved westbound along taxiway Tango One, Stu finally hung up his phone.

"Well, you do good work," Stu said to Todd. "We found the negative of the photo that was made of you and Mrs. Thomas. We also found photos of Mrs. Thomas and several other men, some of which are fairly graphic in nature and could never be shown on television like yours was. She apparently was very, uh, friendly...."

"She was a good person and a good friend of mine, in spite of her reputation."

"They also found Javelin Maintenance Manuals, flight schedules, electronic test equipment, soldering irons, and detailed plans on how to make a device to corrupt the stall warning system of the Javelin. The only thing better would be a signed confession. Lastly, James just arrived at the aircraft. He and our guys are checking the aircraft that was supposed to go to Raleigh. So far, they have removed the panel cover from Station One Ten and found a plastic penguin attached to the Signal Summing Device. They're getting finger prints as we speak. As a matter of fact, that's probably the aircraft right there with all the vehicles surrounding it!"

Todd had already noticed the ruckus about five hundred yards ahead. "Yea. I think you're right, Stu."

"They think he got away from the ramp area, but we have two agents ready to arrest him when he works his way back to his car in the employee lot."

Todd smiled, then the smile disappeared. "It's a pity that the bastard was ever born. He killed a plane full of people including my best friend, Scott. Then he killed his own wife. Jeez. I'd love to have thirty seconds alone with him."

The tiny Cessna angled off the taxiway and onto the large, empty ramp. At first, one of the rampers didn't know what to think when he saw a small plane heading his way. He spoke into his radio, then crossed his hands above his head, indicating to Todd that he should stop.

Two other pilots were walking behind the ramper in the direction of one of the two airplanes parked at the far west side of the ramp. They stopped and looked at the Cessna, wondering what it was up to.

Al didn't notice the Cessna. But he did notice the pilots walking towards either his plane or the one just to his left. He dashed up front, buckled himself in, and slouched low in the seat, just to be ready. He watched the pilots who stood and watched the Cessna with fascination.

The ramper, twenty yards closer to the Cessna than the two pilots, heard something over his radio then motioned with a big sweeping arc of his arm to bring the Cessna to the far right side of the south facing ramp, around the Raleigh plane and the two planes further west. Todd gave the ramper a thumbs up, then added a little power and swung the Cessna to the left and then in a big right circle around the three Javelins.

The pilots continued walking towards Al's plane. Al still didn't take notice of the Cessna crossing in front of him. When Al was convinced it was *his* airplane that they were heading for, he quickly flipped on the boost pumps, then pressed the right START button on the overhead panel. The propeller in front of the right wing immediately began spinning. When the RPM gauge climbed through ten percent, he pushed a lever forward to introduce fuel, just like the maintenance technician had done.

Todd saw the pilots stop and stare at the airplane that was starting up. Todd glanced in front of the airplane. There was no ramper out in front! Someone had to indicate to the pilot that it was safe to start the engines, then remove the chocks and the Ground Power Unit cable from the airplane. Wait, there were no chocks! The rotating beacon wasn't turned on! *Who was starting up that airplane?!*

"NO!" Todd yelled, then slammed on the brakes to the Cessna. His plane had moved too far behind the Javelin for him to see inside the cockpit, but he knew who was in there. He pulled the mixture handle, which killed his engine, then he set the parking brake and leaped out before the propeller on his Cessna even stopped.

"That's him!" he exclaimed as he ran around to the front of his Cessna, then around the back of the Javelin towards the passenger door.

Stu struggled with his seat belt and shoulder harness. By the time he got himself unbuckled, the Javelin had already begun to roll forward.

Todd grabbed the handle to the Javelin's rear door and yanked it hard as the airplane began to move. The door, dampened by pneumatic actuators, came slowly down. Todd was now running along side it as the plane accelerated. He leaped at the half opened door then reached for something to hold on to. His body rotated down as the door moved to its fully opened position.

Finally, he braced his foot against the step rail and thrust himself forward just as the plane swerved wildly to the right and onto the taxiway. He was inside.

With the speed of a halfback, he sprinted up the aisle and grabbed the red Feather Lever on the center console. He turned it ninety degrees, then yanked it up, right as Al delivered a blow to Todd's face with the back of his fist. The engine immediately began to spool down, yet the aircraft continued to zoom down the taxiway.

Blurred from the hit, Todd raised himself up, reached with his right hand, and flipped off the airplane's hydraulic valve switches. Without hydraulic power, Al would not be able to steer. The airplane immediately began to veer off toward the grass.

Another back-handed slug came back towards Todd, but hit harmlessly on Todd's chest. Though still blurry-eyed from the single shot to his face, Todd could see Al unbuckling his seat belt so he could defend himself or possibly grab a weapon. Todd dropped down at the entrance to the cockpit, executing a half twist in the air down to his all fours, facing backwards. He then reached between his legs to the cockpit's center console as he braced himself, then yanked hard on the emergency brake. The plane's main tires locked up, sending Al into the yoke and the glare screen.

Todd quickly reversed himself and grabbed Al's hair with both hands. He pulled Al back towards him with all the strength he could muster.

The plane had skidded to a stop just after entering the grass along the left side of the taxiway. Al was dazed from the sudden stop, and let out an ear piercing scream when he was dragged from the cockpit by his hair. Todd slung him down against the seat backs of Row One, then slugged him in the face no less than ten times. All of the pent-up anger of the past week was released with those punches.

When he was convinced that any more punches would probably not be felt, he punched him once again.

Sweating heavily and breathing hard, he reached over to the cockpit, threw a few switches to de-power the aircraft. Then he dragged Al to the back of the airplane, opened the door, then hurled him down the stairs and onto the grass next to the taxiway.

Still breathing hard, he looked down at the motionless man at the base of the aircraft's steps.

Todd pulled on his shirt to see if any fresh blood was appearing, then stood tall in the doorway of the airplane just as four or five vehicles stopped and men got out yielding weapons. Todd raised his hands slowly, indicating he was unarmed. In the distance, he could see Stu Varney jogging along the taxiway toward him.

He remained on the airplane steps with his arms slightly raised for about fifteen seconds until someone near one of the cars finally took charge and came forward. "Hold your arms straight out and come down the steps—slowly!" a man wearing dark sunglasses yelled.

Todd did as he was told.

"Now lay down on the grass, arms and legs extended! Move!" Again, Todd did as instructed. An arriving crowd of police and investigators converged on him and Al, who were no more than three feet from each other. Todd was frisked and handcuffed, as was Al, who only then began groaning.

Three men lifted Todd up to his feet and turned him in the direction of a police cruiser, as more and more vehicles began arriving.

"Let him go!" Stu yelled as he arrived, panting and sweating. When he worked his way through the maze of people, he held up his badge and said, "I'm Stu Varney, head of the Sabotage and Air Piracy Division, FBI. You can undo his handcuffs. He's on our side."

A group of rampers and mechanics lined the edge of the taxiway at the west end of the ramp and strained to see down the taxiway.

More cars arrived at the aircraft, some with yellow lights atop them, others with blue. Soon, there were thirty or forty officials surrounding the plane.

"R.C.?!" Kelly shouted as she appeared from the ever-growing crowd. She raced toward him.

"K.W.!" he roared as his eyes watered with joy. An officer was still unlocking his cuffs when she leaped on top of him and hugged him wildly. Finally, the cuffs opened and he returned the hug.

"It's over. It's really over, K.W.," he said quietly as he buried his face into her shoulder and squeezed her. After a moment, he looked up and saw James Hatch, beaming.

With Kelly in tow, Todd bounded over to James and introduced her. "James, this is my wife Kelly. Kelly—James."

Kelly spoke first, "James, I can't tell you how much your trust has meant to us." She shook his hand warmly and smiled.

"Well, if I'd *seen* him, I probably would've had second thoughts," James replied with a smile as he surveyed a disheveled but ecstatic Todd.

Sweating, unshaven, and completely exhausted, Todd grinned, "Sorry, but lately I've been having bad hair days."

• • • •

The now larger crowd of onlookers that lined the edge of the Bands ramp stepped back slightly as a parade of two police cruisers, a Bronco, and an unmarked police car whizzed by. Some fifteen other vehicles still surrounded the Javelin which was leaning off into the grass.

Suddenly, the unmarked car swerved out of line and stopped, just beyond the crowd. Stu got out of the passenger-side door, walked up to a man in the crowd, and angrily flashed his badge. Kelly and Todd peeked from behind the car's tinted glass.

Stu pointed as he walked. "Are you Gary Heinmann?"

The man with the bruised face and gauze-wrapped fingers nodded nervously as he stared at the badge.

"I am Special Agent Stuart Varney of the FBI. We are investigating a call that you made to a Mrs. Kelly Grant earlier this week. Do you recall making such a call?"

"I, uh,...."

Stu interjected: "You know, son, it is a violation of Federal law to make prank or offensive phone calls...."

Some rampers and pilots moved away from Gary, isolating him.

"....Conviction of such offenses may lead to fines of five thousand dollars and imprisonment of five years, or both."

Gary stood silently, horrified and numbed.

"However, the Grants are willing to drop the pending charge against you if you reciprocate and drop your charges against him. If you do not, I will personally assist Mr. Grant in obtaining a full conviction and a maximum fine. Do you understand?"

"Yes, sir."

"You have until close of business today to drop all charges," Stu said, then turned away from Gary and walked back to the car.

As he neared, he smiled slightly at Todd and Kelly and winked.

• • • •